THE HEARTLAND DIARIES

BY FRANK MIELE

COLUMNIST, REAL CLEAR POLITICS
WWW.HEARTLANDDIARYUSA.COM

2018

Volume 1: Why We Needed Trump, Part 1:
Bush's Global Failure: Half Right

Volume 2: Why We Needed Trump, Part 2:
Obama's Fundamental Transformation: Far Left

Volume 3: Why We Needed Trump, Part 3:
Trump's American Vision: Just Right

2019

Volume 4: The Media Matrix:
What If Everything You Know Is Fake

Volume 5: How We Got Here:
The Left's Assault on the Constitution

Volume 6: What Matters Most:
God, Country, Family and Friends

Volume 7: A Culture in Crisis:
Reviews and Reminders from the War Upstream

**Collected from the author's 18 years as managing editor
of the Daily Inter Lake in Kalispell, Montana.**

Frank Miele

Heartland Diary Volume 4

HEARTLAND DIARY VOLUME 4

THE MEDIA MATRIX

What If Everything You Know is Fake

BY FRANK MIELE

HEARTLAND PRESS
KALISPELL MONTANA 2019

THE MEDIA MATRIX
WHAT IF EVERYTHING YOU KNOW IS FAKE

ISBN: 978-1-7329633-3-7
FIRST EDITION

LIBRARY OF CONGRESS CONTROL NUMBER: 2019901413

HEARTLAND PRESS
KALISPELL, MONTANA

DEDICATED
TO THE JOURNALISTS
WHO STRIVE FOR FAIRNESS,
STICK TO THE FACTS
AND FOLLOW
THE GOLDEN RULE OF OUR PROFESSION

*'TELL THE STORY OF OTHERS AS YOU WOULD
WANT YOUR OWN STORY TOLD.'*

Acknowledgements

Thanks to Richard Spencer for his continues support, which has gone far beyond writing the introduction to the Heartland Diary USA series (now incorporated as the afterword of this volume).

Also, my heartfelt thanks to my colleague Brant Horn for agreeing to write a foreword for this new volume. His encouragement and advice throughout the many years of our joint employment at the Daily Inter Lake was crucial in the final shape of many of the essays included here. I also appreciate his taking time to record his own memories of our fruitful collaboration in the foreword.

I also again have to acknowledge my debt to the publishers of the Daily Inter Lake for giving me the opportunity to write the collected columns in the "Heartland Diaries" over the course of 14 years and to Hagadone Montana Publishing Company for giving me permission to reprint them in this form.

Of course, as any author will understand, I owe a deep debt of gratitude to my wife, Yuzhao, for her continued patience with what surely seems like self-absorption to anyone who has not lived with a writer. She rightly qualifies for sainthood, and I would be remiss if I did not mention so.

—FDM, March 2019

Foreword

'AN UNFLINCHING DEMAND FOR ACCURACY AND BALANCE'

BY BRANT HORN

I had the pleasure of working with Frank Miele at the Daily Inter Lake, a small daily newspaper located in Kalispell, Montana for nearly 15 years. Frank, as the managing editor, created the product that I, as the circulation director, marketed and distributed. Although we have very different personalities and disparate strengths, together we made a good team that successfully grew the readership and distribution of that small newspaper from Y2K through the beginning of the Great Recession in 2007. It is true that the readership of the paper declined after 2007, but the Daily Inter Lake continued to outperform the newspaper industry in general, and also outperformed similar sized community newspapers across the nation. I attribute the success of the Daily Inter Lake through those years to Frank Miele and his consummate drive to publish an unbiased newspaper that fairly covered all of Northwest Montana, not just the pieces he liked.

From our first introduction, I knew Frank Miele was a man I could work with. I found him to be congenial, very well read, exceedingly intelligent and brutally honest. Although the desk in the small managing editor's office was perpetually cluttered, literally covered from edge to edge with heaps of paper and newsprint, Frank always found time to interrupt his work and hear out every hare-brained scheme that I, as a young, brash and sometimes clueless circulation director, cooked up. I wanted to borrow from William Randolph Hearst's model of sensationalism, that became known as "yellow journalism" to make to product more compelling and Frank simply wanted to build the reader's trust with honest, even keeled and accurate reporting.

I once demanded that Frank instruct his newsroom to use lurid words in headlines: words like "bloody," "death," "sex" or "mayhem." Often times, I implored Frank to lose the cute front page "stand alone" photos of children, wildlife and mountains and replace them with more exciting pictures of fires, car wrecks and bikinis. When I made wild suggestions such as these, my friend would abruptly call me an idiot and throw me out of his office. And off I would skulk with my head hanging low and my fragile ego damaged. The point is that Frank rightfully didn't care about feelings nearly as much as he cared about producing the most honest and respectable newspaper he could muster, and that meant not indulging me and my stupid ideas.

Every now and then even a blind squirrel finds a nut. And so, sometimes I did bring a good idea to Frank. When I did, he took quick action. I asked him to work with the editors to make sure photos weren't cut off at the fold on page one. I asked him to try to get headlines above the fold. These things he did, and did well. On 9/11, I made the unthinkable suggestion that the Daily Inter Lake publish an "extra" afternoon edition of our morning paper. Our publisher, Tom Kurdy, was overseas, and Frank made the command decision to go ahead with it. The extra edition was a smashing success and bolstered our position as a news leader in the community.

Aside from finding creative ways to produce a daily newspaper with an ever-shrinking budget, perhaps the most difficult aspect of Frank's job as managing editor was to publish an unbiased newspaper in today's leftist media climate. In this task, Frank was unrelenting. As if moved by gravitational-like forces, a newspaper's coverage will continually drift to the left, unless that drift is actively and deliberately countered via effective leadership. This, Frank did masterfully.

Of course, local newspapers cover state, national and world news; and of course, the Daily Inter Lake did not produce such content. Like all other small newspapers, we relied of the Associated Press for non-local content. Any discerning reader will quickly find that the AP slants hard to the left, oft times not even trying to be objective. Obviously then, just the simple act of running AP stories pushes a newspaper's content leftward. As a result, Frank insisted that "any editor who just runs AP stories without first editing for bias is not doing his job." I remember during the Bush years he used this example as a bare minimum: "When the AP story claims, without support, 'George Bush is stupid', at least change the copy to read 'some people say George Bush is stupid.'" I recall times that Frank refused to run AP stories on particular national events because the AP did not produce so much as one story on said event that met any standard of journalistic objectivity. There were several times he confronted AP editors with factual and/or bias errors, sometimes winning hard-earned retractions or corrections.

Another obstacle to publishing an unbiased newspaper in the 21st century is hiring reporters and editors that are willing and able to produce such unbiased content. I saw Frank address this as well: he screened applicants, looking for those who were less likely to be idealistic. He coached his staff on now dead staple skills of journalism, skills such as editing out their own biases and treating all people and organizations fairly; even those whom the reporter may not like or agree with.

I'm sure most readers of this book are aware of the distinction between news content and the opinion page in a newspaper. While Frank kept opinion and bias out of the news-hole, he invited all opinions onto the editorial page gladly. I remember very clearly in 2003 when he came into my office announcing the new Montana Perspectives (Opinion) section to be added to the Sunday paper, along with his freshly minted "Editor's Two Cents" column. This addition to the Daily Inter Lake was, singularly and without question, the biggest improvement made to the paper during my tenure as circulation director. The Perspectives section brought a level of reader engagement that I had never observed before in my newspaper career while Frank's increasingly conservative commentary in the "2 Cents" column gave voice to the quiet right-leaning majority in Republican northwest Montana.

I felt fortunate that over the years Frank invited me to give his column one last read on Friday before it was published on Sunday morning. Honestly, getting an advance look at his piece was often the highlight of my work week. Most weeks I would read the piece, learn something new about politics, history or literature and simply tell him to run it. Sometimes I would challenge a premise or suggest a few minor edits, and one week, I simply told him not to print the stupid thing (he ran it over my objections... but I digress).

In very short order, the "2 Cents" column became the most read and most discussed content in the Daily Inter Lake. I spoke with literally hundreds of subscribers over the years who claimed they continued their subscriptions simply to read Miele's column each Sunday. Those columns, which form the substance of this book and the Heartland Diary USA series, informed and educated me, oft times challenged me, and also made my job as circulation director easier, as it gave me something to offer my customers when they complained that all newspapers were just too damn liberal anymore.

In summary, for 15 years, I observed Frank's passion to produce an excellent, unbiased and fair newspaper that earned the trust of the people of Northwest Montana. This he did excellently and professionally. Frank produced a newspaper that I was proud to market; indeed, our community was blessed to have a newspaper edited by him. I give all this as background information to illustrate the rare type of journalist Frank Miele is. His unflinching demand for accuracy and balance is a dying, if not dead, art in American newspapers and it places him among the "old breed" of great American newspapermen.

Whitefish, Montana
February 2019

Introduction

"HOW I TOOK THE RED PILL AND SAW THROUGH THE MEDIA MATRIX"

BY FRANK DANIEL MIELE

In the Keanu Reeves science-fiction thriller "The Matrix," a mild-mannered computer programmer with an adventurous imagination discovers that reality is beyond anything he ever conceived. More importantly, the reality he knows is false, a construct known as "The Matrix." As his mentor Morpheus explains to him:

"The Matrix is everywhere. It is all around us. Even now, in this very room. You can see it when you look out your window or when you turn on your television. You can feel it when you go to work ... when you go to church ... when you pay your taxes. It is the world that has been pulled over your eyes to blind you from the truth."

The part that concerns us today is the Matrix you see when you turn on your television or read your newspaper. That's what I am calling The Media Matrix, and we are so surrounded by it that we often don't even realize that our beliefs and opinions are shaped and molded by an outside force largely beyond our control. Now, before you assume that journalism is the problem, let me offer an alternative view. Journalism is neither the problem, nor the solution — and let's get this straight right away: What happens on CNN, MSNBC and FOX News isn't real journalism anyway; it's entertainment and opinion. But even real journalism in newspapers isn't the solution either. It is just one more manifestation of The Media Matrix — the living, breathing entity that consumes us (and is consumed by us) 24 hours a day.

I am talking about the information envelope that has become our native habitat. It's no surprise that journalists have a hard time fathoming that they often produce what President Trump popularized as Fake News; they live in the same murky Media Matrix as the rest of us — Twitter, Facebook, smart phones, 24/7 cable blather, the endless Towering Babble known as the Internet. Honestly, can you really expect journalists to escape the impact of that swamp of supposition? More likely they are among its worst victims because they — more than most of us — live in the Media Matrix by choice. It is their home field.

So let's think of it this way — Fake News is a symptom of the Media Matrix, and though as individuals we may not be able to cure society of the disease caused by information overload, we may be able to treat the symptom on a case-by-case basis.
That means each of us must become skeptical, cautious consumers of news. President Trump has started many of his supporters on that road, but there is a long way to go to get wide acceptance for the idea. Casual observers assume that Trump is exaggerating the danger to improve his own political position. Opponents of Trump believe that he himself is a manufacturer of Fake News, and thus embed themselves even deeper into the Media Matrix where they are comforted with a steady stream of soothing lies.

People like me who are in the news business but recognize the danger of Fake News are few and far between. To paraphrase the dictum of Jesus, "A whistleblower is not without honor except in his own profession." Journalists are rare who will hold each other to account for their bias and political agenda — mainly because they share many of the same beliefs as the worst offenders even though they would never engage in deception themselves. They give each other the benefit of the doubt, and thus earn the doubt of the rest of us.

I'm an outsider journalist, one who never went to journalism school, but I certainly hope you don't have to be an outsider to see through the Fake News of the mainstream media. Basically, all you have to do is listen to your readers. Instead of telling them what they SHOULD think, find out what they DO think. Unfortunately, most reporters and editors these days seem to think they have a "higher calling," which invariably revolves around a responsibility to tell the readers THE TRUTH instead of telling them THE STORY. Folks, there is no truth except that which is decided by God; the rest of us are lucky just to get the facts straight, but if you are going to be a journalist, that is what you should strive for. Tell the story as accurately as possible, and let the readers come to their own conclusions.

Perhaps because I am an admitted news junkie (see the prologue), it was inevitable that I should one day pop the red pill and see through the Media Matrix. But there was no Morpheus to instruct me. For most of us, we simply use our own conscience as our guide. Right and wrong come from natural law, not from a teacher, and it's important for news consumers to train themselves to hunt down and root out bias in reporting. The more you read, the more you see how reporters have become opinionators. This is especially easy if you have an area of personal expertise which lets you separate the wheat from the chaff, the straight reporting from the slanted propaganda. For me, what opened my mind is when I became a conservative in the wake of 9/11 and thus was treated to the scorn and derision of most of my own industry when I raised questions about bias and distortion in news reporting. I did so fairly frequently in my "Editor's 2 Cents" column in the Daily Inter Lake, as the writings in this book will attest. Although I was crafting opinion columns, not news, I discovered that many in the community were disturbed by the idea of an editor who was a professed conservative. Moreover, as I started to write critically about George W. Bush's immigration policies and Barack Obama's socialism, I noticed that I was becoming a pariah to many in my own newsroom — and this was in heartland Montana! How much more subversive it must seem to be a conservative journalist in New York City or Los Angeles! But remember, the red pill isn't about becoming a conservative; it's about seeking the truth, wherever it lies (pun intended).

If you enjoy the essays in this collection, please visit me at www.HeartlandDiaryUSA.com or follow me on Facebook @HeartlandDiaryUSA or on Twitter @HeartlandDiary.

Kalispell, Montana
February 2019
frank@HeartlandDiaryUSA.com

PROLOGUE

THE IMPORTANCE OF NEWS

April 10, 2005

All right, I ADMIT IT!

I am a news junkie. I'll spend 10 hours working at the newspaper, and then head home to rest and relax — and promptly turn on CNBC, Fox News, CNN and MSNBC — sometimes virtually all at once — to see the same stories discussed ad infinitum.

Sometimes the stories are of world significance such as the war in Iraq; sometimes they are of no significance at all such as the latest poll showing how many people think Martha Stewart should be wearing an ankle bracelet as part of her house arrest — or is it a tiara?

In some cases, one story totally dominates television news coverage. The past three weeks, for instance, the deaths of Terri Schiavo and Pope John Paul II have gotten so much screen time that even the war in Iraq has seemingly been forgotten.

But those are exceptions. Once those stories are done, I will be content to dwell again on the intricacies of the Michael Jackson trial, the oddities of Midwestern weather, and the latest flap-doodle over who bollywhacked who. It may seem trivial at first glance, but the news is not about seriousness only; it is ultimately about the cascade of humanity careening from birth to death like a billion ping-pong balls dropped over Niagara Falls. Each individual ball reveals nothing on its own, but in context with all the others, it discloses the shape of the maelstrom we call life.

I've read Thoreau's proclamation in "Walden" that, "To a philosopher all news, as it is called, is gossip, and they who edit and read it are old women over their tea," but that argument has never persuaded me — and not just because I am an editor (or because I like tea).

It seems as though Thoreau was living in some alien place — or ivory tower — a world where you could invent a philosophy so abstract that it never even got a whiff of real human life. After all, what Thoreau first calls news and then denounces as gossip is really no less than the collected experience of humankind, and how exactly do you do without that in a philosophy?

Thoreau "the philosopher" apparently had little inclination for taking account of the comings and goings of the common people, whom he likened (in the same famous chapter of "Walden") to ants. He says also, "If we read of one man robbed, or murdered, or killed by accident, or one house burned, or one vessel wrecked, or one steamboat blown up, or one cow run over on the Western Railroad, or one mad dog killed, or one lot of grasshoppers in the winter — we never need read of another. One is enough. If you are acquainted with the principle, what do you care for a myriad instances and applications?"

This sounds good on the printed page. Thoreau was nothing if not a persuasive writer. But think about it for a minute. What exactly would we do all day long if we considered everything that happened around us to be inconsequential because it has happened somewhere else sometime before? Even fishermen — so easily amused — would be bored. After all, they wouldn't need the application of repeatedly casting a filament line into murky water on the off chance of catching a rainbow trout. They would simply need to know that such a fish had been caught once before, and they should then start to feel full in the belly just with the smug satisfaction of their own knowledge. If you are already acquainted with the principle of pan-fried fish, what do you care about lemon butter or spices?

But maybe Thoreau was wrong. Perhaps there is something we can learn by paying attention to our world and its habitants. At the very least we will be endlessly amused. And I hope readers of this paper would agree with me that every house fire, or murder, or robbery is a new one, and that we should not dismiss them as Thoreau urged. Every news story ultimately is about a person, and if that makes it gossip, then so be it.

Is not what Thoreau dismisses as gossip actually something that could more politely be called the conversation of life? And do we not all find considerable value in that conversation because it provides us with a forum to ponder the ironies, the frailties, and the inspirations that confront us every day? Is not everything ultimately worthy of the gaze of a worthy intellect? Is it not true, as Thoreau's benefactor Emerson once said, that "the world globes itself in a drop of dew"? I believe it is.

So if our gaze from time to time is distracted by this trial or that death, or even by this divorce or that relapse, do not automatically assume we have lost our way. An alert observer can always learn something new about human nature no matter where he is looking — except perhaps his own navel.

Even Thoreau, that "sad Hindoo of Concord," realized that his no-news-is-good-news "philosophy" did not have a hold on the world. As he himself acknowledged, "Yet not a few are greedy after this gossip."

Count me in.

And now that we've established the importance of news, could someone please tell me where I put that sports section? Ah, baseball! Now that really is a bit of gossip worthy of a philosopher!

The Media Matrix

BIAS, ARROGANCE AND NBC: OR, I REPEAT MYSELF

August 14, 2005

Bernard Goldberg just came out with another book, and it is raising hackles in all the right places.

Goldberg is the author of "Bias" and "Arrogance," in which he took on the self-appointed guardians of the truth in the mainstream media, especially at CBS, where he used to work as a reporter.

His new book has the pungent title "100 People Who Are Screwing Up America," and while you could make the case that Goldberg has become just as arrogant as the people he writes about, you have to forgive him because he is both entertaining and educational.

He also gets under the skin of people like Michael Moore (No. 1), Howard Dean (No. 20) and Eminem (No. 58), and you have to give him credit for that.

A lot of Goldberg's targets are liberals like those three, but there are also people from the opposite end of the spectrum such as Michael Savage (No. 61) and David Duke (No. 66), who also deserve a thumping. The thing that most of these people have in common, of course, is that they are oblivious to criticism and consider themselves incapable of screwing up anything, even a lightbulb.

Now, the reason I am telling you about Bernie Goldberg is not to promote his book, but because I got so frustrated last week watching an episode of "Hardball" on MSNBC that I am unofficially extending Goldberg's list by one.

No, it's not Chris Matthews — the contentious, sophomoric, self-important host of "Hardball," though he certainly merits a chapter or two in the revised edition of "Arrogance."

Instead, it is guest host David Gregory, NBC's chief White House correspondent, who demonstrated himself to be unqualified to be any kind of reporter during an interview in which he was abrasive, confrontational, rude and just plain stupid.

The subject of the interview was Katherine Harris, the Florida Republican who has announced that she is going to try to get a promotion from the House of Representatives to the U.S. Senate.

Harris is a lighting rod for liberal criticism because of her role in the historic 2000 presidential recount, when she was Florida's secretary of state and had the responsibility of certifying the election result. And if the sparks flying off of Gregory are any indication, then he is a flaming liberal.

His approach was to intimidate, harass, and virtually slander his guest — along with the president and his brother, Gov. Jeb Bush. The introduction set the lurid tone for what was to follow, as Gregory said that Harris had been "vilified for insuring President Bush's victory, lampooned for her appearance. Now she's back, this time without support from the Bushes and running for the Senate."

This is the beginning of one of the most biased, slanted, unfair interviews I have ever seen. So much so that I was actually getting sick to my stomach watching it, feeling bad for Harris because I knew she had to maintain her calm demeanor even though she probably wanted to spit at Gregory right between the eyes.

It was quite instructive to watch Harris keep trying to steer Gregory back to reality, while he just as vehemently took back the helm and like the insane Captain Queeg spun his vessel in pointless circles.

First she explained that Gov. Jeb Bush had said she would be a formidable candidate, and that she was grateful for his support.

Then Gregory "hit back" and read a quote from Gov. Bush that said, "I hope Congresswoman Harris runs a strong race. She'll be a good candidate, and Bill Nelson is very vulnerable."

Gregory apparently thought this was a negative comment, and wondered why it was not an "endorsement."

Harris didn't take the bait, and tried to talk about the campaign, but the reporter wasn't interested.

"I want to get to some of those issues," he told Harris in a curt brush-off. "But I'd like to pin you down on this point, because I think ... it strikes a lot of people that there doesn't appear to be an endorsement here."

Oh really? And what makes that news exactly? Does Gregory think that Gov. Bush owes Harris an endorsement? Is he suggesting that there should be a quid pro quo in effect for Harris's role in what Gregory called "insuring President Bush's victory"? Is he alleging collusion in the 2000 presidential election?

Because if any of those things are true, then Gregory has no business interviewing Harris or anyone else. His personal opinions don't have any place in an interview with a newsmaker, and if he can't be objective, then why is NBC allowing him to lurk around the White House?

Harris tried to set him straight, by pointing out that "it is unusual to have endorsements" during a primary because a governor and other party leaders like to maintain neutrality on races between different candidates within their own party.

At this point, Gregory just started making things up, and I was squirming in my seat, waiting for Harris to unscrew the smile off her face and tell Gregory to take a flying leap.

"Congresswoman," said Gregory, "Let me just interrupt you, because when the president's senior adviser, Karl Rove, and Gov. Bush of Florida spoke to you about your bid for the Senate, what is it that they said to you?"

She explained again that the governor had been "very gracious" and that she had not talked to Rove at all since her bid for the Senate had been announced.

Gregory at this point must have decided to use his "super top secret anonymous sources" to pin Harris down because he asked a question that implied he knew a lot more than he was telling:

"Isn't it true — isn't it true that the White House and even the president's brother, the governor of Florida, have discouraged you from entering this race?"

Whoa! Isn't that one of those "When did you stop beating your wife questions?" they teach you not to ask in Journalism 101? Gregory is obviously already convinced he knows the answer before he asks the question. But if he knows it to be true, shouldn't he tell us what evidence he has? And if he doesn't have any evidence, shouldn't he treat the interview subject with a little more respect?

Apparently not in the world of NBC News.

During this entire inteview, Gregory was like a rabid dog spinning around in circles, with his tongue lolling out of his head and foam spilling from the corners of his mouth. Although Harris tried to talk about her accomplishments and focus on her race with Sen. Bill Nelson, Gregory had no interest except in finding controversy where there was none.

"But just — just to be clear here, for the record, you're saying that nobody within the White House, nobody within the Republican Party in Florida ever discouraged from you entering into this race?"

Harris once again assured him there had been no such discussions.

Gregory got flustered: "And do you — do you — do you expect..."

HARRIS: So, we are moving forward. We have positive — David, we have positive comments.

(CROSSTALK)

GREGORY: I understand.

(CROSSTALK)

GREGORY: I understand that.

(CROSSTALK)

HARRIS: ... from the Republican National Committee.

GREGORY: And I want to get to that. Let me just — let me just go through my questions. I will be happy to get to your agenda items. I just want to clear this point up, because there might be some confusion, based on what's been publicly written about this and, as I say, my — my own information. Are you saying that, because this is just the primary, that you expect President Bush to campaign with you in advance of this election?

HARRIS: No. I think, because it is a primary, I wouldn't have expected any endorsements whatsoever...

GREGORY: Does the president owe you? Do you expect him to campaign with you down the stretch?

HARRIS: Why in the world would you ask if the president owed me? I simply followed the letter of the law. That's it... And I don't know why there's—I think we can move on and not create controversy — try to create controversy where none exists.

GREGORY: All right. I'm certainly not trying to do that. I'm just trying — I'm just trying to — to — to get — to nail this down...

And a minute later, Gregory made the following comment, which has to be the most hilarious example of unintended self-deflating irony that I have seen in a long time:

"You said, at one point, you thought the national media was trying to make you foolish. Do you still believe that's the case?"

Harris had the remarkable restraint not to laugh in Gregory's face, and simply once again said that all she cares about is taking her message "to the people of Florida."

Well, I think the message we ought to be sending is to NBC. If David Gregory is the best that network can do by way of fair journalism, then NBC ought to give its acronym a new meaning: "Negative, Biased and Controversial."

It doesn't matter what you think of Harris. She may or may not have done the right thing in the 2000 election. But I would hope you would treat her with respect and dignity, and if you were a reporter, I would hope that you would do your job the way it's supposed to be done — fair, balanced and businesslike.

In other words, I would hope you would not act like David Gregory, who is not just screwing up America; he's screwing up journalism — and that's something I don't tolerate.

MEDIA MADNESS

October 16, 2005

What kind of news media do we want?

It's a question we had better ask ourselves pretty seriously pretty quickly because in the 21st century, it is just possible that the so-called fourth estate holds more power than all the other estates put together.

These days you can think of the other estates as the executive, judicial, and legislative branches of government — the places where power is invested by the people. The fourth estate is journalism, where power is wielded in the name of the people.

It's a term that dates back to the 1700s when the political philosopher Edmund Burke distinguished between the three levels of the British Parliament and the "Reporters Gallery" that kept watch on them from above.

The idea, of course, is that the people had a representative, in the form of journalists, who would look out for the public welfare in the workings of government.

It is a good idea, and we at the Inter Lake take seriously our obligation to shed light on public policy and to open the doors of any back rooms where officials might be trying to hide from public scrutiny.

But there also comes a time, and we recognize this too, where the media — whether in the form of a newspaper or a pack of cable TV pundits — becomes a pain in the "paparazzi."

You can particularly see that in the way the press handles the president of the United States. Rest assured, this has nothing to do with partisan politics. It started well before President Bush took office, and President Clinton probably more than anyone was the victim of the ever-increasing snoopiness of the press. But Clinton, at least, had himself to blame. He was too stupid to keep his pants zipped.

This president, on the other hand, is criticized not for lapses of judgment or morality, but for such things as needing a potty break. I'm not sure how many of you were subjected to this ridiculous example of a press that has run amok, but in brief, it turns out that the president needed to use the bathroom while he was at the United Nations, and he scribbled a polite note to that effect. A photographer with a telephoto lens happened to intercept the note, and suddenly the TV talking heads in all earnestness were trying to decide if the president's use of the toilet was a sign of weakness!

It seems that as part of the legacy of Bill Clinton, there is now no bodily function beneath the attention of the White House press corps and probably no sneeze in the White House too small to be considered a symptom of avian flu.

Fact of the matter is that the national news media — in particular the cable news channels — thrive on controversy, and they will go anywhere to find it, or to manufacture it if need be. Indeed, some of those reporters go to such great lengths to shed light on dark places that they might sometimes be mistaken for suppositories.

Two recent examples will suffice:

First, let's consider the attempt to bring down the Harriet Miers nomination to the Supreme Court by imputing conspiratorial motives to Karl Rove in his briefing of Focus on the Family founder James Dobson.

In particular, Dobson was criticized for saying this: "When you know some of the things that I know — that I probably shouldn't know — you will understand why I have said, with fear and trepidation, that I believe Harriet Miers will be a good justice."

Well, whoop-de-do.

The pack of wolves jumped on that statement like a side of beef. The "smoking gun" was Dobson's acknowledgment that he knew some things about Miers, as he said, "that I probably shouldn't know." The all-knowing media interpreted that to mean that Karl Rove, the grand poobah of the White House, had given Dobson a secret handshake (over the phone no less) to assure him that Miers would vote to overturn Roe vs. Wade.

I, for one, just shook my head and pondered how stupid and blindered some high-paid Washington journalists could be. Doesn't anyone out there know how to read? Dobson's statement was not some nefarious admission of skulduggery among a conservative cabal; it was rather a humble recognition that Dobson had received special privileges as a result of his position of influence, and that he felt a little ill at ease about it.

How do I know that? Because, thank goodness, I do know how to read. And Dobson plainly was not talking about some underhanded, undercover effort to sneak an anti-abortion vote on the high court because the very first thing he says is "when you know what I know" about Harriet Miers, you will support her, too. In other words, he had early information about Miers' background that would soon become available to all. Namely that she was a loyal friend to the president, a member of an evangelical Christian church, and had shown spunk and determination in her advancement past the gender-based glass ceiling. Based on that background briefing — not on Karl "Rasputin" Rove's high sign — Dobson had determined that she was a candidate for the court that he as a conservative could support.

Imagine that.

The second example of media folly requires less explanation, but it is just so typical of how the self-important press has twisted its role of "public watchdog" into "yapping puppy" that it needs to be mentioned.

This one concerns the president's conversation via satellite hookup Thursday with 10 soldiers from the Army's 10th Infantry Division stationed in Iraq. The president was using the opportunity to publicize the constitutional referendum in Iraq as well as to boost the morale of the troops.

The conversation itself got almost no attention from the media, but when it turned out that a White House staffer had prepped the 10 soldiers on how the conversation with the president might go, it was seen by CNN, FOX and MSNBC as one more chance to portray President Bush as a doddering fool.

Never mind the fact that presidential meetings with the public have always been subject to advance preparation. Never mind that the advance preparation amounted to little more than figuring out which soldier would answer which type of question. Never mind that even a Time magazine reporter admitted that such preparations are not unusual. It was still, as this same reporter said, a chance to bolster "the perception that this administration relies too much on spin."

Wait just a doggone minute! Who relies too much on spin? The president? How about the hordes of reporters who manufacture controversy in order to ensure that they will get a guest spot on "Hannity and Colmes" or "Hardball"?

It's almost enough to make you turn in your press pass and start "selling postcards of the hanging," as Bob Dylan put it in his masterpiece song about the collapse of civilization in "Desolation Row." But to paraphrase another poet, John Donne, "Don't ask for whom the noose falls; it falls for thee."

Maybe Oscar Wilde said it best, as he often did:

"In old days men had the rack. Now they have the press. That is an improvement certainly. But still it is very bad, and wrong, and demoralising. Somebody — was it Burke? — called journalism the fourth estate. That was true at the time, no doubt. But at the present moment it really is the only estate. It has eaten up the other three. The Lords Temporal say nothing, the Lords Spiritual have nothing to say, and the House of Commons has nothing to say and says it. We are dominated by Journalism."

What is scary is that Wilde made that remark more than 100 years ago. Maybe the problem we are facing today is not so new after all. But I still think if we want to avoid a bad end, we might consider taking down the noose and turning it into a lasso to rein in a reckless press.

LIONS AND TIGERS AND MIERS, OH MY!

October 23, 2005

Maybe this column has become too gloomy.

Is that possible? I don't know what got me so worried about the future of our country, Western society and the Seahawks, but it seems like lately every time I sit down intending to entertain my readers with a witty piece of fluff about doing laundry or raking leaves, some national crisis intervenes. Hurricane Katrina. Illegal immigration. Harriet Miers.

Hold on there. Harriet Miers?

Aunt Harriet?

Are you kidding?

Is this woman really a danger to our republic? Other than the damage she could do if she becomes a fashion trendsetter, I mean.

Well if you believe George Will, she is. George is the conservative commentator you've been reading on the Opinion page of the Inter Lake for most of the last 20 years. He is something of a trendsetter himself. Since the day he first wore a bow tie on national TV when he was a young sprite, at least two other people have donned the sporty symmetrical triangles on their collar. Neither has ever been heard from again, but I gather Tucker Carlson on MSNBC doesn't think he will share their fate.

But that is for another column.

For this column, I want to focus not on Will's wardrobe, but on his war paint. Read his histrionic column about the nomination of Ms. Miers on Page D2 now, and then return here for a reality check.

All right, let's start with the first paragraph: Mr. Will describes "the perfect perversity" of the Miers nomination and says that it "discredits, and even degrades, all who toil at justifying it."

My goodness, didn't we wake up on the wrong side of the royal bed this morning!

Will sets up a number of straw men and then knocks them down by huffing and puffing like the big bad wolf. It seems that everyone who supports the Miers nomination is doing so for selfish reason or for stupid ones. Only Mr. Will and his Ivy-League educated cronies know what is good for the rest of us.

Well, pardon my spittoon.

You will notice, if you read George's column carefully, that he never actually explains why Miers is unqualified to serve on the bench, merely establishes through polemic that he loves women, disdains analysis, and sees himself as a "thoughtful conservative" as opposed to Neanderthalers like George Bush.

It turns out that, according to Will, "Thoughtful conservatives' highest aim is not to achieve this or that particular outcome concerning this or that controversy. Rather, their aim for the Supreme Court is to replace semi-legislative reasoning with genuine constitutional reasoning about the Constitution's meaning as derived from close consideration of its text and structure."

Now, my rhetorical question for Mr. Will is this: Just what exactly have you learned about Harriet Miers that makes you sure she is incapable of "genuine constitutional reasoning about the Constitution's meaning"? Why are you so convinced that she is incapable of "close consideration of its text and structure"?

Elsewhere in your column, you demean those who laud her "for her ability to analyze and strategize" and "to get all the facts together."

But aren't those just the qualities you would want in someone who is doing a "close consideration" of the text of the Constitution?

Mr. Will may not think he is a sexist, and he lamely points to his admiration for Margaret Thatcher ("some of my best friends are women") but the fact of the matter is that George Will provides no evidence from Miers' background, her career in the law, or her public service that she is not qualified and capable. He just assumes so, and if that is not sexist, it is certainly prejudicial.

Is it not just possible that the person most likely to accomplish a return to the original intent of the Constitution is someone who has not been co-opted by the system of pontificating academics and bench-sitters who Will so obviously admires?

The Constitution, in case you have not read it recently, is one of the most plain-spoken, straightforward documents ever to be produced in service of any political venture. I personally would feel more comfortable turning it over to anybody down at the Grange hall for safekeeping than to any number of Harvard lawyers.

What worries me is not Aunt Harriet staring at the simple words of, say, the Second Amendment and seeing them for what they are, but some pot-bellied good ol' boy of the legal profession who has learned to obfuscate and foggify by seeing everything through a prism of 200 years of befuddled precedent.

You can't have it both ways. If you want the Constitution to be interpreted the way it was originally intended, then you are much better off hiring someone for the job who will look at the original document, and not the intervening opinions of those who tainted the Founders' vision with what Will calls "semi-legislative reasoning."

Mr. Will is right about one thing. We would be better off with a judge on the Supreme Court who cared about the Constitution more than anything. But what he doesn't know is whether Harriet Miers can be that judge.

And unless he stops yelling long enough to hear what she has to say at the Senate Judiciary Committee hearings, he will never find out.

'WITH ALL DUE RESPECT?' DOH!

November 6, 2005

Does anyone really think that television reporters make any effort to keep themselves out of the story?

Maybe that's true at the local level, but as soon as you give reporters a 24-hour-a-day venue for them to hear themselves talk, it's as if the newsroom turned into that late-night coffee shop in "Friends."

Hour after hour on cable news, we are subjected to an endless combination of news reporters and so-called anchors sitting on the couch "chatting" with each other just like Rachel and Phoebe about what a news story "really" means and about who is sleeping with whom and generally voicing their uninformed opinions about matters both big and small.

If a reporter does a story about an issue, then by God she must have an opinion about it, and by God the public won't rest until they find out what she "really" thinks. And if there is an anchor at the couch, then by God he must know more than the reporter, but "that" is another story.

I think this is called the danger of overexposure. Probably everyone in the world really does have an opinion about everything, but we were much better off when we didn't have to hear them. These television reporters have absolutely no credibility left. They are so smug and so self-important that it really doesn't matter if they are liberal or conservative. Some unintended bias is only natural. But what makes these reporters insufferable is that they really "think" that "what they think" matters. They have forgotten that as reporters they are meant to convey other people's stories, not to become the story themselves.

All this would be slightly amusing — another instance of the endless vanity of man — were it not for the huge power that the cable news companies wield in shaping public opinion. Were that power simply used in informing the public of the various sides of complicated issues, then it must be seen as a public service.

But if reporters become advocates for a particular point of view, then they are doing no one any good, except their own egos. These reporters occupy a position of trust — or should — and they ought to be smart enough to keep their mouths shut when they are not doing what they were hired to do — report.

Except they really were hired to be good looking and stylish, weren't they? Or to have a little edge? Or because they were a little bit lippy? And irreverent? And maybe just a wee bit smarter than the rest of us?

All right, maybe not smarter. But they sure act like they think they are.

Which brings us to my latest candidate for Pseudo-Journalist of the Year — CNN's Kyra Phillips, the host of "Live From" on CNN.

I was home minding my own business having a late lunch one day last week when I had the misfortune of seeing what one Internet blogger called the "completely bizarre heated exchange" between Phillips and Sen. Chuck Grassley of Iowa.

Seems that Grassley had agreed to appear on the show to discuss the failed nomination of Harriet Miers to the Supreme Court, but when he got on the air, Phillips was in the midst of an emotional meltdown worrying about those rich American tourists stranded in Cancun following Hurricane Wanda.

It got her "thinking" about what the federal government could be doing for all those people. Then she heard from President Bush speaking live in Pompano Beach, Fla., where Wanda had gone after it left Mexico. He was explaining to the people of Florida that "the federal government, working with the state and local governments, [is] responding as best as we possibly can."

That apparently was more than Phillips could take. She told Sen. Grassley that their conversation about Harriet Miers could wait. She had something she wanted to say, and by God she was going to say it.

"I thought we learned a lot of lessons from Katrina," said Ms. Phillips. "DOD [the Department of Defense] had to step in and help out. Things got done. Now we're seeing problems here in Florida. We're seeing problems with Americans stuck in Mexico.... Do we need DOD? Do we need to call in DOD and get military help here [in Florida]? Because there are people that don't have water, don't have power, don't have ice, and they're getting frustrated."

Oh me, oh my. No ice! What is a hurricane victim to do?

Apparently, according to Phillips, the best thing to do under those circumstances is to declare martial law and send in the tanks — I mean the tanks that have been specially equipped with ice-makers, of course.

Sen. Grassley hurriedly tried to bring her up to speed on the history of the United States and why the military is excluded from a direct role in civilian affairs, except in dire emergency, and even that under specific circumstances, but Phillips was having none of it.

Grassley explained there is an ongoing "major discussion" in Congress about "the extent to which we ought to repeal some laws that go back to Reconstruction that limit what the military can do domestically" so that the military could be the lead agency in a natural disaster. Grassley further explained that "never before" would Congress have even considered allowing the military to step in and take an active role on American soil, but because of the uproar over FEMA's shortcomings in Katrina, it was being discussed.

Phillips was livid: "Why is it just being discussed though? We're bringing live shots day in and day out of these people desperate for water and ..."

Grassley cut her off before she could again terrify the American public with the idea of an ice shortage, and tried to explain to her the importance of the so-called "Posse Comitatus Act," the law which greatly restricts use of the military for law enforcement in the United States.

"Oh, but sir, sir, we saw Gen. Honore come in there to Canal Street [in New Orleans] and bring food and water and tell people to put down their guns. And finally we saw people off the streets and they stopped dying on the sidewalks in New Orleans. Now, you know, how long do we have to wait in disgust until we start seeing people dying in Florida? All due respect, sir."

Well, just a doggone minute. That was NO due respect. That was shameless pandering, and hysterical preaching, and by the way just how many people ARE dying on the streets of Florida anyway? And does Ms. Phillips really not understand the difference between a normal hurricane and what happened in New Orleans? Is Ms. Phillips so tightly wrapped inside her stiffly coiffed head that she can't get any oxygen? IS SHE HALLUCINATING?

I nearly called 911 to get some emergency assistance for Ms. Phillips, but before I could pick up the phone, I saw that Sen. Grassley was heroically trying to give Phillips a reality transfusion to bring her down from her self-induced panic attack.

The increasingly frustrated Grassley tried to explain to her the difference between the National Guard and the U.S. Army, and for a moment it looked like Phillips was going to be OK. She seemed to vaguely grasp the notion that Gov. Jeb Bush had the power to call in the National Guard whenever he wanted to, but then she started on another emotional meltdown. Apparently being in Command Central at CNN was too much for her. Day in and day out, she had to watch these disturbing images of real Americans who were experiencing REAL LIFE! The horror! The horror!

"Sir, I don't know if you can see these live pictures — not the live pictures right now — but these are, this is videotape from throughout the day today and yesterday and the day — I mean, long lines for gasoline, people waiting in line for water, waiting in line for ice. People arguing, shouting...

"This just — you would think we would learn so many lessons from Katrina, and it seems like we're seeing this all over again. Obviously, or I don't know, maybe the scale is like what we've seen in some ways in Louisiana. But it's happening. It's happening before our eyes and these people need help."

At this point, you had to be really proud of old Chuck Grassley for not screaming at Phillips, "Kyra, there is only one person around here who needs help, AND IT'S YOU!"

Instead, he did the equivalent of a quick slap to the face to try to bring her out of her hysterical panic: "I'm going to stop this, because there's no sense in me having a confrontation with you... and I'm not going to make public policy on television."

The senator should have made his exit right then and there, because he had made his point, and it was a beauty, but unfortunately the interview stretched on for a couple more minutes while Grassley searched in vain for a way to get Phillips to understand why it would be illegal to send American troops into Mexico to help those rich tourists stranded on the beach down there in Cancun.

Afterwards, Grassley apparently retreated to the relative sanity of Capitol Hill and left Kyra Phillips in the middle of her private hell at Command Central, where CNN was busy providing "videotape and live shots of a lot of desperate people... not getting water and ice and resources."

For good measure, at the end of the segment, just to demonstrate that she had learned nothing by talking to her guest, she asked the following inane questions:

"Does the state of Florida need the National Guard? Does DOD need to step in? Is military help necessary? We saw what happened during Katrina and after Katrina there in New Orleans and parts of Mississippi and Alabama, where the military came in and got things done. Is that something that needs to happen in this area? That's a question that remains."

One other question that remains is this: How long will the American public tolerate the pandering, preening twaddle that passes for journalism on the cable news networks? It's not just Kyra Phillips, and it's not just CNN. The same kind of whiny, policy-steering lunkheads can be found on FOX and MSNBC.

Bottom line: If they want to determine national policy, let them do what all the other self-important fools do — run for Congress (with all due respect to Sen. Grassley, of course!).

CHEWING ON CHENEY'S ANKLES

February 19, 2006

If we needed evidence that there is a total disconnect — a short circuit — between what happens in Washington, D.C., and what happens in the rest of America, we certainly got it last week.

The vice president of the United States shot a friend of his, a 78-year-old man, in the face and shoulder with birdshot. They were hunting quail, and the friend — Harry Whittington — made the mistake of retrieving a bird without announcing where he was. Then Vice President Cheney made the mistake of shooting him while following a covey of quail with his 28-gauge shotgun.

You know all this.

It's what is called an accident.

You also know that after the shooting was announced, reporters in Washington, D.C., were up in arms, demanding to know why they weren't informed of the story more quickly, and why the story first appeared in the Corpus Christi Caller-Times. One reporter even had the temerity to ask, "Has [the vice president] offered his resignation?"

That is what is called a lynch mob.

I just shake my head in absolute befuddlement that our country has come to the point where our main source of amusement is inflicting pain and humiliation on others, especially if they are "public figures."

But perhaps I should not be surprised. This is, after all, the same species that gave us human sacrifice and "The Jerry Springer Show," so inflicting pain on our fellow humans may be second nature for us.

Of course, some people may not think Dick Cheney is human. I get the feeling that the pack of bloodthirsty hounds in the White House press room thinks he is an old buck, and that if they run him hard enough he will tire and falter and they will bring him down by biting at his ankles.

Meantime, life outside the press room goes on as normal. Police do their investigations. Doctors do their tests. The patient works on his recovery. Both the shooter and the man shot and their families pray together and singly. They pray for healing, but they also pray for patience.

Yes, patience. That is what they all need now as a trying, hard personal time is turned into a public spectacle.

Certainly, everyone understands the need for an investigation by the proper authorities whenever a shooting occurs. There is nothing wrong with expecting that the vice president should not get special treatment because of his office.

But there is something wrong with expecting the vice president not to be afforded the same courtesies that we would all expect if we were in the same circumstances. He should certainly be allowed the same privacy to compose himself at a time of great sadness and stress that we would want. And he certainly should not be demonized as a bad person because of an accident.

But some people don't get it.

Starting with the Washington press corps, and then followed by Democratic pundits and politicians and even a few Republican ones, it became a kind of parlor game last week to construct fantastic conspiracy theories out of the substance of rumor and innuendo. Cheney and Whittington, it was noted, were hunting with women who were "not their wives." Drinking had taken place, and it was very possible the vice president was "impaired," even though he only had one beer at lunch several hours earlier. There may not have been a "delay" in getting the story out so much as a "cover-up."

All week long, the allegations (or whispers) from the self-important poobahs of the Potomac grew more and more absurd, until finally you just wanted to vomit up all the poison that you had ingested and get clean of it somehow.

But perhaps somewhere in all this ugliness there is a lesson we can learn. Perhaps the fact that this was a hunting accident provides a metaphor which can help us to understand our own human foibles better.

In that spirit, it is interesting to note that the concept of "sin" refers to "missing the mark" in the sense of an archer falling short of a target. To sin is therefore to be human, to err, to fall short of perfection. It is indeed a universal condition which nonetheless many think they can cloak over in themselves.

Maybe it is the same in this modern-day parable of the shooter and the shot. It seems that Dick Cheney missed his target, fell short of his intention of doing the right thing, just as the sinner so often cannot live up to his good intentions.

Christ warned us, "He that is without sin let him cast the first stone," against the sinner, but judging by the number of people throwing stones at Dick Cheney, that same sense of humility and forgiveness is in short supply when you change the message to "He that has never made a mistake, let him cast the first stone."

Perhaps I'm in a better position than the rest of you to identify with the vice president in this situation since I too shot a friend in a hunting accident. It was when I was about 13 years old, at a time when my best friend and I used to like to take BB guns and pellet guns into the woods to shoot at sparrows and other small birds.

I was walking behind my friend in the brush when he released a branch that hit my arm and caused me to pull the trigger on the gun I was carrying. Fortunately it was only a pellet gun, but through my own carelessness in not engaging the safety, I shot my best friend in the base of the skull. He cried out and stopped in his tracks and for the longest time I thought I had killed him. Fortunately, the CO_2 cartridge that powered the pellet gun was nowhere near as powerful as gun powder, and my friend survived my stupidity with no more than an ugly raised red welt at the base of his hairline, though at first we thought it was a bullet hole.

You probably can't imagine the horrible feeling you get when you do something so incredibly stupid and put another person's life at risk by shooting them accidentally.

In my case, the risk was minimal. In Cheney's case it was extreme. But in both cases, we did what human beings often do — we made mistakes, felt horrible about it, and tried to do what was right afterwards.

"He that has never made a mistake, let him cast the first stone."

MORE MAINSTREAM MEDIA MADNESS

March 26, 2006

Leave it to the mainstream media.

Whenever I despair that I may not be able to think of a topic for the next week's column, I can always count on some reporter in Washington, D.C., or New York to do something boneheaded.

This week, I got lucky. The mainstream media went into a near-fatal frenzy of arrogance. It was like the march of the liberal lemmings into the Sarcastic Sea. Everywhere I turned there was one more example of self-important big city know-it-alls exercising their god-given right to look down their noses at the rest of us. And this doesn't even count the nightly sniveling of the sophomoric Keith Olbermann on MSNBC.

So for at least the next two weeks, I'm going to take a look at some representatives of the mainstream media who apparently think the main stream is veering ever leftward, and that they are obliged to enlighten us about the dangers of the Neanderthal right.

First up is Jennifer Loven, who most of you have never heard of. I too had never heard of her until last week when someone sent me an article she wrote for the Associated Press called "Bush Using Straw-Man Arguments in Speeches."

At first I thought it was a "news analysis" or opinion piece, but it turns out that it was supposed to be a straight news story, the news apparently being that Jennifer Loven looked up from her navel long enough to notice that President Bush understands and uses a common tool of rhetoric called the "straw man" argument.

Here is how her story starts out:

> "Some look at the challenges in Iraq and conclude that the war is lost and not worth another dime or another day," President Bush said recently.
>
> Another time he said, "Some say that if you're Muslim you can't be free."
>
> "There are some really decent people," the president said earlier this year, "who believe that the federal government ought to be the decider of health care ... for all people."
>
> Of course, hardly anyone in mainstream political debate has made such assertions.

Loven then goes on to imply that Bush is somehow being sneaky by using "straw-man arguments" in his ongoing dialogue with the public about his policies. A "straw man" argument, in case you don't remember Philosophy 101 — is when you create a weak argument, one that is easy to refute, and attribute that position to your opponent, just about the time you knock it down.

Loven decided it was big news that she had discovered this "straw man" device being used by President Bush in his speeches, so she wrote an entire "news" story about her "objective" interpretation of Bush's rhetoric.

Of course, it wouldn't be appropriate to say the president is a "lying sneak" — which is what she apparently believes to be "objective" truth — so she dressed up the story by using two professors to buttress her argument that the president is engaging in what one of the professors — Wayne Fields of Washington University in St. Louis — calls "a bizarre kind of double talk."

Fields then goes on to say, "It's such a phenomenal hole in the national debate that you can have arguments with nonexistent people. All politicians try to get away with this to a certain extent. What's striking here is how much this administration rests on a foundation of this kind of stuff."

Huh? What say? The entire Bush administration rests on a foundation of straw-man arguments because the president on occasion uses the rhetorical device of beginning a sentence with "some"?

There are two fundamental problems with this approach to reporting the news. First, it is analysis, not news. Second, it is wrong.

The reporter has no business writing this kind of story in the first place. If she is going to be an objective reporter, she is there to tell what happened and not to tell us what we are supposed to think about what happened. And if she is going to engage in analysis, she had better make sure it is so labeled.

But even more importantly, if she is going to "educate" us with her thoughtful analysis, she had better at least be right. The only thing worse than a pompous know-it-all is a pompous fool, and Loven is vying for the title. After all, the argument she makes in her "story" is based on the unproved premise that Bush has used this particular rhetorical device more than other politicians. She offers no statistical analysis to back this up, just anecdotal evidence.

But significantly, in the examples cited by Loven, the president is not refuting a weaker argument at all, but a stronger argument, so it is not a straw man in any case.

Take the line about Iraq, for instance. Yes, there are those who say we should withdraw from Iraq on a timetable, rather than immediately, but their position has been noted and countered, not ignored. The president has repeatedly explained why he doesn't think an announced timetable for withdrawal is appropriate.

But that certainly doesn't mean he should avoid the more radical arguments of the anti-Bush caucus in Congress such as Rep. John Murtha. Indeed, Murtha's arguments are much more forceful than those of the "timetable" advocates, and thus demand a response. Back on Nov. 17, 2005, Murtha threw down the gauntlet and told the president "the emerging government [in Iraq] must be put on notice that the United States will immediately redeploy."

That is another way of saying "not ... another dime or another day." So the president was not mis-stating or overstating his opponent's argument. Rather than ignore Murtha and marginalize him by saying he is out of the mainstream, the president responded to his criticisms, as he should. John Murtha is no straw man, and he must be taken seriously. The president was wise to do so.

The same is true for those who have raised the other arguments that Bush responded to with the statements quoted in Loven's story. The problem for Loven isn't the argument; it's George Bush. She just doesn't like him.

You don't have to take my word for it. Do a Google search of her name, and you will discover that she has a history of writing stories that are slanted against the president. In another masterpiece of unacknowledged analysis, for instance, Loven wrote "President Bush Twists Kerry's Words on Iraq" in September 2004. That was about the same time when Dan Rather was not just "twisting" but actually inventing from whole cloth President Bush's military records.

It is of particular concern to me that Loven writes for the Associated Press, which of course is the main source of national news in the Inter Lake, but I'm not going to let it ruin my day. Despite her abysmal example, I remain confident that AP reporters in general understand their responsibility for fairness and strive to meet it.

(Author's Note: Please excuse the preceding paragraph, which was my attempt at extending an olive branch to the Associated Press — an olive branch which they proved unworthy of receiving in subsequent years.)

REPORTING, OPINIONS
AND 'JUST PLAIN RUDE'

April 2, 2006

Last week's column on the mainstream media elicited many responses, most of which agreed with me that East Coast reporters have a tendency to skew the news with their own left-leaning viewpoints.

A few people chided me for being a member of the mainstream media myself.

Of course, I do consider the Daily Inter Lake to be part of the mainstream media in Northwest Montana, and we need to be scrutinized by our local readers the same way I am attempting to scrutinize certain national voices. I welcome that scrutiny and the opportunity to talk to our readers about their concerns regarding coverage of particular stories. We understand that we are a community newspaper, and have an obligation to reflect the community in certain fundamental ways.

There is nothing wrong with being mainstream; the problem is when the mainstream media becomes arrogant and boastful, trying to impose its views on everyone else instead of acting as a conduit for all viewpoints.

I'm not sure how anyone could disagree, although a few people tried to get the mainstream media off the hook by pointing out that I myself was expressing an opinion.

That's certainly true, but with a significant difference — I am not a reporter. As a columnist, it is my job to have an opinion. The same thing applies in my role as an editorial writer when I am expressing the opinion of the Inter Lake's editorial board. And to be fair, I enjoy reading well-argued opinions very much because they show me new ways to think about issues and can be quite entertaining as well. So I am not proposing doing away with opinion.

But reporters have an obligation to maintain an objective approach to the stories they cover. That's not to say they don't have opinions, but if they are going to have credibility as reporters, they need to keep those opinions out of their stories. Instead, we've grown used to reporters becoming talking heads on television, where they speculate incessantly about the meaning of stories or the outcome of stories or the virtue of the people they write about.

And that means those reporters have not the slightest fig leaf of objectivity to cover the very public part they play in the national debate. That of course has led to a loss of credibility not just for them, but for the national media as a whole, and by extension all the media.

As a rule, opinion writers should limit their opinions to matters that they don't also cover as reporters. Reporters should limit their reporting to the facts and to the opinions of others. In the past, reporters typically understood this distinction, and made an effort to keep the line clear.

But that has not always been the case. Consider, for instance, the case of Helen Thomas, the "dean" of the White House press corps.

She was the top Washington reporter for UPI for many years, and loved to insert herself and her opinions into the stories she wrote, but now she is an avowedly left-wing columnist. That gets her off the hook for having opinions, but it doesn't justify her disrespectful performance a few weeks ago during President Bush's March 21 press conference.

Rather than asking a question of the president to elicit information, Thomas asked a question for the purpose of grandstanding and making a political point. Don't forget this is the woman who called George W. Bush "the worst president ever," so we have no reason to expect objectivity.

But I still don't understand where a political disagreement gives someone the right to be just plain rude. Unfortunately, Thomas isn't just rude, she is gleefully rude, and in this case she accused the president of going to war with Iraq for secret reasons and then of lying to the American public about why we went to war.

Here's her question, in part:

"Mr. President, your decision to invade Iraq has caused the deaths of thousands of Americans and Iraqis, wounds of Americans and Iraqis for a lifetime. Every reason given, publicly at least, has turned out not to be true. My question is, why did you really want to go to war?"

The president, being a gentlemen, did not accuse Thomas of impersonating a journalist, but instead responded firmly but graciously to her canard. After first taking exception to her premise that he "wanted war," he assured the American people that he had learned the lessons of September 11 and that no American president could ever again take the chance of doing nothing while those abroad are plotting attacks against us.

He also reiterated that Saddam had the chance to avoid attack by disarming and disclosing the nature of his weapons programs under U.N. Resolution 1441. "And when he chose to deny inspectors, when he chose not to disclose, then I had the difficult decision to make to remove him."

This notion bothers Thomas and other Bush's critics because stockpiles of weapons of mass destruction were never found, but nonetheless the United Nations had laid down the law with Saddam and he chose to play chicken with the arms inspectors instead of coming clean. President Bush made sure Saddam lost that game of chicken by acting swiftly and decisively.

Of course, nothing the president said really interested Ms. Thomas. She wasn't at the press conference for the purpose of interviewing the president; she was there to embarrass him. I'm sure she doesn't get her marching orders from the Democratic Party, but she seems to know the parade route by heart.

Let's face it. In the strictly partisan struggle which has befallen our nation, facts are ultimately less important than talking points. The spin machines are waiting in the wings to twist everything for maximum political advantage, such as claiming that what the president said was a lie. Thomas was just helping matters along by starting with the premise that President Bush, like Cretans, is always a liar.

But maybe that is the premise of all Democrats, or at least the vocal ones. A reader, for instance, wrote to me to complain that the president was distorting history when he talked about Saddam's response to Resolution 1441. Here is the president's comment again:

"And when he chose to deny inspectors, when he chose not to disclose, then I had the difficult decision to make to remove him."

The reader was sure the president was lying.

"That's not what happened," he wrote. "We got the resolution passed. Saddam called our bluff and allowed the inspectors in. President Bush pressed ahead with the invasion. Saddam did not deny inspectors — just ask U.N. inspector Hans Blitz — at the time of the invasion he said the inspections were working, and that Saddam did not have WMDs."

No one can disagree with the notion that Saddam did not have WMDs at the time of the invasion, but that does not mean he was in compliance with 1441. Let's look at the facts.

Former chief U.S. weapons inspector David Kay reported to Congress on Jan. 28, 2004: "In my judgment, based on the work that has been done to this point of the Iraq Survey Group, and in fact, [as] I reported to you in October, Iraq was in clear violation of the terms of Resolution 1441."

In that October 2003 report, Kay had said, "We have discovered dozens of WMD-related program activities and significant amounts of equipment that Iraq concealed from the United Nations during the inspections that began in late 2002."

The report makes very interesting reading for anyone who thinks Saddam was a misunderstood pacifist during the stretches when he wasn't ordering mass murders of Iraqi civilians — or for anyone who insists that "Bush lied, so people died."

Perhaps Helen Thomas could even look it over before she embarrasses herself in public again. But you know that won't happen. She enjoys the spotlight too much.

'OUR CRACK TEAM OF EXPERTS ASSURES US …'

April 30, 2006

How would you like to see this headline in tomorrow's newspaper: "Inter Lake hires team of doctors and scientists to inspect local restaurants."

I can assure you that you won't ever see such a headline, but one reader recently suggested he thought that's just what we should be doing. The reader was unhappy with a story we did about the county health department's inspection of a local restaurant. In his guest opinion, he argued that the inspection was poorly done and that the Inter Lake should have known it was poorly done.

The implication was that a newspaper like the Inter Lake ought not to report anything which it does not independently verify as true.

This would elevate the status of the Inter Lake to something like the ancient Oracle at Delphi, which would be nice. People would know they could open our pages to find out everything from where they should eat lunch (Bob's Pizza Shop, 56th and Wabasha) to whether or not there are weapons of mass destruction in countries of dubious distinction (dang, that one would have come in handy a few years ago).

This unfortunately would severely tax our resources (eight news reporters, five editors, three photographers, two news assistants, and three sports reporters or editors). To start with we would need a bureau in every major city in the world. While some of the photographers would probably start packing their bags tomorrow, a few more sedentary souls in the newsroom would probably complain about the change of school districts for their kids (where is Dubai again?).

But of course, just having a reporter on hand to check the accuracy of what we are told would not be enough in many cases. We would also need to hire a staff of experts on everything from DNA to virtual reality (Dr. Henry Lee meet Paris Hilton — oh wait, she is our expert on bad judgment). Before we reported the latest crash-test results on motor vehicles, for instance, we would need to spend millions of dollars on cars, trucks, crash-test dummies, a test facility, and crash-test smarties (the engineers who could tell us what it all meant).

Or maybe, just maybe, we can keep doing it the way we do it now, which is to find stories about interesting people doing interesting things and tell you about them. Of course, some of what people do that is interesting is not particularly pleasant. War, for instance, and murder investigations, for another — and yes, even restaurant inspections.

Some of what we report will be inaccurate, occasionally because we make a mistake, but far more frequently because we are reporting stuff that is happening now, right now, every day, up to and beyond deadline. It means today's theory may be tomorrow's trash. Information is slippery stuff, and though we follow standard procedures to keep it as accurate as possible, we also know — and expect our readers to know — that every "opinion" in the newspaper is subject to doubt, even the official ones of police authorities or bureaucrats.

Most of those people are highly qualified professionals, who take every precaution to make sure they know all the facts before they comment in the newspaper, but "facts" are slippery things, too. As the reader who didn't like our restaurant inspection story pointed out, a "mouse turd" may just be a leaf of Chinese tea. The question is, do you want to take the Inter Lake's word for it or the word of the people who are paid to do the inspections?

I suppose there is a certain amount of glamor in reporters poking through garbage cans looking for evidence of crimes, and certainly reporters are called upon regularly to ferret out information from government and public sources. But there is a limit to how much investigative journalism makes sense, or should even be tolerated.

After all, the underlying premise of investigative journalism is that if you pick up enough rocks, you will eventually find something disgusting under one of them. The trouble is that if you spend too much time looking at the "dirt" under the rocks you just might miss the world under the "dirt." Turns out there is a whole planet out there, full of interesting stories that don't need to be investigated; they just need to be told.

To me, that's the fundamental mission of journalism — to make a record of the world we live in day by day. The word journalism in fact comes from the Latin word diurnalis, and literally suggests the intent of keeping a daily record.

That task, as you might well expect, is formidable. If done well, it leaves little time for "muckraking," as investigative journalism was once known. And besides, "muckraking" can be dangerous when it is done with an agenda. Sometimes, "truth seeking" reporters approach stories with a sanctimoniousness that makes you think they should come to work in white robes.

Here at the Inter Lake, you will not see too much of that, I hope.

As much as possible, we want to report the news, not make it. We will do that by covering your friends and neighbors, your cities and neighborhoods, your schools and your legislators. From time to time, we will even cover a restaurant inspection if it rises to the level of general interest.

When that happens, we hope you will judge us not by what the inspector from the health department said, but by how well we told the story. Did we make clear what the importance of the inspection was? Did we tell both sides of the story, allowing a chance for rebuttal if warranted? Did we explain the process used in the inspection? Did we follow up so that our readers were informed when the restaurant got an excellent rating at its next inspection?

I think if you go back you will see that we did all those things.

The Inter Lake, you see, has no stake in whether or not a particular restaurant passes its health department inspection or not. But the public does have a stake in knowing what the health department is doing on its behalf. In this case, the newspaper's role was simply to pass along to the public what county officials were doing as employees of the taxpayers. If the taxpayers don't like it, then they should do something about it.

But it's not up to the newspaper to withhold the story from the public, and it's certainly not up to us to do our own independent inspection of the restaurant's kitchen. That would go well beyond the function of the newspaper as a place to get information, and turn us into outright busybodies.

I'm perfectly willing to let the national media have the corner on that market.

AND NOW FOR A FEW DISSENTING OPINIONS

June 25, 2006

You may have noticed a new ad running in the Inter Lake the past few days promoting this column.

It features an unfortunately large picture of yours truly and some glowing quotes from readers. In order to supply the quotes, I needed to scour through several hundred e-mails I've received in recent months.

Fortunately, lots of them had kind things to say about me and this column, for which I am grateful. But just in case anyone thought I might get a swelled head as a result of being complimented, I wanted to take a few minutes this week to acknowledge not those who cheer me, but those who chide me.

One of my favorites took several hundreds words to tar and feather me as a fascist toady of "King George," but then ended with the always popular debating technique of insulting my appearance: "If you are going to plaster your picture all over a public forum," said this reader from east of the mountains, "please have the decency to get a nose-job."

Fortunately, my mother braced me for such thoughtful analysis when I was 5 year old, teaching me to say in response:

"As a beauty I'm not a great star,
There are others more handsome by far,
But my face, I don't mind it,
Because I'm behind it —
'Tis the folks in the front that I jar."

So there! Mother always knows best.

And while we are on the face, let's move from the nose to the I's:

A certain letter-writer who shall remain nameless recently took the author of this column to task for using the first-person pronoun too often. Admittedly, it is not easy for the person who writes this column (and you all know who he is) to avoid the first-person pronoun insofar as this is a personal column, but one can see now that the challenge is worth it. Alas, even if the author were entirely eyeless like Samson in Gaza, he would still have to pray for the strength to say "I" on occasion — as in "I apologize."

Of course, most people who are unhappy with me don't resort to personal attacks (or personal pronoun attacks, for that matter). Instead, they stick to debating the actual points of my columns, as the lady in the hospitality industry who wrote to call me "an egotistical, arrogant jerk" and told me I should brush up on my reading of the New Testament. She might want to consider a brush-up on her Superhost training.

But clearly the most entertaining of the responses I've gotten from around the world to my column have come from my good friend (note gentle sarcasm) Mike from Seattle, a former Montanan who apparently grew up in Bozeman.

In one of his early letters, he started out by accusing me satirically of being one of those "wise Montanans" who doesn't like "big city know-it-alls," and then proceeded in letter after letter to demonstrate why that is so.

Here are some of his choice epithets for me: "dreadfully pedestrian writer," "mean little SOB," "kind of wacky." But he wasn't content to lash out at me alone; he decided to shoot for bigger game, so he tied me up with the "Christian right" and opened fire:

"We ... find you guys a little scary — we suspect you'd string us all up if you had the energy or smarts to figure out how to do it... It's all so damn dreary, fearful and joyless; I guess the promise of heaven is about the only way to drag yourself through the day."

And although he isn't a physician, he decided to play one for my benefit, diagnosing me as suffering from severe depression because I often write about problems in our society with a sense of pessimism: "Talk to your physician, it's very treatable. I mean this as someone who truly cares about helping others."

Thank goodness for "big city secular liberals," as he calls himself and his friends. If it wasn't for their caring concern and love for me, I would still not know that my "dark, dark, nihilistic, depressing description of the world is really a textbook example of depressed thinking... It's a simple chemical imbalance and absolutely nothing to be ashamed of."

And I thought I was just being cute... but then how do I explain the nose?

LOYALTY YES, BUT TO WHAT?

July 9, 2006

Loyalty is generally considered a virtue.
Disloyalty is generally considered a vice.
But one must sometimes choose between conflicting loyalties, and one's choices on such occasions go a long way toward defining a person's character.

For instance, a person might have a great love for his or her country, and yet have a greater love for God. If such people hold in their heart a religious belief that war is immoral, then they are granted a conscientious objector status and exempted from combat duty.

Are these people disloyal to the United States? Not at all, but they had to choose between two loyalties and decide which would be paramount. By choosing God over country, they have declared who they are.

In the famous Victor Hugo novel "Les Miserables," another kind of choice is posed. Jean Valjean steals a loaf of bread to feed his starving family. He is a good man who respects the law, but his loyalty to his family prevails. This is the first of many choices Valjean makes, each of which reveals the complexity of his character. Sometimes his loyalty to principle leads him into error, sometimes to salvation.

So it is with all of us.

Thus, we are perhaps wrong to consider loyalty in itself a virtue. It is instead a test of virtue. We are all loyal by nature to something — family, country, god, self — and usually to many things. How we sort these loyalties out provides a kind of snapshot of the soul. That which we are loyal to, and that which we betray — what better way to take the estimation of a man?

I broach this philosophical matter at the start of my weekly column because I am about to be disloyal — to my profession.

It seems that many journalists have decided — based partly on expediency and no doubt partly on altruism — that they have the right to print anything, and especially anything which involves the government.

While this principle works well in general, it should not — in my opinion — be universally applied. There are frequently matters discussed in the corridors of power which should not be aired publicly, and for a variety of reasons.

One of the most self-evident is seen in the government's role as criminal investigator. Allegations of wrongdoing are often brought before local police, sheriffs or the FBI, but not until the allegations have been investigated or otherwise substantiated should they be considered fair game for journalists.

But, of course, reporters do on occasion get word of some juicy scandal or police investigation that seems to be of immense popular interest, but with just one problem — the police aren't sure of all the facts yet, or aren't ready to make an arrest.

On the local front, not too long ago, a wealthy businessman was accused of soliciting prostitution and other crimes. This newspaper was aware of the investigation months before any charges were filed. You could make the case that our readers had an interest in knowing what their government was doing, and also had an interest in knowing that a potential predator was in the community, but yet the Inter Lake did not publish any stories about this matter until such time as the warrants were served and the police were ready to make their case.

Were we disloyal to our readers? Were we disloyal to journalism? Or were we loyal to standards of fairness, decency and good citizenship? I would argue the latter.

Unfortunately, in the age of pack journalism, where getting the red meat — er, I mean the story — first is so important, sometimes those standards are forgotten.

Everyone remembers the case of the Atlanta security guard who was vilified by the press as the Olympic bomber when he was in fact the Olympic bombing hero. Such cases would be repeated many times over were the press to have untrammeled access to all of the false accusations made in police stations every day.

On a much grander scale, the government protects not just reputations but also our very lives when it keeps secret a variety of classified information gathered in the course of intelligence-gathering and spying. And of course it also keeps secret the programs through which this classified information is gathered, in order to prevent the enemies of this nation from learning how we watch them.

In times past, such top-secret information had been considered unprintable. The elected and representative members of our government were entrusted by the body politic with the grave responsibility of doing the work of protecting the public in whatever way was deemed necessary. The idea of violating that trust would at one time have been considered treasonous, especially if it aided an external enemy of the state.

But today, reporting on secret government programs has become something of a competitive sport for the mainstream media. USA Today revealed the existence of a National Security Agency program to track terrorists by analyzing calling patterns in a massive database of phone records. The New York Times wrote an earlier story revealing the existence of a program to eavesdrop on telephone and e-mail communications between people in the United States and those abroad — again meant to locate terrorists and prevent them from killing people.

People use a variety of justifications for printing these stories, often falling back on the "freedom of the press" guaranteed by the First Amendment. But like all freedoms, this one is not absolute, but includes certain responsibilities. Thus we have laws against libel to protect reputations from being smeared with false information, and we have common sense — which ought to prevent publishing some information (whether true or not) because it will harm individuals or the nation beyond any value to be found in the story itself.

As I say, not everyone in my profession agrees with me. Not even everyone in my own newsroom agrees with me. Indeed, since the Pentagon Papers and Woodward and Bernstein, the Fourth Estate — the unofficial outsider component of government — largely considers itself exempt from any "checks and balances." It is a power unto itself like Milton's self-deluded Satan, who declares, "We know no time when we were not as now;/ Know none before us, self-begot, self-raised/ By our own quickening power..."

But Satan discovered that pride cometh before a fall, and likewise the press could very easily overplay its proud claims of independence and anger the public, which ultimately is the keeper of all power in our system. Indeed, the public does appear to be stirring recently, in the wake of yet another New York Times story, this one telling how the federal government has — through legal means — been monitoring the records of a banking information broker in Belgium in order to track financial transactions used to fund terrorism activities worldwide.

Other newspapers then followed suit, but it is improbable the story would have surfaced at all had it not been for the Times' insistence on ferreting out any and all secret anti-terrorism programs and revealing them to the public no matter how crucial they may be to national security.

Reading the original story by the Times is a somewhat surreal experience, consistent with watching Anthony Hopkins lick his lips at the thought of fava beans in "Silence of the Lambs." Just as a serial killer takes pleasure from finding an innocent victim and then draining that victim of hope and ultimately life, so too does the New York Times revel in its capacity to uncover a legal secret program and drain it of any hope of effectiveness to save innocent lives.

The program, as reported by the Times, "is limited... to tracing transactions of people suspected of having ties to al-Qaida..." and is "viewed by the Bush administration as a vital tool." Indeed, the program is credited with helping "in the capture of the most wanted al-Qaida figure in Southeast Asia."

As one former senior counterterrorism official said in the story, "The capability here is awesome, or depending on where you are sitting, troubling." One imagines that if you are sitting in a cave in Pakistan or Afghanistan, plotting to destroy the Sears Tower or smuggle an atomic bomb into Manhattan, it is somewhat troubling. But apparently it is equally troubling if you are sitting in the editor's office at The New York Times.

Indeed, it is hard to understand exactly what The New York Times thought it was accomplishing by revealing this top-secret program except to inform our sworn enemy of one of the most "vital" tools we use to protect ourselves. The only logical explanation is that The New York Times has determined through some self-serving process that transcends loyalty to nation — and apparently eclipses the obligation to save innocent lives — that it has the right to publish any and all information about the government simply because the government works for the public.

It did not matter to The New York Times that the Bush administration, the chairmen of the 9/11 Commission, and even Rep. John Murtha (a sworn opponent of Bush) all pleaded with the newspaper to keep quiet for the good of the country. All that mattered was that the Times had a secret, and doesn't know how to keep one.

As editor Bill Keller said, "We remain convinced that the administration's extraordinary access to this vast repository of international financial data, however carefully targeted use of it may be, is a matter of public interest."

A matter of public interest? What? Isn't it more a matter of public interest to preserve and protect one of the most successful programs available to fight terrorism? Doesn't the editor really mean it is a matter of prurient interest? Isn't he really licking his chops like Hannibal the Cannibal — greedy for another bit of bone and gore?

Shouldn't the lead of The New York Times story really have been this: "A formerly highly successful anti-terrorism program conducted in secret by the Bush administration to protect the citizens of this country was crippled today with publication of this story."

Isn't that the real news?

But Keller and his counterpart at the Los Angeles Times wrote a self-defense recently which says, "Our job, especially in times like these, is to bring our readers information that will enable them to judge how well their elected leaders are fighting on their behalf, and at what price."

Not a word was uttered by those editors to explain how they balance this "job" with their ability to cripple vital national security programs. Not a word was uttered about what price the country will pay as a result of the New York Times' decision.

These editors are indeed loyal to their job, but whether they are loyal to their country you will have to judge for yourself.

I can, however, tell you one thing. On the off chance that I were ever to learn details of a program that might help to track down and kill Osama bin Laden or any of his murderous thugs, you have my word on this:

My lips are sealed.

'OUTING' THE OUTRAGE: NEWS ONLY MATTERS IF IT HURTS BUSH

September 3, 2006

Where is the outrage now?

Can anyone explain why no one seems to care that former State Department official Richard Armitage has been "outed" as the source of the leak that put Valerie Plame's name and job (CIA agent) on the front pages of every newspaper in the country?

Can anyone explain why Armitage, whose identity as the leaker was known to the FBI nearly three years ago, has not been indicted for blowing Plame's cover? Wasn't that the whole point of the endless investigation by Special Prosecutor Robert Fitzgerald?

Can anyone explain why Plame and her husband, former ambassador and current blowhard Joe Wilson, are not adding Armitage to their lawsuit against Vice President Cheney, his former assistant Scooter Libby, and presidential assistant Karl Rove? Can we really believe their lawsuit is not just a political ploy when they cherry-pick defendants who are closest to the White House and exclude the ones that are most culpable?

The facts of the matter are myriad, and highly technical, and — in truth — of minimal interest to anyone except the most dedicated conspiracy theorist, so I am going to keep this column's focus simple:

Where is the outrage? Where are the endless hours of analysis and hand-wringing on cable TV? Where is the demand for someone to be held accountable?

OK, those simple questions deserve a simple answer — there is no outrage and no demand for accountability because the latest (and most crucial) revelation in what has come to be called "the Plame affair" didn't hurt President Bush and didn't make Karl Rove or Dick Cheney look bad.

Admittedly, there is no great significance to the fact that Armitage talked to columnist Robert Novak and reporter Bob Woodward and revealed to both of them that Wilson's wife was a CIA agent. She wasn't a covert agent and hadn't been for many years. Anyone who wanted to know that she worked for the CIA could have followed her home from work at Langley Field on any given day. I think it is safe to say that foreign powers do that on a regular basis.

But the fact that Armitage's identity as the so-called "leaker" was known three long years ago IS significant. That means Fitzgerald's investigation should never have even happened. The FBI knew the answer to the crucial question before the investigation even started, and had concluded there was no criminal wrongdoing!

You would think that would light a little spark of outrage among the scandal mongers of the cable brigades, but it has only merited a few brief mentions and has now apparently been relegated to the ash can of history after a few short days.

I mean, I understand that at a time when we are fighting two wars on the ground, plus a long-term war of civilizations, plus are losing the war to secure our borders, the Plame affair is pretty much a non-story.

But when this particular non-story got started (of the many non-stories that are hyped everyday by CNN, Fox and MSNBC), the media was happy to dissect hundreds (maybe thousands) of theories and counter-theories about how President Bush and his cronies had "lied" the American people into war and then "gone after" the Wilsons to punish them for "telling the truth." It was all terribly useful in the campaign to diminish the president's credibility, and it never mattered whether the allegations were "true" or not.

Today, we have the rest of the story. President Bush didn't lie. There was no campaign by the White House to "punish" Joe Wilson for his own lies. The special prosecutor has been the one on the witch hunt all along. Yet it appears that the media now puts the story's importance somewhere between the national debt (over $8.5 trillion, by the way) and the surrender of U.S. sovereignty to the North American Union (which President

---

Bush did lie about, by the way). In other words, you will hear hardly a peep about it.

Let's give credit where credit is due. The Washington Post did write an editorial correctly noting that Armitage was essentially an opponent of the war in Iraq and that he was therefore a philosophical ally of Wilson. Clearly he did not leak the CIA information about Wilson's wife to hurt the couple, so the oft-repeated charge that there was a well-engineered White House campaign to punish Wilson makes no sense. A few other media outlets have also been responsible in reporting the facts about Armitage's role in talking to Novak, but there has been little attention paid to the way this whole non-story was manipulated from the start to smear President Bush (including by the Washington Post, by the way).

Were there people in the White House who didn't like Joe Wilson? You bet. People in D.C. like Cheney, Rove and others were talking about Wilson and Plame because Wilson had put himself in the news by making his allegations that the president had lied in the 2003 State of the Union address.

You remember the infamous complaint about those 16 words where Bush said that British intelligence had reports that Iraq had been seeking to purchase uranium yellowcake from Niger in the 1990s. Turns out Bush was right. Nothing in those 16 words is inaccurate, and we now know the British reports were correct, even though the White House backed away from them after Wilson went public with his allegations. Christopher Hitchens has done extensive reporting on this matter, and you can read his stories at slate.com if you want to learn more about how Wilson "fixed" the intelligence and facts in his op-ed around his dislike of the Bush war policy.

Naturally, once Wilson went public with his false accusation, people in the White House were busy dissecting his motives. In addition, the fact that his wife had played a crucial role in Wilson being assigned by the CIA to visit Niger to investigate the original claims that Iraq had purchased uranium "yellowcake" would not have been irrelevant (even though Wilson lied about that, too).

But you do not have to envision a smear campaign to understand why people, many well outside the White House, were closely examining Wilson's credibility. He had, after all, accused the president of the United States of lying. That's not mashed potatoes.

Once Wilson had launched himself from obscure semi-retired ambassador to know-it-all pontificator of anti-Bush propaganda, he should have expected to have his life and motives analyzed. But anyone who thinks there has to be a nefarious purpose to discuss people's private lives probably has never spent a great deal of time around the watercooler.

And the "watercooler" in Washington, D.C., essentially means the entire federal empire. Gossip is the currency of the realm there, and it is used by both bureaucrats and media pundits the way wampum was used by Native Americans for hundreds of years — as a token of importance and rank.

The mainstream media's outrage over the release of "classified information" in the Plame case has always, therefore, carried the stink of hypocrisy. It is the mainstream media's own policies and practices which make the release of classified information an everyday event.

So if there is going to be any outrage, perhaps it should be saved for those almost weekly occasions when the New York Times publishes our national security secrets on its front page. If the media giants spent as much time investigating how they themselves had come to possess and publish classified documents as they did on how Valerie Plame's name went public, they would be doing us all a favor, instead of just themselves.

OLBERMANIA: IS HE EDWARD OR MAX?

November 5, 2006

I hate to admit it, but it's been fun to watch the on-air nervous breakdown of Keith Olbermann the past few months.

Olbermann, the obscure self-absorbed pundit who started as a twitchy loud-mouthed sports commentator and then slowly evolved into a chimpanzee, has been engaged in a long-running performance as a newsman on MSNBC.

He is witty in a smug, superior demeaning sort of way, and if you enjoy watching a 5-year-old child rip the legs off of spiders, then you might get a kick out of watching Olbermann make his nightly announcement of who the worst person in the world is for the day.

It's also entertaining to watch him trot out his sycophantic corps of Olbermann lickers for their nightly analysis of the news from a far-out left viewpoint. The scary thing is that half of these left-wing advocates are masquerading as even-handed journalists by day — people like Howard Fineman of Newsweek and Dana Milbank of the Washington Post. But there they are like those bobblehead puppies nodding in silent ascent in the back window of the car up ahead that's veering leftward into oncoming traffic — yes Keith, yes Keith, whatever you say Keith.

But lately Olbermann has fallen into the delusion that he is a serious newsman, or worse yet the conscience of the nation — apparently in the mistaken belief that he is channeling the spirit of the dear, departed newsman Edward R. Murrow. We should have known that Olbermann was a little close to the edge when he started signing off his nightly program with Murrow's trademark "Good night and good luck," but it seemed like a harmless homage until K.O., as he is known, decided to go for the knockout.

Apparently, he decided that if Murrow had brought down Sen. Joe McCarthy with his television reporting, then it was fair game for Olbermann to go after even bigger game — President Bush. So he has unleashed his churlish snarling grin on the Bush White House and delivers a nightly rebuke of Karl Rove, Donald Rumsfeld, Tony Snow, Dick Cheney or President Bush himself for daring to carry out policies offensive to Citizen Olbermeister.

Here's how Olbermann, who was anointed "the best news anchor on television" by The Nation magazine, introduced his story about Sen. John Kerry apologizing for his tasteless joke last week about the military forces in Iraq:

"Thus does Senator John Kerry apologize, and the White House says he did the right thing, and presumably it's case closed. And presumably, now the president will apologize to the troops for creating a war with no plan, no exit strategy, and no hope, for mocking them in a tuxedo while they died in Iraq."

We hope that simple straightforward, um, "not fair" and "not balanced" reporting by Olbermann will convince all good Americans that if this is what "the best news anchor on television" sounds like, then we had all better follow the advice of John Prine and blow up our TVs.

But the daily harangues and harumphs from Olbermann were just appetizers for those who enjoy watching a man at the end of his tether. It was not until August when Olbermann launched the first of his "special commentaries" that we were able to appreciate the grandiosity of Olbermann's dementia in full.

First was his attack on Donald Rumsfeld, in which Olbermann miraculously turned Rumsfeld into Neville Chamberlain and himself into Winston Churchill, and then went a step further and accused the government of the United States of being fascists. He cutely cited his hero, Edward R. Murrow, at the end of the piece, and quoted this passage from Murrow, "We will not walk in fear, one of another. We will not be driven by fear into an age of unreason...," without showing the slightest awareness that he himself was the poster boy for the Age of Unreason.

His second "special commentary" blamed the president for the fact that there is no memorial or building yet in place at the site of the World Trade Center, notwithstanding the fact that the building project and memorial are in the hands of others. The commentary lasts about 15 minutes and is worth seeing in its entirety for its shrill polemic and its false dichotomies," but I can boil it down to about eight sentences:☐   "Five years later this space... is still empty.

"Five years later there is no Memorial to the dead.

"Five years later... this is still... just a background for a photo-op.

"It is beyond shameful...

"Who has left this hole in the ground?

"We have not forgotten, Mr. President.

"You have.

"May this country forgive you."

Camera pulls back from Olbermann's quivering lip to look out over Ground Zero and then Olbermann turns it over to President Bush as he is about to address the nation on the solemn occasion of the fifth anniversary of Sept. 11. "The best news anchor on television" has just introduced the president of the United States to the nation with the words, "May this country forgive you."

Clearly anyone who has the audacity to say that Fox News is biased has never had the stomach-churning opportunity to watch MSNBC.

The most recent "special commentary" came just this past Wednesday, in which Olbermann managed to call the president dishonest, stupid, and evil: "There is no line this president has not crossed, nor will not cross to keep one political party in power. He has spread any and every fear among us in a desperate effort to avoid that which he most fears — some check, some balance against what has become not an imperial, but a unilateral presidency."

Thus K.O. continues his assault on the mantle of Edward R. Murrow. By God, he will wear that thing sooner or later, no matter how much bigger it is than his shoulders, not matter how unseemly it is to posture for personal advantage when the fate of the nation is in play.

"Good night and good luck," says Olbermann, but he might be modeling himself after the wrong TV predecessor.

If you examine closely those shifty eyes of his, the nervous tics, the staccato stentorian self-adulating speech patterns, you may be surprised to find that Olbermann is not channeling Edward R. Murrow at all, but rather another famous TV personality — Max Headroom.

Do you remember the computer-generated out-of-control quip-loving punster of the 1980s television show? Max was the on-air alter ego of a legitimate news reporter named Edison Carter who got killed, sort of, and wound up having his memory turned into plasma electrons, sort of, which found a way to hijack a television network known as Network 23 and to become the "conscience of the nation," sort of, when he is not engaged in lurid self-obsession.

"...This is Max Headroom on Network 23. And I — and I — and I know right now you're looking at me and you're thinking Wow, Wow, he could become a star. So, so, before you get the wrong idea about me, let me just say very humbly... you're right. I could."

Yes, there is a strong family resemblance between Headroom and Olbermann, and there is also a similarity between the abysmal ratings of MSNBC and Max's Network 23:

"Hel-Hel-Hello, and welcome to N-Network 23. Live and direct, it's Network 23 — the network where t-t-two's company and three's an audience."

I suppose there is just a slim possibility that Keith Olbermann is in fact some sort of computer-generated reincarnation of Edward R. Murrow created by feeding all of Murrow's television shows and writings into a computer and spitting out the nasty Max version.

Or perhaps Olbermann is just a smarmy, self-absorbed overgrown baby who is the "best news anchor on television." But if he is, then "good night and good luck."

We are going to need it.

WE LIVE IN STRANGE TIMES

December 3, 2006

Everyday, it's something.

One day, you get up and there's a blizzard outside. Maybe the pipes have burst. Your car won't start. Or worse yet, your car starts and you get in an accident at the first intersection.

Some days, it's like that. Nothing goes right.

Another day, you wake up and turn on the "Today" show. No blizzard. No burst pipes. No accidents. Just the "Today" show. So why do you feel even worse after watching one hour of Matt and Meredith than you did on that day earlier in the week when hell froze over?

I suppose it's not Matt and Meredith's fault. They are likable enough people, and as far as infotainment shows go, "Today" is not half bad.

But unfortunately, any TV show, newspaper, or column that is talking about the real world these days is likely to have the same effect on you as the flu — it makes you want to crawl back into bed, pull the covers over your head and shiver.

That's because we live in strange times.

Wednesday was a case in point.

The top news of the day was that the New York Times had leaked a memo written to the president of the United States by his national security adviser, Stephen Hadley. In the formerly top-secret memo, Hadley had criticized Iraq's prime minister, Nouri al-Maliki, as a leader who was either ignorant or incapable.

This kind of leak would be bad enough any day, but it came the day before President Bush was to meet with Maliki in Jordan. The story aired on the "Today" show above a headline that read "Leaked Memo — White House: Doubts about Maliki."

Matt Lauer brought in NBC's political expert Tim Russert to explain the importance of the leaked memo and noted that the president was said to be "displeased" that the memo had been leaked.

I was hoping Russert would jump on that one, and confirm that we should all be "displeased" when a top-secret memo written to the president of the United States is leaked, especially when the leakage is timed to do maximum damage to the president's foreign policy. I was hoping to hear Russert say, "Well, Matt, this is just one more instance of the New York Times putting itself in charge of national security and doing what it wants without regard for the law or the effect on this country."

But of course I didn't expect to hear anything like that. Indeed, to listen to the story on NBC, you would never even know that leaking top-secret government memos is a federal offense, and that when it is done to damage national policy in a time of war, it could easily be considered treasonous.

Russert did note that, "I don't think it's by coincidence. There are people in the administration who want to send a message to Maliki," but he didn't call for an investigation into who had leaked the memo. He did not say anything about the media having a responsibility to keep quiet about secrets it learns which might harm our national security. In fact, I'm pretty sure he doesn't know such a responsibility exists, and maybe it doesn't anymore.

In fact, the longer I watched the "Today" show that morning, the more I became convinced that our country has lost its mind. Here are some of the additional highlights of the news report from that morning, which in one way or another make me think common sense is no longer an American virtue:

• The Supreme Court heard arguments brought by a coalition that the Environmental Protection Agency ought to be forced to regulate so-called greenhouse gases as pollutants in order to prevent global warming. Should the court agree with the coalition, it would basically have arrogated to itself the power not just of the judiciary, but also the legislature and the executive branch. Essentially, we will not need to have elections anymore. We will just let men and women in black robes tell us what is good for us. Call it the nanny court. Certainly this will be the first case of court-decreed "global cooling" in the history of the planet, and once they demonstrate their omnipotence by saving the planet, I'm sure the rest of us will be happy to cede our few remaining human rights over to the control of the court for our own good.

• But the legislative branch still has a few tricks up its sleeve. Case in point: In Louisiana it is now illegal to smoke in the car if you are driving with your children. The "Today" show report was fair enough, and provided an accurate account of the law's intentions and impacts, but the content of the report was more proof that the nanny state is taking over control of our lives. Parental responsibility be damned. Children must be saved from their parents first and foremost, and who better to do it than Uncle Lawmaker.

• One last story from the nanny files: Blind people are complaining that the government is discriminating against them because money in different denominations all looks and feels the same... For a brief second, I thought I was watching a Monty Python skit, but no — this is real life. People really do expect the government to do everything for them to make them feel better about their lives, no matter what the cost or what the actual benefit.

• I suppose this next report is also about the "nanny government" — and in particular one unintended consequence of legislation that was passed to make life easier for another group of handicapped citizens — in this case, deaf people. "Every month on your phone bill, you pay a fee to help the deaf communicate by phone," said Lisa Myers as she introduced this story.

In fact, the government collects $92.5 million a year to pay for Internet relay services, which allow the hearing impaired or disabled to send phone messages by typing their messages. Unfortunately, "operators are required to read any message sent no matter how vile or obscene."

As this report showed, the problem is absolutely grotesque, forcing operators to pass on vulgarities, X-rated phone sex or hate speech, and to read scripts prepared by con men trying to defraud businesses or individuals.

If you or I were in charge of that program, it would be stopped in a day. But the government can't figure out how to prevent phone operators from being turned into pimps and accomplices. These poor operators have no choice but to repeat the vile filth sent to them or to quit their jobs. To warn the FBI or police is against the law, and "to ensure the privacy of deaf people, the FCC prohibits the phone company from keeping any records."

Absolutely idiotic.

But by no means the worst story of the day. That high honor goes to the much-teased segment on whether the movie "Borat" is responsible for the breakup of Pamela Anderson and Kid Rock's marriage. I can't imagine who actually cares about this story, but as part of the ongoing "People" magazinification of the news business, Matt and Meredith and the gang at NBC are supposed to be absolutely fascinated. Who knows? Maybe they are.

Long story short, but not quite as short as the marriage, Anderson and Rock filed for divorce on Monday after 121 days of wedded bliss (possibly drug-induced). The problems in paradise apparently began when Anderson and Rock attended a screening of "Borat," the satiric, role-playing, reality-based docu-comedy about the faux Kazakhstani journalist portrayed by British comedian Sacha Baron Cohen.

The success of "Borat," and what it tells us about ourselves, will have to wait for another column, but suffice it to say that humor based on hurting other people and belittling them is not a high art form (despite what Michael Richards may have thought when he yelled racial epithets at his audience during a comedy show). As for whether "Borat" was responsible for the breakup of Anderson and Rock's marriage, I am not sure. Apparently, one of the central gags in the film is that Borat is obsessed with Anderson (famous for "Baywatch" and a sex tape with her first husband, Tommy Lee). But this should not have surprised Kid Rock, as presumably half the male population (all of it under 30?) is obsessed with Anderson.

It is somewhat odd that Ms. Anderson dragged Mr. Rock to the film in the first place without telling him that her lascivious slutty nature would be a recurring gag in the movie. But it is even more odd that Mr. Rock did not already realize that his wife's lascivious slutty nature was a recurring gag in his own life. And it is most odd of all that a morning TV show designed for the whole family would even cover the story, but that is where we are as a country.

And for that we cannot blame the "Today" show or its stars, Matt and Meredith and Al and Ann. It is not Borat's fault, and it is not even Pam and Kid Rock's fault. As Shakespeare said, lo, those 400 years ago, "The fault, dear Brutus, is not in our celebrities, but in ourselves." Or something like that.

TURN THE CHANNEL? ARE YOU KIDDING?

May 6, 2007

All information is not equal.

You would think we would know that by now, but all education is not equal either. In fact, it seems like our modern education prepares us more to be consumers than connoisseurs of information. A connoisseur of wine can tell the difference between an exquisite wine and a merely good one. A consumer, on the other hand, just likes the burning sensation in his belly and the empty sensation in his head.

Knowledge is much the same way.

There is truth, and there is untruth. There is valuable information, and there is dangerous information. There is information which can save lives, and there is information which can destroy lives.

Only a fool would treat all information as of the same value, but more and more the ability to discern what is helpful and what is hurtful is being robbed of us by what can only be called information overload. Cable television, the Internet, the endless chatter on our cell phones, talk radio, e-mail. Everywhere we go, we are learning more and more. So much, finally, that we can't really be expected to take the time to find out which parts of what we know are true, and which parts are false.

Every week, for instance, dozens of people e-mail me chain letters which someone sent to them with a headline clamoring URGENT ... PASS THIS ON TO EVERYONE YOU KNOW ... VITAL ... OUR FUTURE IS AT STAKE ... and there wasn't even any fine print anywhere that said "may not be true." Time after time, I have researched the claims of those e-mails and found them to be half-truths or non-truths, usually blatant lies. I try to send them back to whoever sent them to me with a note about our individual responsibility to become better informed.

But who am I kidding? The Internet fake-news machine is not going to shut down because I caution one stray forwarder of phony e-mails. Nor for that matter is society going to become civil just because one parent teaches his or her children how to say please and thank you. Both accomplishments are better than surrender, but surrender may be inevitable. Thanks to the deification of mere information, there is no longer any reason to get a story right before spreading it around. There is no reason to think about consequences, and there is no need to be respectful or courteous. I say what I like, and if you don't like it, turn the channel.

That indeed sums up the problem.

"Turn the channel" has become a mantra for cultural surrender-monkeys. No matter how bad it is; no matter how vile; no matter how dangerous — turn the channel. And one after the other, we become numb with frustration and fear and do what we are told — "Turn the channel" and everything will be OK.

Except everything isn't OK — because plenty of people don't want to turn the channel. They want the violence and sex and smack talk. It turns out the lowest common denominator is lower than any of us thought.

Our culture is collapsing all around us, and we are only fooling ourselves if we think we can avoid the inevitable consequences as one tradition after another falls to the ground. The truth is, we aren't avoiding injury; we are avoiding responsibility. If you wonder why another young man went crazy and shot up a campus, it's because we turned the channel, but he didn't. If you wonder why young girls are having sex before they even reach puberty, it's because we turned the channel, but they didn't. If you wonder why the waiter at your favorite restaurant insulted you or why the next driver over just flipped you off, it's because you turned the channel, but they didn't.

Or maybe you didn't turn the channel either. If you look at the ratings, none of us has been.

Take the strange case of Rosie O'Donnell, for instance. Just last week, she announced her timely departure from ABC's "The View." I call it timely because "it was about time" that she lost her platform to spout anti-American propaganda on national TV.

But she didn't go because she was unpopular. She used her time in the national spotlight to mouth support for terrorists, disdain for Christians and hatred for the president, but no one was turning the channel. As long as she insulted Donald Trump's hair, she was everyone's favorite loudmouth. Indeed, her presence on "the View" sent the ratings soaring, which just encouraged her to be more and more outrageous.

Finally, in late March she announced that the World Trade Center attack was an inside job:

"I do believe that it's the first time in history that fire has ever melted steel," she said. "I do believe that it defies physics that World Trade Center tower 7 — building 7, which collapsed in on itself — it is impossible for a building to fall the way it fell without explosives being involved. World Trade Center 7. World Trade Center 1 and 2 got hit by planes — 7, miraculously, the first time in history, steel was melted by fire. It is physically impossible."

She probably thought she could say anything she wanted and no one could ever prove her wrong, but as usual she forgot about the hand of providence. Just a month after her pontification, a gasoline truck exploded beneath a section of the San Francisco-Oakland Bay Bridge highway ramp. Due to the high temperatures caused by the burning fuel, the concrete and steel structure collapsed.

If Rosie were an engineer, she would have known that steel doesn't have to melt to lose its structural integrity, but one thing Rosie O'Donnell doesn't know anything about is integrity.

Nor, from what we can tell, does ABC, or CBS, or NBC — because O'Donnell will be back on TV in some fashion sooner rather than later. So far as we know, the only reason she is not there right now is because ABC was not paying her enough to say things that don't make sense, but ARE provocative.

Which brings us to the point.

Samuel Johnson said that "Patriotism is the last refuge of a scoundrel," but that was in another time and place. Today, in the United States, more and more, it seems like the First Amendment is the last refuge of the scoundrel.

Everyone claims it as their own — Don Imus, Al Sharpton, Larry Flynt (the publisher of Hustler magazine) — and because it is a bedrock of our republic, everyone is afraid to consider whether it has any cracks in it that could cause the foundation to crumble.

Last week, the Federal Communications Commission released a report that said violence on TV is bad for children and that Congress ought to do something about it. This has the "First Amendment Refuge" crowd hopping mad. According to them, it's all right to put anything on TV because consumers can "turn the channel."

That was the conclusion of an editorial in the Los Angeles Times, for instance, which said:

"The ultimate filter is the on/off switch, which not only shields children from violent programming but tells networks and advertisers to offer different fare. If the report's findings about the effects of TV violence on children are true, then the biggest wake-up call should be to parents, not regulators."

Unfortunately, this is the equivalent of telling each of the people in front of the 2004 tsunami that they were in charge of their own flood control. There is simply no way for a parent to monitor and filter media content in anything like an effective way. We can educate our children, and hope for the best, but we cannot follow them around 24 hours a day.

Heartland Diary Volume 4

Even more significant, however, is that any parent who does successfully prevent his or her children from imbibing the filth on the national airwaves has accomplished nothing. The filth is not just on the TV; it is in our culture. Turning off the tap in one kitchen may prevent contaminated water from entering the home, but if the reservoir is itself polluted, then how will any home be made safe?

It is not just violence on TV that is the problem; it is the continuing collapse of any kind of standards. NBC airs its "To Catch a Predator" shows about men attempting to have sex with children during what used to be called the "Family Hour," from 7 to 8 p.m. Daytime TV is filled with the worst kind of trash about sexual adventurism and secular dysfunctionalism, and the cable networks engage in a non-stop stream of tradition bashing that can only serve to destroy the anchors that hold us together as a society.

The reason we have to start thinking about some reasonable controls on our information overload is that for the past 50 years, our society has been engaged in a great experiment to see whether self-restraint and the greater good could prevail over self-centeredness and private demons. That hypothesis has now been proven wrong, definitively.

Apparently, too many of us forgot to turn the channel.

WHY WE WENT TO WAR WITH IRAN: TALES FROM THE FUTURE

June 17, 2007

Probably some people think the reason we went to war against Iran is because they dropped several nuclear bombs on Israel in 2012.

That makes sense in a simple, straight-forward cause-and-effect universe. When President Ahmadinejad finally made good on his promise to obliterate Israel, what choice did we have?

It was either attack Iran or wait for the next strike, this time against the United States.

But what most people don't remember is that there was a good chance to use non-military intervention in Iran before Ahmadinejad had solidified his power base and before he controlled the nuclear technology that he eventually unleashed on the world.

Indeed, back in 2007, the Bush administration had engaged in a classic political war against the tyrant by beginning to encourage his country's oppressed millions to weigh the cost in human dignity, economic stability and intellectual freedom of living in the shadow of a madman.

This involved the typical three-pronged approach of all such destabilization efforts:

1) a propaganda campaign to counter the government-approved media with stories that expose government lies, honor government victims and inspire government opposition;

2) the cultivation of sources in the media in Iran and elsewhere in the Middle East to run negative stories about the regime, in order to encourage a groundswell of opposition; and

3) the use of international forces responsive to the United States to manipulate Iran's currency and weaken the Iranian economy in order to provoke dissatisfaction and eventually rebellion.

Of course, such measures are only undertaken as a last resort to avoid confrontation and war, and the Bush administration clearly did not want another war after its disastrous entry into Iraq four years before.

Likewise, the Democrats were theoretically eager to avoid another war — one which was widely understood to have the potential to be much more deadly than the U.S.-Iraq War — so there were reasons to hope that a united national policy would indeed destabilize the Ahmadinejad government before it acquired nuclear weapons and became a world threat.

Unfortunately, what no one counted on was Brian Ross, and the toll that naked ambition charges to innocent bystanders when they cross the bridge from ignorance to knowledge.

Ross, you see, was the always unforeseen fly in the ointment. The ABC newsman had learned about the non-military campaign against Iran and reported it to the world as if it were completely just and justified to reveal secret American foreign-policy plans to not only the American public, but to what can only be termed our enemy.

Here is a little of what he said that fateful day back in May 2007:

"Current and former intelligence officials tell ABC News that Mr. Bush has signed an official presidential finding authorizing the CIA to carry out what is known as a black or covert operation against Iran." He then went on to describe the three-part plan outlined above.

Of course, those of us who know about the history of TV in those days are not surprised that an American reporter would take actions to subvert the foreign policy of his country. And it was one more clear sign of the virtual collapse of American civilization that there was no arrest of Ross, and virtually no public discussion of why treason is a bad thing.

If such a thing had happened 75 years before, there is no doubt that Ross would have been thrown in jail, either under arrest himself as a traitor or to be questioned about the identities of the "current and former intelligence officials" who had betrayed their oath of office.

Ironically, there was another television show being aired in the same era as Brian Ross's report which offered the perfect formula for how to deal with spies and traitors. It was called "To Catch a Predator," and featured NBC news reporter Chris Hansen setting up sting operations to trap men who were illegally plotting to have sex with children.

It's too bad that no network in those days had thought to establish a show called "To Catch a Traitor." Hansen or some other suave host could have lured "current and former intelligence officials" out of the shadows of their anonymity and into the light of day so that we citizens could watch them spilling their guts about top-secret government policies.

Perhaps if someone had rounded up the criminals in the CIA and other intelligence agencies before Ross got hold of them back in 2007, the country could have avoided a devastating war in which millions lost their lives. Or maybe such a show could have targeted reporters who put their own careers ahead of the good of the country.

Because what Ross seems to not have noticed is that as soon as he reported on a "covert" operation against Iran, it ceased to be covert. And as soon as it ceased to be covert, it ceased to be of any value. The enemy took the necessary steps to avoid destabilization, Ahmadinejad remained in power, and Iran continued to develop nuclear technology.

President Bush certainly could have taken military action against Iran in the final year of his presidency, but he was already weakened politically by attacks on his Iraq policy. So consciously or unconsciously, he opted in 2008 to leave the Iran mess for the next president to deal with.

Probably, the next president could have taken military action in 2009 or early 2010 that would have put Iran on notice that its nuclear ambitions would not be tolerated. But the next president was just as afraid of the media as President Bush was. Instead of military intervention, negotiation was the course of the day.

And that gave Ahmadinejad all the time he needed to complete the manufacture of enriched uranium and weapons-grade plutonium.

Was there an alternative to war?

Yes, but Brian Ross decided not to allow it.

HEY NEWSWEEK: WHY NOT JUST CALL US HERETICS?

August 12, 2007

If you wanted to see an example of biased journalism, a good place to start would be the Aug. 13 cover story in Newsweek about global warming.

The issue's cover says "Global Warming Is A Hoax," but there is an asterisk, which leads to the statement "Or so claim well-funded naysayers who still reject the overwhelming evidence of climate change."

In other words, Newsweek has an agenda to promote global-warming hysteria, and they don't feel any need to give equal time to a point of view they disagree with. Indeed Newsweek's author Sharon Begley denounces global warming skeptics as "deniers," a term which I think establishes the pseudo-religious quality of the global warming crusade as well as anything.

We are indeed reaching the point where "science" has become the equivalent of religious dogma, and "deniers" of the "received truth" (from the Intergovernmental Panel on Climate Change, in this case) have the same status as the poor saps who dared to tell the Congregation for the Doctrine of the Faith (previously known as the Inquisition) that church dogma was wrong.

Although "deniers" of the faith of global warming cannot yet be executed, they can be excommunicated — from the one true church of government funding for scientific research — and that threat of lost funding has marginalized skeptics of global warming to the point where they probably feel a little like Galileo under house arrest.

Newsweek complains that some of the scientists who do not recite the Catechism of Climate Change, as declared by the Intergovernmental Panel, have taken what can only be considered 20 pieces of silver from the Whore of Babylon, also known as ExxonMobil. To quote Newsweek, "Since the late 1980s, this well-coordinated, well-funded campaign by contrarian scientists, free-market think tanks and industry has created a paralyzing fog of doubt around climate change."

The language is virtually identical to that used by the Catholic Church to describe the damage done to "true faith" by anyone who dared to use the lever of science to pry people out from the confines of ignorance. And just as the Inquisition would try to link heretics to Satan, so too does the modern inquisition against global-warming skeptics — for in this day and age there is surely no greater demon than ExxonMobil, is there?

But for just one moment, let us ask the obvious question: What difference does it make where I get the money to do my scientific research, if indeed it is scientific research and not just propaganda? Obviously no difference at all. The earth is still going to be revolving around the sun, regardless of who paid for my lunch.

Nor does it matter how many scientists say something. Consensus is not the equivalent of truth in the scientific realm — otherwise the sun really would revolve around the earth because that is what everyone believed for thousands of years. Consensus can be developed around error just as easily as around truth because all that consensus reflects is the human tendency to groupthink. It is an aspect of politics, not science. Indeed, consensus in science is meaningless unless there is first a Galileo, an Edison or a Pasteur to lead the way.

Can anyone name the Galileo of global warming?

I didn't think so.

But yet, there is Newsweek shaming the millions of people who don't buy the official dogma of the Church of Climate Change and denouncing them as "deniers," as if the science behind global warming is supposed to be unquestioned, unchallenged and unerring like the Bible or the pope (take your pick).

Well, there are many people who refuse to recite the Catechism of Climate Change, but yet Newsweek and other outlets of received truth insist that there is no room for doubt. A few examples will suffice: We are not supposed to notice that climate change has been happening for millions of years. We are not supposed to notice that the earth has witnessed a cycle of warming and cooling since it was created, and that the last ice age ended just 10,000 years ago. We are not supposed to ask whether the global warming that has been taking place for the last 10,000 years (long before the Industrial Revolution) may simply be continuing because of planetary conditions beyond the control of man. We are not supposed to notice that the issue of global warming has conveniently been replaced with the issue of climate change so that fear about the climate can now incorporate any kind of anomaly, whether it is hotter temperatures or cooler ones. We are just supposed to shut up, get in line, and march in lockstep to the official irrefutable undeniable indisputable conclusions of people who say they are way smarter than the rest of us.

Well, sorry, but I've never been very good at toeing the party line. So pardon me while I raise my voice of doubt.

Mankind always sees itself as at the center of the universe. It always has, and it probably always will. Thus, virtually each tribe in the world has a creation myth that describes how God created them as a chosen people. People also have a tendency to blame themselves for the effects of nature. In the past this was usually manifested as a belief that God had sent the rain or the drought or the snowstorm as punishment for some human sin or failing. Likewise, people would engage in propitiatory acts ranging from dances to human sacrifice in order to convince the gods to send the correct amount of rain or sunlight or provide the correct conditions for good hunting or farming.

Given the psychological tendency to see weather as human-caused (as a mechanism of reward and punishment), is it any wonder that most people see changes in weather today and think that mankind must be responsible for it?

Of course not.

But please don't tell me, as Newsweek had the audacity to do, that "warming of the climate system is unequivocal." The only thing unequivocal is the past, and what we know from the past is that if there had not been global warming 10,000 years ago, we would never have developed agriculture, which would have meant we would never have developed cities, which meant we would never have created universities, which meant we would not have had to listen to people complaining about how warm it is today.

As for the future, I suppose it would be nice to know more about it.

But rather than wait for scientists to accurately predict what the weather will be like in 100 years, I think I'll set my sights a little lower. I'll be happy if the weather forecaster can accurately predict what the weather will be like next weekend for the fair.

Until he can do that, I think I will sit out this panic, put a few more charcoals on the greenhouse-gas emitting barbecue grill, and sit down for a good read about the trial of Galileo.

WHAT PART OF SECRECY DON'T THEY UNDERSTAND?

October 14, 2007

In its continuing effort to get the word "secrecy" stricken from the American lexicon. the New York Times earlier this month reported on several so-called classified documents related to the government's tactical decisions about how to fight the war on terror.

This is not the first time The New York Times has reported on "top secret" government documents, programs, or war plans. The paper's argument, of course, is that the government works for "we the people" and therefore "we the people" should know everything the government is doing.

The problem is that whatever "we the people" know, "they our enemies" also know. Information is fungible; once it is in circulation it cannot be contained in a discrete "safe" form. It can instead be applied by anyone for anything at any time. And like magnesium, it burns brightest (and most dangerously) when it is in the open air.

This principle has been understood since the dawn of time, and thus secrecy has been an important component of all human dealings, whether in government or elsewhere. People have acquiesced to the need for secrecy because of their understanding that sometimes knowledge is deadly. "Loose lips sink ships" was literally true during World War II, but it remains metaphorically true today in all regards. When the New York Times leaks the U.S. government's plans to counter insurgencies in Afghanistan or Iraq, it is putting in danger our troops, our policies and those governments.

Of course, the Times wants you to think that it is protecting you from the government by releasing these secret legal opinions issued by the Justice Department on the matter of what is and isn't appropriate for interrogation techniques used on terror suspects.

The fact of the matter is it is not protecting you from anything. Rather, it is providing comfort to our enemies both by girding them with information and by fomenting public discord over policies that may not be tasteful but are nonetheless vital. It is also misleading you into thinking you are somehow at risk because of these policies. You are not.

The government is not going to waterboard you; it is not going to head slap you; or pretend to drown you. Even if you are insanely sympathetic to people who want to blow up our tall buildings and sacred national monuments, the government is going to have no interest in you whatsoever until you cross the line and begin to plot to do harm yourself or try to contact those who will.

But the government does have an interest in such people — a legitimate interest — and we should all have an interest in helping the government to accomplish its goals of finding and thwarting people who want to do us harm.

We do all have such an interest, but the New York Times wants to convince us we have a greater interest in hamstringing our government to protect the rights of terrorists. To the New York Times, secrecy is the enemy, not terrorism.

But in fact, secrecy is not in and of itself a problem. Oftentimes, it is justified, wise and valuable. It is a tool, which like any tool can be used or abused. But just as some people want to ban all guns, some people want to ban all secrets, at least in government.

I suppose it's human nature to want to know the things we are not meant to know. Even at the very beginning of the human story, in the book of Genesis, we are told how very easy it was for Satan to persuade Eve, and then for Eve to persuade Adam, that God didn't know what he was doing when he declared the fruit of the one tree to be secret.

I suppose, in a way, Satan was the first proponent of "open government." God, of course, as the divine commander, had the need and authority to declare certain information to be classified. He encoded that information in the form of, let us say, an apple, and told Adam and Eve that for their own good, for the good of everybody, it was best if they did not know what was in there.

At first, they were perfectly happy not knowing what was in that apple — a small, tiny finite fruit — because, after all, they had everything else in the world. Literally everything. They had a quality life, a good life, and did not even question whether it was appropriate for God, the divine ruler, to tell them it was best — for their own good — not to eat the apple.

But Satan, in the form of a serpent, was "more subtle than any beast of the field." In fact, he thought he was smarter than everyone else, and had used reason and logic to conclude that God's government was oppressive and dictatorial. Satan was obsessed with the idea that God had the power to decide for other beings what was in their best interest, and determined to give power to people to decide for themselves what they wanted to do, how they wanted to live, and what they wanted to eat.

So he told Eve about the forbidden fruit: "God doth know that in the day ye eat thereof, then your eyes shall be opened, and ye shall be as gods, knowing good and evil."

And that was essentially the truth. Adam and Eve's eyes WERE opened. They DID know good and evil. They WERE better informed than before, but the question is, "Were they better off?"

The New York Times thinks it can determine for all of us what will make us better off, but the New York Times was not elected by anyone. At least the government — which determines officially what is and is not secret — has been put in place by us. It works for us. The New York Times works for the board of directors of the New York Times.

If the New York Times is going to do away with secrecy, we suggest they begin at home. Let's get a full public disclosure of all salaries at the Times, as well as a complete record of all contributions made by or on behalf of the employees of the Times. It would certainly be interesting to know whether any reporters covering particular beats have a conflict of interest, wouldn't it? In addition, it would be useful for the New York Times to publish a full and accurate transcript of all editorial board meetings as well as meetings to determine what is and isn't in the nation's best interest. That might shed a little light on whether the paper really does have a liberal bias, don't you think? After all, the argument used for open government also applies to the New York Times, doesn't it? The newspaper declares itself a representative of "we the people," and thus should owe a full accounting to "we the people" as well.

Except of course they value their privacy, which is just another name for secrecy.

And what's good for the New York Times should be good for the rest of us, too.

'SECRETS, LEAKS AND POLITICAL CORRECTNESS': A PARABLE FOR OUR TIMES

October 21, 2007

Last week, I wrote about the New York Times' crusade to uncover and publish top-secret information and made the case that secrecy is in fact oftentimes a good thing, not something to be rooted out and destroyed.

That column generated quite a few comments from people who were worried that I was advocating torture. I didn't actually, but I do advocate whatever is necessary, including a little secrecy, to keep us safe and to help us prevail in our war against Islamic terrorists.

Some people say this is not Christian, that it just promotes "us against them" thinking. Apparently they didn't get the memo about the wheat and the chaff. In fact, Christian thinking is all about "us vs. them," except that Christ was trying to increase the "us" and decrease the "them" by persuading people to "repent and sin no more."

Interestingly, Christ is perhaps the best example in history of how important secrecy is — not just in private life, but also public life. Probably, when the "whistleblower" Judas leaked inside information about the Jesus movement to the Sanhedrin, he intended to shed light on what he thought were misguided policies, but can't we all agree that, in that case at least, a little more secrecy would have been a good thing?

Indeed, as any student of the Bible could tell you, the New Testament is filled with examples of how important secrecy is. Starting in the Gospel of Mark, the earliest of the Gospels, there is a recognized "secrecy theme" which exhibits itself in a variety of ways. Whenever Jesus heals the lame or blind, for instance, he warns them not to tell anyone else what has happened. You might say that Jesus was hoping to avoid the paparazzi, and since paparazzi literally means swarming flies, you would not be far wrong. He probably thought he could work best in an intimate setting, without a bunch of gawkers trying to get a glimpse of him.

Of course, we know that did not work. People were climbing on rooftops to see him, clinging to tree branches, and reaching out to touch the hem of his garment. They all wanted the same thing — to know his secret.

But Jesus wasn't always talking — at least openly. Many times, he preferred to preach in parables. Over and over, he would walk amidst the people and tell them stories that seemed to make no sense. Even his very disciples were puzzled by them. Jesus was not swayed to change his approach, however; he actually taunted those in the crowd who were unable to comprehend his words: "Let those who have ears to hear, hear!" he shouted. He then huddled with his disciples and told them what the parables really meant, probably infuriating the crowd.

In a similar setting today, there would have been people holding up signs complaining, "The parables are for everyone, not just a few!" and "Jesus unfair to mentally challenged!"

If the New York Times had been there, 2,000 years ago, reporting on the ministry of Jesus Christ in Israel, perhaps we would have gotten a story something like this:

> JERUSALEM — Jesus of Nazareth, an itinerant preacher from Galilee, has secretly told his private council that he is planning for full-scale war against the forces of evil, and that deaths could number in the hundreds of thousands, yea millions.
>
> Jesus would not respond to numerous questions from the crowds on this matter, but he has actively begun to plan for his ascension to the throne of David, sources close to the rabbi told the Times.
>
> Although Jesus commonly calls for blessings on the peace-makers, he is reportedly working behind the scenes to envelope the world in a stormy conflagration similar to that worked in Sodom and Gomorrah in years past.
>
> Asked whether he was the messiah foretold in ancient scripture, Jesus dodged the question, responding only "Whom do men say that I am?"

The rabbi has been careful not to identify himself as the messiah, perhaps to avoid prosecution for blasphemy, but sources say that he has repeatedly used various code words to signal his followers about his "true identity."

Reportedly, one of his disciples known as Simon Peter did confront Jesus at one point while they were on a fund-raising tour through the towns of Caesarea Philippi, saying "Thou art the Christ."

According to at least one source present, Jesus told Peter and the others within earshot that they were never to repeat this again to anyone. Some of those gathered with Jesus at the time said they felt threatened and harassed, and believe that they were being warned not to testify against Jesus in a court of law.

Most of Jesus' followers say that he has a secret teaching, which is only available to a few, whom he calls the Chosen Ones. Although he does preach regularly about salvation and a coming day of judgment, Jesus is withholding from the public certain useful information said to be written in a book he carries. This Book of Life supposedly contains a record of all the deeds and misdeeds of those on Earth, with an appendix indicating the place of habitation for each in the next life.

The publishers of the Times have confirmed that they will file a Freedom of Information lawsuit with the Sanhedrin to force Jesus to hand over the Book of Life and any and all related papers, documents and scrolls such as would be necessary to decipher said Book, along with an accounting of any war plans that have been made in secret with his council.

• • •

And so it goes. If it were not for the New York Times, I suppose we might never get to the bottom of that story either. Let those who have eyes to see, see.

WHY NOT ASK CANDIDATES WHAT THEY BELIEVE?

December 23, 2007

As we prepare to celebrate the birth of Christ, it is worth looking around and considering what Christ would think of the mess we have made.

First of all, because of his insight into the nature of man, we have to assume he would not be surprised. There is no indication anywhere in the New Testament that Jesus was naive. On the other hand, there is also no suggestion that he would just shrug the mess off and tell us to do better next time. Instead, he would expect us to do better this time.

Jesus had fairly high standards, for himself and for his followers. He told us to pick up our own cross and follow him — and that meant being willing to suffer for our beliefs, being willing to die for them if necessary, and always remembering to put our own will in second position to the will of God, just as Jesus had to do.

Jesus was no chicken. He didn't join any armies, and he didn't lead the expected war against the Roman Empire that some of his followers wanted, but he took a stand. He didn't just go along to get along. He said what he believed, and believed what he said.

Perhaps, most importantly, he had a moral code that gave him strength, substance and certainty. Indeed, the moral code he lived and died by was so powerful that it ultimately changed the world, shaped Western civilization and helped our founders create the nation we live in today.

Unfortunately, that moral code — like the cross itself — is now foolishness to the Hollywood elite and a stumbling block to our politically correct leaders. More and more we see Christians mocked for their beliefs, or pressured to keep quiet. Former Gov. Mike Huckabee, for instance, had to explain repeatedly to the mainstream media last week why his Christmas greeting advertisement in Iowa had "hidden" Christian symbolism.

Not the "hidden" Christmas tree plainly visible at his side. Not the "hidden" words coming straight out of his mouth which explained that "what really matters [about Christmas] is the celebration of the birth of Christ." No, it was the bookshelf in the background that looked like a cross to some viewers that made media pundits see deviltry in Huckabee's Christmas ad.

Turns out these folks were convinced the "floating cross" was an attack on former Gov. Mitt Romney, who is a Mormon. Oddly enough, no one has explained how the cross symbolism hurts Romney, whose church is officially known as the Church of Jesus Christ of Latter-day Saints and who has publicly professed that Jesus is his personal savior.

Probably, the people making such allegations are actually trying to kill two candidates with one well-aimed stone. It is unlikely they are trying to protect Romney from Huckabee, but rather trying to protect the nation from what they perceive to be two kookie religious zealots who will use their "moral code" to govern with principle rather than simply by doing what is convenient or popular.

Indeed, it has become something of a truism of late that we should not select our political leaders because of their religious beliefs. Even Romney gave a speech this month in which he said, "A person should not be elected because of his faith nor should he be rejected because of his faith."

Certainly, it is plain in the Constitution of the United States that "no religious test shall ever be required as a qualification to any office or public trust under the United States." That is a wise and useful prohibition. We the people should be able to elect whoever we want, and should not see our favored candidates excluded because of their faith or lack of it.

But there is a difference between a requirement for office and a requirement for what each individual voter expects of the candidates they will support. There, it seems vital that the electorate should consider the moral qualifications of the candidates, and specifically the moral code or world view that each candidate subscribes to. After all, it is the beliefs which a candidate has before being elected which will inform his or her choices after taking office. If you want abortion to be legal, for instance, you should not vote for someone who believes abortion is murder. If you want to improve border security, you should not vote for someone who believes that all people have a God-given right to migrate wherever they choose.

Some people will say that a person's religion is a private matter, and of course it is. But when you run for public office you shed a certain amount of privacy, and what matters to the public is not what a candidate will do in church, but what they will do in public as a result of their belief system. If our democracy is going to have any meaning, then voters must consider what moral creed a candidate follows.

Toward the end of that same Sermon on the Mount where Jesus advised us to "judge not lest ye be judged," he also had this to say of false prophets: "You will know them by their fruits. Grapes are not gathered from thorn bushes nor figs from thistles, are they?" In other words, he taught us that in place of haughty judgment we could substitute wise discernment, and recognize that not all those who come to lead us are suitable for the job. Even those in "sheep's clothing" may inwardly be "ravenous wolves."

It is foolish to think that when choosing our public leaders we should not consider their moral character. Who would want to elect immoral leaders, after all? Yet in large part, moral character is shaped by one's religion or one's decision not to follow a religion at all. This doesn't give a free pass to those who profess to be religious. As Jesus implied, it is often those who pretend to be religious who are the most dangerous among us. But likewise it does not mean we should select our leaders based on some kind of religion-free criteria.

Don't forget, our national leaders are moral leaders as well as political leaders. And it is easy to see that moral character does matter to the American people by looking at the presidencies of Richard Nixon and Bill Clinton, among others. Nixon and Clinton were perhaps the most skilled politicians of the last half-century. Nixon was one of the most successful presidents in our history when it came to pushing an agenda through Congress, yet he was ultimately forced to resign in disgrace because of a moral failing. President Clinton did not accomplish as much as Nixon, but he governed over a period of prosperity and optimism and had great personal popularity, yet he too was disgraced by a moral lapse and was only the second president in our history to undergo the ordeal of impeachment.

As we select our new president, in this coming year, in seems we should first think about our own moral values, then ask which candidate will promote those values in his character and his policies. This does not mean voting only for candidates who are of the same religion as us, or who have the same world view, but it does mean realizing that we can't just pretend our values don't matter. If we don't publicly vote for our values and embrace them, they are not values at all. They are window dressing.

'LYING LIARS'
AND POLITICALLY CORRECT TRUTH

February 3, 2008

A few years ago, Al Franken wrote a little book called "Lies (and the Lying Liars Who Tell Them): A Fair and Balanced Look at the Right."

As the title makes clear, Franken was only interested in skewering Republicans in his book, which was not really "fair and balanced," but which was funny. Since Franken is now running as a Democrat for the U.S. Senate from Minnesota, it is unlikely he will be available to do an equal opportunity book about the Democrats, or as he would put it "the left."

I've done a few columns in the past about members of the media, but not so much to call them liars as to demonstrate that their so-called objective news reports are often slathered with a dripping sloppy mess of preconceptions and smarmy snickering condescension. The issue isn't whether they lie or not; the issue is whether we should simply put a label on all cable news channels that reads "For Entertainment Purposes Only — Do Not Use as a Source of Information."

And the problem isn't just the liberal media outlets such as MSNBC, where famously you can watch Bush-hater Keith Olbermann interview people even further to the left of himself in order to get answers to such pressing questions as "Has the president just lost his mind?" ("Well, yes, Keith," says the boot-licking sycophantic guest, "but more importantly the nation has lost its collective mind for putting up with this president's endless supply of bull puckey.")

All right, maybe the problem is the liberal medial outlets such as MSNBC, but it is also conservative Fox News, where the parade of preening, prattling, fawning co-anchors is non-stop from morning till night, each one more self-important than the next. It's true that Fox has a wider variety of guests on the air than MSNBC, but it doesn't matter because ultimately all of the news and all of the discussion on these "news" networks is pre-digested pabulum that is intended to prevent you from having an original thought.

All that matters is ratings, as Bill O'Reilly has observed. And ratings means that we get such Howard Beale-inspired claptrap as "body language" analysis of newsmakers and sweeps-week segments on "Spring Break Girls Gone Wild." And we also get endless recyclings of stories that probably never should have been "cycled" for national consumption in the first place. You know the ones — death in Aruba, missing in Spain, assassinated by car accident in a tunnel in Paris, dismembered in a neighborhood to be named later.

Meanwhile, the important business of government goes on. The deficit grows. The illegal population soars. The lies continue.

Ah yes, the lies. That's where we started this meditation, wasn't it? So let's look at the most famous lie of the last two weeks:

"Jesse Jackson won in South Carolina twice in '84 and '88, and he ran a good campaign. And Sen. Obama is running a good campaign."

But the curious thing about this lie is that it wasn't a lie at all — it was just (sorry about this, Al Gore) an inconvenient truth. It was so inconvenient, in fact, that the mainstream media tried to use it to turn Bill Clinton (the "first black president," remember?) into a racist for saying it.

Indeed, the national media spent several days glibly telling the public that the Clintons were playing the "race card" in order to scare white voters into being afraid of Hillary Clinton's major opponent for the Democratic presidential nomination, Barack Obama, who is indeed black.

But what exactly was the race card? And who told the lie?

Turns out the race card was played by the black voters of South Carolina, 81 percent of whom voted for Obama compared to just 17 percent for Clinton. The only way that makes sense is if the black voters were voting for Obama largely on the basis of his skin color. After all, there is barely a smidgin of difference between Clinton, Obama and John Edwards on the issues.

And the white vote shows that very clearly: Clinton won 36 percent of the white vote and Obama won about 25 percent, with about 39 percent going to Edwards, who won the state in the 2004 primary.

If the black vote had been as color-blind as the white vote, the winner in South Carolina would probably have been Edwards again, but instead blacks voted overwhelmingly for Obama because they identified with him, not necessarily because they thought he would do the best job.

That's why Bill Clinton was entirely justified in comparing Obama's victory to Jackson's in 1984 and 1988. Both men's victories were based on winning huge support among blacks while losing among whites. Indeed, in 1988, Jackson only got 7 percent of the white vote, yet won the state. That doesn't mean Obama's victory can be dismissed, but it has to be put into context. There are very few states where Obama can count on similar sizable black voting majorities. He needs to win the white vote to gain the nomination. Saying so doesn't make you a racist. Bill Clinton is not a racist; he is a realist.

Unfortunately, the media chose to inject race into the campaign as an issue, using Bill Clinton's comment as the starting point for endless finger-pointing and falsehoods that wrongly implied to voters that Clinton had done something despicable, deceitful or underhanded. He just said what the politically correct media was largely afraid to say. (Credit here to political analyst Craig Crawford who had the temerity to stand up to Olbermann on MSNBC and insist that Clinton's comment was "race free.")

Let's face it. There are plenty of lies to go around in national politics, and "lying liars who tell them." Just consider the enormous, bald-faced lie that John McCain has been telling about Mitt Romney supporting a timetable for U.S. withdrawal from Iraq. Romney never said that. But don't take my word for it; check it out for yourself.

That's something the national media doesn't expect you to do, and which the politicians count on you not to do. But if you expect to play an informed role in the next election, it is something you simply have to do.

CAUGHT BETWEEN BARACK AND A HARD PLACE

February 17, 2008

Call it Obamamania. Call him the Kool-Aid Kandidate. But please, let's call the whole thing off.

The love affair between Barack Obama and the rest of the world has just gotten crazier and crazier.

Two incidents last week are worthy of note. In the first one, MSNBC's blatherer-in-chief Chris Matthews embarrassed himself by gushing about Obama like a schoolgirl with a crush on the team captain.

After watching the speech by Sen. Obama following his primary victories in Virginia, Maryland and D.C. on Tuesday, Matthews told his co-host Keith Olbermann, "I have to tell you, you know, it's part of reporting this case, this election, the feeling most people get when they hear Barack Obama's speech. My, I felt this thrill going up my leg... I mean, I don't have that too often. No, seriously. It's a dramatic event. He speaks about America in a way that has nothing to do with politics. It has to do with the feeling we have about our country. And that is an objective assessment."

No, seriously. He really thinks that is an "objective assessment."

But of course Matthews is right about one thing. Obama does speak about America in a way that has nothing to do with politics. Politics is about policies, about ideas, about programs — but Obama's speech is all about platitudes and puffery and pretense. Just read the speech that gave Matthews "restless leg syndrome," and you'll see what I mean.

A cynic such as myself could go through the entire speech and point out how Obama's big-sounding words mean absolutely nothing, or could mean just the opposite of what they appear to mean. Here, for your edification, are some of the leg-tingling moments from the speech, along with translation into language even Chris Matthews could understand: • "Today the change we seek swept through the Chesapeake and over the Potomac."

Translation: "Today I got more votes than Hillary Clinton."

• "We know it takes more than one night — or even one election — to overcome decades of money and the influence, bitter partisanship and petty bickering that's shut you out, let you down and told you to settle."

Translation: "The reason I am winning election after election is because I have more money than Hillary Clinton, but as long as I say I am against politicians, no one seems to notice I am one of the best of them."

• "We have given young people a reason to believe, and brought folks back to the polls who want to believe again. And we are bringing together Democrats and independents and Republicans; blacks and whites; Latinos and Asians; small states and big states; Red States and Blue States into a United States of America. This is the new American majority."

Translation: "I have told people what they want to hear, or just allowed people to hear whatever they want to hear, because when I talk no one really hears anything except the sound of my voice lulling them to sleep."

• "At a time when so many people are struggling to keep up with soaring costs in a sluggish economy, we know that the status quo in Washington just won't do. Not this time. Not this year. We can't keep playing the same Washington game with the same Washington players and expect a different result — because it's a game that ordinary Americans are losing."

Translation: "When I say 'the same Washington game with the same Washington players,' I mean I am not a Clinton. When I say 'soaring costs,' I mean more entitlements. When I say 'sluggish economy' I mean higher taxes. When I say 'expect a different result,' I mean 'more of the same.' "

• "It's a game where lobbyists write check after check and Exxon turns record profits, while you pay the price at the pump, and our planet is put at risk. That's what happens when lobbyists set the agenda... It's a game where trade deals like NAFTA ship jobs overseas and force parents to compete with their teenagers to work for minimum wage at Wal-Mart. That's what happens when the American worker doesn't have a voice at the negotiating table... and that's why we need a president who will listen to Main Street — not just Wall Street; a president who will stand with workers not just when it's easy, but when it's hard."

Translation: "I may not speak the same language as Hugo Chavez, but I sound a Venezuela is good for the United States. Let?s nationalize the oil companies."

• "It's a game where Democrats and Republicans fail to come together year after year after year, while another mother goes without health care for her sick child. That's why we have to put an end to the division and distraction in Washington, so that we can unite this nation around a common purpose, a higher purpose."

Translation: "If I get elected, I will transfer the wealth of this nation from the rich to the poor, because there are more poor people than rich people, and therefore more votes."

• "It's a game where the only way for Democrats to look tough on national security is by talking, and acting and voting like Bush-McCain Republicans, while our troops are sent to fight tour after tour of duty in a war that should've never been authorized and should've never been waged. That's what happens when we use 9/11 to scare up votes, and that's why we need to do more than end a war — we need to end the mindset that got us into war."

Translation: "Some Democrats believe in a strong defense, but I am not one of them. It's easy to get the Democratic nomination by acting like I am against war, so I am going to do it. All you know for sure is that I think the most dangerous thing in the world is electing a Republican as president of the United States."

• "It's time to stand up and reach for what's possible, because together, people who love their country can change it. Now when I start talking like this, some folks tell me that I've got my head in the clouds. That I need a reality check. That we're still offering false hope."

Translation: "Some people are on to me — they know just how dangerous I am — but with my reputation as a golden orator, I can drown them out. The truth cannot long stand against a sea of sonorous platitudes."

• "Now we carry our message to farms and factories across this state, and to the cities and small towns of Ohio, to the open plains deep in the heart of Texas, and all the way to Democratic National Convention in Denver; it's the same message we had when we were up, and when were down; that out of many, we are one; that our destiny will not be written for us, but by us; and that we can cast off our doubts and fears and cynicism because our dream will not be deferred; our future will not be denied; and our time for change has come."

Translation: "Vote for me, and you will have a future. Vote for Hillary Clinton, and tomorrow will never come. Vote for John McCain, and you will burn in hell."

Regarding that last sentiment, it appears at least one McCain supporter is taking it seriously, which brings us to the second seriously wacked incident of Obamamania last week. On PBS, Mark McKinnon, a top adviser to McCain and former adviser to President Bush, announced that he will quit McCain's campaign if Obama is the Democratic nominee.

Although McKinnon said he supports McCain 100 percent and disagrees with Obama on fundamental issues, he doesn't seem to think issues matter as much as charisma. Like a good Kool-Aid drinker, he said: "I would simply be uncomfortable being in a campaign that would be inevitably attacking Barack Obama."

Remarkably, McKinnon is a guy who just two weeks ago was blasting Rush Limbaugh and other conservative talk show hosts for not getting in line behind McCain as the presumptive GOP nominee.

He asked "Isn't it better to get behind a Republican you may disagree with from time to time than work for an outcome that puts a Democrat in the White House with whom you will disagree all of the time?"

Translation: "I am one of those evil lobbyist types who Barack Obama claims to hate... but can we expect to see people like me and other typical political hacks in the Obama administration next year? YES, WE CAN!

INTO THE BLACK HOLE OF POLITICAL CORRECTNESS

March 16, 2008

I first ventured into the bizarre world of politically correct presidential politics six weeks ago when I wrote about Bill Clinton being scolded by the national media for comparing Barack Obama's success in South Carolina with Jesse Jackson's success there 20 years before.

We heard that Clinton had "played the race card," and he was castigated by the national media for having somehow done something dastardly, when all he actually did was tell the truth at a time when many Democrats did not want to hear it.

The same thing happened last week when liberal Democrat Geraldine Ferraro made the mistake of questioning whether Obama was the right person to be elected president in 2008, or whether he was just the right man in the right place at the right time to get elected.

Those are, of course, two very different things, and if we were reasonable people we would be able to have a reasonable discussion about the differences. Ferraro, who supports Hillary Clinton, raised the prospect in an interview with the Daily Breeze of Torrance, Calif., that ' If Obama was a white man, he would not be in this position. And if he was a woman (of any color) he would not be in this position. He happens to be very lucky to be who he is."

Ferraro is certainly not the first person to consider the possibility that Obama has become a nearly unstoppable force in the Democratic Party in large measure because of who he is — not because of what he stands for. This seems almost like a foregone conclusion, when you consider all the better qualified candidates who were easily trounced by Obama. And it clearly plays a part in the political pundits' pronouncement that Obama cannot lose the nomination now without ripping apart the Democratic Party. The so-called superdelegates are supposed to be able to vote for whoever they wish to vote for, but they are being warned that if they "steal" the nomination from Obama, black voters will revolt and throw the election into doubt. And, of course, Obama would not have a lead in the delegate race today at all were it not for the fact that he has been receiving 80 percent or more of the black vote, which is the core Democratic vote in many states.

That certainly sounds like "who" Obama is matters at least as much as what he says.

As noted, Ferraro is just the latest of several liberal Democrats who have found out that race, not Social Security, is now the deadly third rail of American politics.

Ferraro is not just any liberal Democrat either; she is the former front woman for the advancement of women in politics, replaced only in the current year by Hillary   Clinton. It was Ferraro who was the first woman to appear on a major political party's presidential ticket, albeit on the bottom of the ticket, when she ran with Walter Mondale in 1984.

And Ferraro is wise enough to admit that she was picked to run as vice president solely on the basis that she was a woman. "In 1984 if my name were Garard Ferraro instead of Geraldine Ferraro, I would never have been chosen as the vice presidential candidate," Ferraro told Diane Sawyer on "Good Morning America."

Sawyer was one of several reporters who tried to paint Ferraro as somehow saying something inappropriate, which made the news coverage appear almost to be a sequel of the "Saturday Night Live" sketch where members of the press fawned over Obama and savaged Hillary.

In this case, however, even Sen. Clinton was taking Obama's side, calling Ferraro's comments "regrettable." It's too bad Clinton doesn't have the courage to acknowledge the truth of Ferraro's comments, because she has no chance to win the nomination unless she can counteract the notion that Obama "deserves" to win.

Of course, not everyone agrees with me. Keith Olbermann, the paid political consultant masquerading as a journalist on MSNBC scolded Hillary Clinton quite loudly in one of his "oh so special" comments Wednesday night, noting that her "insensitive reaction" to the words of Ferraro was "slowly killing the chances of any Democrat to be president."

"Not that there's anything wrong with that," as we would expect Jerry Seinfeld to say after making such a politically unbalanced remark. But Olbermann has long since given up any pretense of fairness in his reporting — he is merely a mouthpiece for Democractic Party propaganda. No wait, I need to give credit where credit is due. Olbermann is not just a mouthpiece; he is actually a very inventive rhetorical assassin who doesn't just mouth the party line, but oftentimes originates it. In large part, he is to the Democratic Party what Rush Limbaugh only thinks he is to the Republican Party.

Earlier on his show, Olbermann had interviewed Eurgene Robinson of the Washington Post who noted correctly that "Geraldine Ferraro says, you know, she's been called a racist and Bill Clinton was called a racist," but then he argues that "Nobody calls her a racist. Nobody called Bill Clinton a racist.

What was said is that what she's - you know the sentiments she expressed, what she said was arguably a racist thing to say. But that's about action, that's about words. It's not about her essence or her being."

Of course, Robinson was doing what most television commentators do — he was saying what he thought he could get away with, and within 30 seconds of saying he knows that Ferraro is not a racist, he said that Ferraro's comments were "clearly meant to belittle and denigrate Obama because of his race."

Huh? Come again? Sounds racist to me, if that's really what she meant to do. And apparently it sounded racist to Keith Olbermann, because he concluded his special comment by demanding that Hillary Clinton distance herself from Ferraro's "words, and the cheap, ignorant vile racism that underlies every syllable of them."

Yet hold on here. Let's take another look at the words that caused all this controversy - "If Obama was a white man, he would not be in this position. And if he was a woman (of any color) he would not be in this position. He happens to be very lucky to be who he is."

Vile? Ignorant? Racist? Not even close, but the more that the mainstream media tries to inoculate Barack Obama from the legitimate conversation about who he is, how he became who he is, and where he wants to take the country, the more they will damage the cause of race relations in this country. You cannot run for president in this country without being able to absorb criticism and demonstrate convincingly to the public that the criticism is unfounded.

Ronald Reagan didn't have to convince anyone to vote for him on the basis of race, but he did have to persuade people that he was not too old to be president. People questioned his fitness for office on the basis of his age much more overtly than anyone has used race as a factor in the 2008 election. But Reagan did not condemn people for their "age-ism" or demand that people stop asking questions about his age. He just used his age to his advantage by making Walter Mondale squirm (and even laugh) as the elderly president cajolingly responded to a debate question: "I will not make age an issue of this campaign. I am not going to exploit for political purposes my opponent's youth and inexperience."

Too bad, none of today's candidates (white or black, man or woman) have the grace or wit of Ronald Reagan. Instead of a humorous rejoinder to an obvious poke, what we get today is defensive self-righteousness and finger-pointing.

Within two days, Ferraro had been forced to resign her honorary position with the Clinton campaign, but to her credit she refused to be silenced even though she had been marginalized.

And by the end of the week, a new controversy had erupted — the words of Barack Obama's longtime pastor had come to light blaming America for AIDS, importing illegal drugs, and promoting white supremacy. In one now famous quote, the Rev. Jeremiah Wright Jr. even called on God to damn America for its profligate ways.

No word yet on whether it is racist to point out that Barack Obama has called Wright a mentor, a consultant and a "sounding board" for more than 20 years. Let's wait a week and see whether this, too, falls into the category of things best left unsaid in Democratic politics. It seems like the black hole of unmentionables is growing by leaps and bounds, but eventually we have to come out the other side, don't we?

ANALYSIS OF THE ANALYSIS OF THE 'ANALYSTS'

April 27, 2008

It's not every day that the Daily Inter Lake is cited in the New York Times, but that's just what happened in an April 20 story about the role of military analysts in wartime news coverage.

No, the Inter Lake was not lumped in with Fox News, MSNBC, CNN and the other networks as one of the big players in shaping public opinion about national policy. In fact, we were just as surprised to see our name in the article as anyone was.

Turns out that retired Maj. Gen. Paul Vallely of Bigfork, the host of the "Stand Up America" radio show, was one of the analysts featured in the 7,500-word story, which questioned whether America was being misled by these analysts "whose long service has equipped them to give authoritative and unfettered judgment about the most pressing issues of the post-Sept. 11 world."

Reporter David Barstow summed up the problem he perceived as follows: "Hidden behind that appearance of objectivity, though, is a Pentagon information apparatus that has used those analysts in a campaign to generate favorable news coverage of the administration's wartime performance, an examination by The New York Times has found."

In other words, military analysts with long military careers or Pentagon associations tend to support the current military in wartime. This to me is not news. In fact, anybody who spent a few minutes thinking about it would realize that the reason the networks want these guys as analysts is because they do have connections to the Pentagon. Inside information is the only kind of information that networks want to pay for.

Our readers and the readers of the New York Times can debate that point, of course, starting with an op-ed today by Franklin Schroeter of Somers which appears elsewhere on this page. For the record though, the Inter Lake doesn't have paid military analysts, and we usually rely on our own readers for their considerable insights on our opinion pages rather than turning to experts.

If on the other hand our readers are considered to be experts in their field, then we are doubly appreciative of their contributions. We certainly have our share of lawyers, doctors and government officials who contribute letters to the editor, as well as truck drivers, teachers, business owners, clerks — well, you get the idea. We also have, thanks to the retirement allure of the Flathead, more than our share of generals, including Gen. Vallely.

Vallely and his frequent co-author, retired Lt. Gen. Thomas McInerney — another of the analysts mentioned in the Times article — have submitted many op-eds to the Inter Lake since 2005, of which we have run some if we thought they were of general interest (pun noted, but not intended). They almost invariably are on topics related to the war on terror, the war in Iraq or the Mideast in general. Their letters are welcome, as are the letters diametrically opposed to them by generals, veterans or just plain folks who oppose the war in Iraq, fear the Pentagon or despise the president. That, we think, is what makes our opinion section so diverse, lively and entertaining.

As for the citation of the Inter Lake by the New York Times, it wasn't exactly central to the story. In fact, it looks like the reporter combed through his list of news outlets looking for something low-key and out-of-the-way to use in comparison to the trumpet blare of Bill O'Reilly when writing about how the military analysts were viewed by the Pentagon.

"[T]he analysts' news media appearances were being closely monitored," Barstow wrote. "The Pentagon paid a private contractor, Omnitec Solutions, hundreds of thousands of dollars to scour databases for any trace of the analysts, be it a segment on 'The O'Reilly Factor' or an interview with The Daily Inter Lake in Montana, circulation 20,000."

Not exactly a claim to world fame for us, but we will certainly accept the mention gladly. After all, I have mentioned the New York Times on more than one occasion, so they owe me.

As for the story the Times referred to, it was a 2005 interview with Gen. Vallely, who at that time was a prominent face on Fox News and still a stranger to most of his neighbors in Bigfork. We wrote a story called "In the Loop," that profiled Vallely as one more of the many people who fell in love with the Flathead on their first visit and decided to move here.

As the title implies, there was no confusion about why Vallely was a valued military analyst. He was "in the loop" because of his long career in the Army and it was noted that when not at home working on his books, he was "jetting off to meet sources from Beirut to Israel to the Pentagon."

The immediate occasion of the story was that Vallely had just returned from a visit to Guantanamo and was being widely quoted in the national media. We thought it appropriate to let our readers know about Vallely's local connection, and asked reporter Candace Chase to do a story on the general.

Clearly, that which came as a shock to the New York Times — the general's close association with the Pentagon — was not being withheld from the Inter Lake's readers. In addition to talking about Vallely's sources in the Pentagon, Chase's article also explicitly spoke of Vallely riding to Guantanamo on the Secretary of the Navy's plane "with other media and congressional representatives."

As for his "appearance of objectivity," Vallely told us "I have no other agenda than to win the war on terror."

If the New York Times thinks that is biased, then perhaps that explains why the Pentagon thought it was important to get their message out through an alternative means than the mainstream media. But ultimately, as the failure to maintain public support for the war shows, the problem is not that the administration worked too hard to "sell" the war to the public, but that it didn't work hard enough.

If the president and the Pentagon believe that going to war is the right decision for our national security, then they had better darn well be prepared to convince us they are right. Otherwise, the casualties, costs and consequences of war will inevitably pile up and "enterprises of great pitch and moment," as Shakespeare phrased it in another context, will "lose the name of action."

JUST A PAWN IN THEIR GAME

June 1, 2008

It is ironic that liberals, who generally don't believe in absolute truth in religion, swear upon it in politics.

You need only look at how anyone who questions the qualifications of Barack Obama to be president is cast into the pit of outer darkness by those who see him as the country's savior. But there is a current case in the news which provides a less sensitive, and perhaps more obvious, example of how making political truth your moral compass results in turning right and wrong upside down.

That is the story of hapless Scott McClellan, who was the left's favorite whipping boy when he was President Bush's bumbling press secretary but is the oracular voice of reason now that he has stuck a knife in the president's back.

McClellan's new book, "What Happened," purports to be a fresh new look at the "truth" of the Bush White House, but in fact just repeats the usual liberal truisms: that President Bush is a moron, his advisers are evil manipulators, and anyone who thinks differently is a fool.

This is manna to liberals and maddening to conservatives. Questions of competence that worried everyone a couple of years ago when McClellan was near the throne are now deemed irrelevant by the left because they can't look a "gift defector" in the mouth. Questions of character that should be as obvious as a crack in the mirror are left unasked, presumably because a witness's credibility is only as good as his character, and McClellan clearly doesn't have any — character, that is.

Of course, the idea that there could actually be "right" and "wrong" of a higher source than politics appears not to have occurred to the Daily Kos bloggers or the TV news anchors. For them, right and wrong is as simple as Democrat and Republican — in that respective order, of course, and thus McClellan is now "persona grata," and is being rewarded with money, fame and the semblance of power for coming to see the political light and telling tales out of school.

In the legal world, such payments for damning testimony would be called suborning perjury, or at the very least bribing the witness, but this is not a real trial; it is a show trial — or a "show business" trial. No one really cares about the truth of the matter; what's really crucial is the overnight ratings (good), the Amazon dot.com standings (better), and the denouement (Bush gets bashed in the end).

The notion that there might be some reason to question the veracity of a man who is a self-confessed moral coward (inability to tell the truth when it actually matters), a disloyal confidant (this one needs no explanation) and a paid informant (see above) does not seem to have occurred to McClellan's new friends. But these are the same folks who are excited to discover that there is more than one religion because they think that gets them off the hook from having to subscribe to any of them.

Don't be fooled into thinking there is a war between Republicans and Democrats. There isn't. That is just a disagreement. The real war is between people who are willing to say and do anything to gain power, and those who aren't.

So don't be too hard on McClellan. He is just one of many pawns in this game. And you can't really blame the guy for selling his soul for a million bucks, can you? After all, they usually go a lot cheaper than that.

THE PERSECUTION OF MARK STEYN, OR WHY I AM GLAD I'M NOT CANADIAN

June 15, 2008

I don't have it too bad.

I've been called a coward, a moron, a bad journalist, and worst of all a bad writer for having the audacity to express my opinions in this column, but at least I have never been arrested or put on trial for telling the truth.

That distinct honor has been reserved for Mark Steyn, the Canadian author who lives in self-imposed exile in New Hampshire.

Many of you have probably never heard of Steyn, which is a pity because he is one of the funniest, most insightful and well-rounded social critics since H.L. Mencken. He is also one of the most persecuted authors since Emile Zola published "J'Accuse" in 1898.

Zola wrote to save one man, the falsely prosecuted and convicted French captain, Alfred Dreyfus, from a conspiracy of small-minded Army officers; Steyn, on the other hand, writes on a practically daily basis to save small-minded Western civilization from itself. In his column, he typically muses about the great issues of our day — self-serving chaos in Washington, open borders in the Southwest, the incredible shrinking virtues of Hollywood, and the imminent demise of the West under the plodding, determined, insistent, grinding crush of Islamic domination.

It can truly be said of Steyn, as it was first said of Zola by the London Times, that his "true crime has been in daring to rise to defend the truth and civil liberty ... [and] for that courageous defense of the primordial rights of the citizen, he will be honored wherever men have souls that are free..."

Except, of course, in Canada.

There he is put on trial by various "human rights" panels for his blatant exercise of free speech, most recently by the British Columbia Human Rights Tribunal. Steyn and the

Canadian newsmagazine Maclean's were recently put through a week-long Orwellian nightmare as Big Brother poked and prodded them to admit the error of their ways for publishing an excerpt of Steyn's best-selling book "America Alone."

The article, entitled "The Future Belongs to Islam," featured this introduction: "The Muslim world has youth, number and global ambitions. The West is growing old and enfeebled, and more and more lacks the will to rebuff those who would supplant it. It's the end of the world as we've known it."

The fact that no less a personage than the Archbishop of Canterbury recently suggested that imposing Islamic sharia law in Great Britain might be inevitable should prove in itself the truth of Steyn's claims. But truth is not considered a defense in "hate crimes."

And the ultimate irony is that the archbishop was criticized by Britain's equality czar for inflaming passions against the very Muslims whom he thought he was helping:

"The Archbishop's thinking here is muddled and unhelpful," said Trevor Phillips, the chairman of the Equality and Human Rights Commission. "Raising this idea in this way will give fuel to anti-Muslim extremism and dismay everyone working towards a more integrated society."

Oh my, it's no wonder that Steyn decided he needed to speak out in defense of common sense and common values. But when he told the truth about what is happening in Europe, Canada and elsewhere, he was sued by the Canadian Islamic Congress for stirring up "hatred" against Muslims and for causing injury to their "dignity, feelings and self-respect."

Of course, Steyn is not entirely alone. There are plenty of people who share his work of speaking out to defend our civilization, which has done more than any other in history to enshrine the idea of human rights, and which now is teetering on the brink of disaster.

But there are also plenty of people, maybe even more, who follow a naive agenda of "hand-holding and polite talk" as the antidote to terrorism, nuclear blackmail, armed aggression and suppression of human rights. It's these folks who get all squishy whenever someone says something that's not politically correct, but just might be factually correct.

Of course, since they often don't have the facts on their side, they sometimes have to resort to ad hominem attacks, threats or just pleas that you shut up. This is particularly true if you write about the neutering of America by folks who think the best way to solve our problems is to pretend they don't exist.

Last week, I wrote a column questioning whether Barack Obama's empty promises suggest that he is just a more mellifluous, hipper, knuckle-bumping version of every other demagogue who has yearned for power and said whatever was needed to obtain it.

That spurred one reader to write about me: "Doesn't he know his words have power? Doesn't he know he has a responsibility to his readers. It's called objective opinion... Do you really think people need or want your foolish, negative, useless comments on anything? Who the hell do you think you are? ... The Media has a responsibility. Didn't they teach you anything about core values and ethics? Your comments are very sad."

She concluded by saying she didn't know why she kept reading my column, week after week, or even how I could keep my job.

Rather than brush aside these heartfelt comments, I tried to answer them reasonably, trying to explain that column writing is never objective and is not intended to be. Indeed, this is the very kind of speech that is meant to be protected by our First Amendment — the right to have opinions. I mean, if Mark Steyn can't say that he thinks Islamic fundamentalism is on the march against the traditional values of Canada and the rest of the West, what exactly can he say? Won't the Canadian government ultimately be poised to say that any criticism of its own leaders is also hate speech?

Here's the relevant piece of law from British Columbia (Section 7-1-b of the Human Rights Code): "A person must not publish, issue or display ... any statement, publication ... or other notice that is likely to expose a person to hatred or contempt."

Such a foolish law would have allowed Adolf Hitler to sue the Canadian government during World War II for its statements that Hitler was a menace to mankind. That's not an exaggeration either. It's the fundamental problem with hate-speech laws — they ban true speech as well as false. Fortunately for us in the United States, the First Amendment protects false speech as well as true, so we don't have the long arm of Big Brother sticking down our throat — yet. But it only takes one poorly decided Supreme Court case to lose the guarantees of a hundred years, or a thousand.

Now it seems like many of my readers, such as the one who wrote to me last week, don't think journalists should have opinions, and of course they are right about that in reference to news reporting, but opinion writing is just as old as news reporting, and it is by definition not objective but subjective. Opinions are the end result of having a human brain. To ban them is to perform a kind of institutional lobotomy, which would have a rather limiting effect on the meaning and practice of free speech.

It would be a funny kind of world really if everyone were to operate on the principles my reluctant reader proposed. "Shut up and 'be objective'" about sums it up.

Of course, how can you ever learn the objective truth unless you listen to different opinions? Are we really all supposed to be born with objective truth stuck somewhere in the back of our cranial backpack. Just add water and watch the truth spew forth like some kind of campers' gruel? I'm afraid that kind of ready-made truth is a little too close to brainwashing for me.

Instead of relying on someone else's idea of who I am supposed to be, I have had to learn to think for myself by reading a variety of philosophers, historians and novelists, among other activities, none of which agreed with each other, but all of which proved that the pursuit of truth should be tireless, zestful and without caution.

I hope I don't ever live in an America where people are expected to "toe the line" of TRUTH, or else keep their mouths shut. Which, I guess, also means I am glad I don't live in Canada.

Good luck, Mark Steyn, and keep up the good fight.

HADITHA: A MEDIA-MADE 'ATROCITY'?

June 22, 2008

The New York Times referred to the deaths of as many as 24 Iraqi civilians in the town of Haditha as the "defining atrocity" of the Iraq War.

If so, then the Iraq War must be particularly unatrocious. After all, of the eight people charged in the Haditha case, seven have seen the charges dropped for insufficient evidence or actually been found innocent, and the one remaining case is no more likely to produce a conviction than the first seven.

Yet there WAS a Haditha atrocity. And perhaps it even was defining of this war and its larger meaning. But the atrocity was not committed by soldiers in Iraq; it was committed in Washington, D.C., by Rep. John Murtha, and by his friends at the New York Times, Time magazine and MSNBC.

Murtha, the Pennsylvania congressman who became a media darling for opposing the war in Iraq despite his own record of military service in Vietnam, is now even more famous for calling American soldiers cold-blooded killers.

In a press conference on May 17, 2006, Murtha said that U.S. Marines had deliberately killed unarmed Iraqi civilians during an encounter in Haditha on Nov. 19, 2005. "Our troops overreacted because of the pressure on them, and they killed innocent civilians in cold blood," Murtha said before anyone had been convicted of anything, before any charges had been filed, and indeed before the investigation was even completed.

Time magazine ran a story on "The Shame of Kilo Company"; the New York Times ran front-page exposes of alleged abuse and coverup; and MSNBC and other cable outlets hyped the story for weeks in an effort to pump their ratings on the adrenalin-spiked news of Marines gone bad.

When it was pointed out to Murtha that he was violating the basic principle of "innocent before proven guilty," he didn't back down. "This is what the Marine Corps told me at the highest level," he insisted to ABC's Charlie Gibson. "There's no question the chain of command tried to stifle the story."

Except that Lt. Col. Jeffrey Chessani, the highest ranking officer charged with covering up the incident, was cleared by a military judge on June 17 of this year, as three other people charged with "covering up" the "massacre" were cleared previously.

But yet there has been no apology from Murtha, and there probably never will be. Turns out that it is a lot harder to admit you were wrong than it is to label American Marines "cold-blooded killers" on national TV.

Chessani plans to file a libel lawsuit against Murtha, and staff Sgt. Frank Wuterich has already done so.

Murtha's lawyers claim that Murtha can say whatever he wants because he is a congressman and thus has immunity from lawsuits, whether he tells the truth or not. Hmmm, maybe that explains a lot about why people don't trust Congress. But it still doesn't explain why Murtha's conscience doesn't work as well as his mouth.

Fortunately U.S. District Judge Rosemary M. Collyer has ordered Murtha to testify in the libel case, despite his lawyers arguing that he had constitutional protection under the "speech and debate" clause.

"You're writing a very wide road for members of Congress to go to their home districts and say anything they choose about private persons and be able to do so without any liability. Are you sure you want to do that?" Collyer asked. "How far can a congressman go and still be protected?"

Apparently quite far, according to Murtha's lawyers, and there's no reason to think that Murtha will ever be held accountable. Nor that the New York Times and Time magazine will pay a price for sensationalizing the story of Haditha when it looked like American soldiers were "cold-blooded killers" but back-paging the story when they were exonerated.

The lesson? Don't believe everything you hear from the mainstream media about how bad America is, and don't get too stirred up when politicians make sensational statements about the evils of the American military. They may just be telling you what they hope is true.

In the wake of the Haditha incident being made public, for instance, CNN's John Vause said, "There is a perception that U.S. forces are brutal and are, at times, trigger happy."

Gee, do you think? Do CNN, MSNBC, the New York Times and John Murtha realize that they are the ones who are creating that perception? Or that their constant drumbeat of anti-American propaganda plays right into the hands of Osama bin Laden, Mahmoud Ahmadinejad and their allies who want to destroy us?

If they do realize it, they should be tried for sedition, and if they don't realize it, maybe they should be tried anyway. Ignorance, after all, is no excuse for betraying your country.

THE PALIN TEST:
A LIBERAL LITMUS FOR THE MEDIA

September 28, 2008

If you were uncertain why people don't like and don't trust the mainstream media, all you have to do is look at the treatment of Sarah Palin and you will get the picture. Reactions to her have become a virtual litmus test for media bias.

Forget about left-wing comedians on MTV or Letterman. They are paid to belittle people who support traditional American values, and they do it very well. Ignore the New York Times, which has an agenda a mile long and a little to the left of Joseph Stalin. That particular devouring leopard will not change its spots, and everyone knows it.

But a few people still cling to a stubborn belief in the fairness of network news the way that Barack Obama thinks small-town Americans cling to guns and religion. But if what happens on ABC, NBC and CBS is reckoned as fairness, then it was also fair to throw the Christians in with the lions. Indeed, the visceral hatred that many liberals feel for Sarah Palin has become engraved on the faces of Charlie Gibson, Katie Couric, Keith Olbermann and other supposedly neutral journalists. (All right, Olbermann really isn't neutral — that was just a joke.)

Gibson's interview, the first that Palin gave after her nomination, was typical of those that followed, and instructive in just how deceitful, biased and dangerous the national media outlets have become.

In particular, if you look at the full transcript of the interview and compare it to the parts that Gibson used on ABC's "World News," you will see two different Sarah Palins. The one sitting across from Charlie Gibson was nuanced, insistent and thoughtful, but the one that Gibson cut-and-pasted in the editing room was a cross between Ma Kettle and Dr. Strangelove.

It is plain that Gibson went into the interview believing that a woman who was governor of Alaska is not qualified to be president of the United States, and he aimed to prove that. Thus, he began by asking Palin if she had "ever met a foreign head of state."

Now, of course, he knew full well that she had not, or if she had it was because of some incidental contact. Governors typically have their hands full managing the affairs of their own "state" without setting up their own "state department" to compete with the one in Washington, D.C.

But that doesn't mean Palin hasn't dealt with foreign countries, and she wisely tried to steer Gibson back to reality by talking about what governors really do. She told him that Alaska's "international trade activities bring in many leaders of other countries," but Gibson didn't want to hear it — and he didn't want you to hear it either. He cut that out of the interview.

Mind you, Palin still managed to get her point across - the answer that Gibson used emphasized that the governor considered her Alaskan experience to be an alternative to "politics as usual." She acknowledged that there are plenty of politicians with a "big, fat resume that shows decades and decades in [the] Washington establishment" who will thus - as she adroitly noted - have had "opportunities to meet heads of state." But Gibson then cut out her coup de grace when she said that Americans "are getting sick and tired of that self-dealing and kind of that closed door, good old boy network that has been the Washington elite."

When moving on to foreign policy substance, Gibson broached the topic of Russia's invasion of Georgia, but he clearly was not prepared for the scope of Palin's knowledge on this topic as he decided to cut out about 70 percent of her lengthy response. Is it possible she sounded too knowledgeable for Gibson to be able to make her look bad? Hmmm, interesting theory.

In any case, this is also the segment of the interview where Gibson's oh-so-cute editing was used to try to make it look like Palin said she understood Russia because it is close to Alaska.

Here's the interview Gibson aired:

Palin: [W]e've got to keep an eye on Russia. For Russia to have exerted such pressure in terms of invading a smaller democratic country, unprovoked, is unacceptable and we have to keep...

GIBSON: You believe unprovoked.

PALIN: I do believe unprovoked and we have got to keep our eyes on Russia, under the leadership there.

GIBSON: What insight into Russian actions, particularly in the last couple of weeks, does the proximity of the state give you?

PALIN: They're our next door neighbors and you can actually see Russia from land here in Alaska, from an island in Alaska.

This segment of the interview has provided comedians and commentators with endless gaglines about how Palin foolishly believes living next to another country provides foreign policy experience. But let's look at what she really said. Here's the unedited interview:

PALIN: [W]e've got to keep an eye on Russia. For Russia to have exerted such pressure in terms of invading a smaller democratic country, unprovoked, is unacceptable and we have to keep...

GIBSON: You believe unprovoked.

PALIN: I do believe unprovoked and we have got to keep our eyes on Russia, under the leadership there. I think it was unfortunate. That manifestation that we saw with that invasion of Georgia shows us some steps backwards that Russia has recently taken away from the race toward a more democratic nation with democratic ideals. That's why we have to keep an eye on Russia.

And, Charlie, you're in Alaska. We have that very narrow maritime border between the United States, and the 49th state, Alaska, and Russia. They are our next door neighbors. We need to have a good relationship with them. They're very, very important to us and they are our next door neighbor.

GIBSON: What insight into Russian actions, particularly in the last couple of weeks, does the proximity of the state give you?

PALIN: They're our next door neighbors and you can actually see Russia from land here in Alaska, from an island in Alaska.

GIBSON: What insight does that give you into what they're doing in Georgia?

PALIN: Well, I'm giving you that perspective of how small our world is and how important it is that we work with our allies to keep good relations with all of these countries, especially Russia. We will not repeat a Cold War. We must have good relationship with our allies, pressuring, also, helping us to remind Russia that it's in their benefit, also, a mutually beneficial relationship for us all to be getting along.

We cannot repeat the Cold War. We are thankful that, under Reagan, we won the Cold War, without a shot fired, also. We've learned lessons from that in our relationship with Russia, previously the Soviet Union.

Oh no, Gibson must have thought! She is actually answering my question in a coherent, comprehensive way! This won't fit in with my plan to score career points by demonstrating to the public how dangerously incompetent she is. What shall I do?

Whether the answer eventually occurred to Gibson or to one of his producers is not known, but the answer was clear —

just cut out all of the parts of the answer that show Palin to have a valid and valuable point of view.

And most importantly, where Palin was using her experience as Alaska's governor to show that she and her constituents have an immediate, proximate interest in good relations with Russia, Gibson intentionally distorted her answer so that she looked like a naive New Age goofball who would peer across the Bering Strait and get a glimpse into the Russian soul.

Which brings us to Katie Couric's more recent interview with Palin on the "CBS Evening News." Couric couldn't let the tasty morsel about Alaska being near Russia drop to the ground without getting a lick in.

Couric asked Palin the following: "You've cited Alaska's proximity to Russia as part of your foreign policy experience. What did you mean by that?"

Of course, you and I both know that Palin should have told Couric directly that she had never said that, but Palin tried to find a polite way to re-direct the question instead. She started out by again talking about the "very narrow maritime border between a foreign country, Russia, and, on our other side, the land-boundary that we have with Canada," but then she clearly became exasperated and said, "It's funny that a comment like that was kinda made to ... I don't know, you know ... reporters.

Couric: Mocked?

Palin: Yeah, mocked, I guess that's the word, yeah.

Mocked is clearly the word that most Americans would have when watching either Charlie Gibson or Katie Couric interviewing Sarah Palin, but Palin again pushed ahead and tried to answer the question. Eventually she said this:

"As Putin rears his head and comes into the air space of the United States of America, where do they go? It's Alaska. It's just right over the border. It is from Alaska that we send those out to make sure that an eye is being kept on this very powerful nation, Russia, because they are right there, they are right next to our state."

Now this is a peculiar statement, and one that Palin might have been keeping intentionally vague because she did not know whether she should speak frankly about U.S. military information she had received as governor.

Turns out that Palin, in her role as commander-in-chief of the Alaska National Guard, has received briefings about Russian military plane incursions right to the edge of Alaskan airspace. That explains why she spoke cryptically of Putin "rearing his head."

The CBS reporter, Scott Conroy, who detailed this in the wake of the Couric interview, however, seemed to be unable to recognize the connection to what Palin had told Couric. Instead of realizing that Palin's comment about "Putin rear[ing] his head and com[ing] into the airspace of the United States of America" was a reference to those recent military incursions, he assumed she was talking about Putin's actual diplomatic visits to the United States. He thus chided Palin for inaccuracy by noting that Putin would have visited Washington by traveling across the Atlantic.

But you don't have to be smarter than a fifth grader to realize that Palin was really talking about Putin's military threat against the United States, and when she asked "Where do they go?" she wasn't talking about Putin's valet and chef, but about his fighter jets and bombers.

Some people are terrified of Sarah Palin. They don't need to be. They should be terrified of Charlie Gibson and Katie Couric and the other ex officio ministers of information who attempt to exert control over what Americans learn and what they don't learn about our government and our leaders.

SARAH PALIN VS. THE MEDIA: THE REMATCH

January 11, 2009

Sarah Palin is back in the news, which not surprisingly delights her fans but also has her enemies licking their chops enthusiastically.

It was inevitable, of course, that Palin would surface again in the national news, but most people thought it would not be for another year or so when she will likely start testing the waters for a run against President Obama in 2012.

But last week's YouTube video release of her reflections on her 2008 vice-presidential campaign turned out to be all the red meat that the media needed to pounce on her again.

Not to say she didn't give as good as she got in this rematch that is as riveting as any of the Ali-Frazier fights and could justifiably be called "The Thrilla in Wasilla."

The action started in Palin's corner when she sat down for a lengthy interview with conservative talk-show host John Ziegler for a film he was making called "Media Malpractice: How Obama Got Elected and Palin was Smeared." The film will not be out until February, but Ziegler released a greatest hits compilation of Palin outtakes on YouTube where she gives her candid appraisal of the national political media as well as such celebrities as Katie Couric, Keith Olbermann and Tina Fey.

Needless to say she is not fond of them because of their attacks on her and her family, but it's at least fitting that many members of the mainstream media are up front about their dislike of her, too.

Olbermann is a good example. On his Jan. 6 show on MSNBC, he declared Palin "The Worst Person in the World" because her son-in law got a job as an electrical apprentice even though he didn't have the required high school diploma (so much for liberal compassion, not to mention Horatio Alger as a model of the American success story).

Olbermann wondered aloud whether Palin had used her influence to get the rules bent, then said he believed her denial but it didn't matter what she said or did anyway, because "the governor is the bottomless pit of political scandals, the all you can eat buffet of political scandals, the endless wedge of Velveeta of public scandals. Governor Sarah Palin, today's worst, and by worst, I mean the gift that keeps on giving and I would be lost without her, person in the world!"

Of course, Olbermann is supposed to be an entertainer, not a newsman, so you have to cut him a wee bit of slack in his manic brand of character assassination, but the same can't be said for MSNBC newsman David Schuster, who did a midday interview with John Ziegler Friday and did the unthinkable — becoming part of the story by declaring on camera that Palin was "clearly unqualified" to be vice president.

Schuster also falsely alleged that Palin was unhappy with Ziegler for taking her quotes out of context, but in fact she was unhappy with newsmen like Schuster. She actually said she was disappointed that the media was taking the quotes on YouTube out of context, not with Ziegler for posting them.

The good news is that Ziegler didn't quietly sit by while Schuster tried to smear Palin further by repeating that she was not qualified to be vice president. Ziegler shot back, "Is that your opinion, David, as an alleged newsperson? As an alleged newsperson, is that your opinion that she was unprepared to be vice president of the United States? Gee, that sounds very objective, David."

But, of course, it isn't objective and yet there is almost no chance that MSNBC will chastise Schuster for his comment, nor will he issue an apology like he did to Hillary Clinton when he said that her campaign had "pimped out" daughter Chelsea Clinton on the campaign trail in February.

The plain fact of the matter is that MSNBC — led by Olbermann, but ably abetted by Schuster, Rachel Maddow and others — enjoys smearing Palin — even out in the open like Schuster did on Friday. The question is how long can they keep throwing low blows and get away with it? Is the American public ever going to step in and referee this mess?

"Thrilla in Wasilla?" This fight is just getting interesting.

PRINCIPLES AND TARGETS: WHEN LEFT MEETS RIGHT

March 8, 2009

Rush Limbaugh has been criticized for saying he hopes the president fails in his efforts to reshape the economy, most recently in this newspaper by columnist Ellen Goodman, who called Limbaugh "a talk radio host who'd rather be (far) right than have his country rescued."

This kind of twisted commentary is what makes one pessimistic about the future of the country. How exactly did Ellen Goodman miss the news that Rush Limbaugh is a conservative and Barack Obama is a liberal (oops, I almost said socialist)? Is there really any logical reason why Limbaugh WOULD support Obama? Does anyone remember liberals like Al Franken and Nancy Pelosi supporting President Bush when he was trying to ensure victory in Iraq? Does anyone remember the sympathetic liberal voices saying, "We need to get behind President Bush as he works to rescue New Orleans and the Gulf Coast from the wreckage of Katrina"? Does anyone remember Chuck Schumer and Hillary Clinton rallying behind Bush's plan to rescue Social Security?

Of course not. But when liberals are in power, criticism of the government is virtually a crime against the state. We need a "fairness" doctrine to shut up those mean old conservatives. Or maybe we should just round up the troublemakers and send them to re-education camps. Heaven knows, there are lots of liberals who would like to send me to one.

But hold on a second. How about we pay attention to what Limbaugh actually said, and not just what Ellen Goodman says he said in her gotcha-style attack. If you only read Goodman's column, you would just hear that Limbaugh doesn't want to see his country "rescued" — not that Limbaugh rejects President Obama's policies because he expects them to bankrupt the country morally and financially.

In particular Limbaugh said: "So what is so strange about being honest to say that I want Barack Obama to fail if his mission is to restructure and reform this country so that capitalism and individual liberty are not its foundation? Why would I want that to succeed?"

Indeed. Why would any of us want that to succeed?

But Goodman equates Limbaugh's defense of liberty with being somehow anti-American. Turns out that dumping capitalism and individual liberty really is "rescuing" America from itself — from its history, its traditions and (as Limbaugh says) its foundations.

Kind of reminds me of those folks around Oklahama who thought highly of Pretty Boy Floyd the bank robber because he "rescued" them by tearing up mortgages while he was robbing banks. Have we really reached the point where looting the national treasury to keep the economy afloat is considered a noble endeavor?

I hope and trust my readers don't think so, but someone really ought to have the courage to say so, and that's where Rush Limbaugh comes in. It is quite apparent that the political structure in Washington, D.C., is corrupt to the core. It doesn't matter if you are Republican or Democrat; as soon as you accept "politics as usual" you are co-opted. As soon as you accept the "system" you are part of the problem.

Rush Limbaugh and a few other media personalities such as Laura Ingraham, Rick Santelli and Jim Cramer don't accept the system. As a matter of principle, they have spoken out against "politics as usual" and taken a stand for common sense, and that's why they are being targeted by the left.

It's not an accident either. It's part of Saul Alinsky's "Rules for Radicals" that he set forth in his 1971 book of the same name. Alinsky was a Chicago community organizer who proudly flaunted his left-wing agenda and left behind a playbook that has been studied and taught by Barack Obama — that other "Chicago community organizer" — along with many other influential leaders.

Indeed, it almost seems like Alinsky's "rules for radicals" are what govern our nation today even more than the U.S. Constitution. When thinking about the undefined "change" Obama promised us before he was elected, consider this.

Alinsky wrote: "Change comes from power, and power comes from organization.... The first step in community organization is community disorganization. The disruption of the present organization is the first step toward community organization. Present arrangements must be disorganized if they are to be displaced by new patterns.... All change means disorganization of the old and organization of the new."

Gee, sounds familiar, doesn't it?

Is it possible that all this chaos in American society today is part of a plan to "change" us once and for all? As you may have noticed, we are in the midst of a revolution that will eventually make the New Deal look like child's play. The Obama administration is intent on increasing the federal government's control of our lives in virtually every arena. Health care? Check. Climate control? Check. Local police? Check. Gun control? Check. Banking? Check. Want to keep your job? Check. Bought and paid for? Check.

The more money Obama and the federal government pour into local and state coffers, the more dependent states and cities become on the federal government. The more you start to rely on your "tax rebate" or "economic stimulus" check to buy necessities, the more dependent you become on a bloated centralized government which like Big Brother "just wants to help you."

President Ronald Reagan summed up the dangers of big government in his farewell address to the nation in January 1989 when he said: "There's a clear cause and effect ... that is as neat and predictable as a law of physics: As government expands, liberty contracts."

That makes me think that at least one former president would join Rush Limbaugh in hoping that President Obama fails. And let's repeat this one last time: Limbaugh never said he didn't want Obama to succeed in "rescuing" the United States; instead he said that he didn't want Obama to succeed in destroying the country by turning it into a European-style socialist state.

But it doesn't matter what Limbaugh really said, does it? Alinsky's "Rules for Radicals" included this unpleasant advice: "Pick the target, freeze it, personalize it, and polarize it."

With George W. Bush gone from the stage, another polarizing figure was needed, and Obama's team has picked out Limbaugh for the job. With allies like Ellen Goodman and MSNBC helping to lampoon Limbaugh, Obama can follow through with one more of Alinsky's tactical rules: "Ridicule is man's most potent weapon."

But ridicule has no effect if the truth is known. That's why it is important to actually study the news for yourself. Never rely on me, Limbaugh, Obama or Ellen Goodman for the facts. Find them out for yourself, and then hold on to them — because they are your lifeline to truth, and to the responsibility which truth brings.

FROM CNN: 'HO HO HO CHI MINH... COMMUNISM STILL CAN WIN'

October 4, 2009

Reporter Carol Costello had a report on CNN's "American Morning" Friday asking whether the time was ripe for a third party in the United States.

That's certainly an interesting topic, and one well worth featuring in a news report, but what was really interesting was that the third party Costello chose to feature was communism.

That seems to tell us more about CNN than about American politics.

No, I don't think that CNN stands for Communist News Network like some people do, but that cable news channel does sometimes seem to have a left-leaning slant (not into Stalin territory like MSNBC, but well over into the Gorbachev range at least).

And if you don't think they lean left, would you do me a favor? Please explain why they picked a communist out as an example of how the country is "ripe" for a third party? Do any of you really believe that communism is about to become a viable grass-roots alternative in Cleveland or anywhere else in America? I don't.

And nobody I know, whether Republican or Democrat, would ever consider voting for a communist for city council, let alone for Senate or president. So how exactly is this a proper focus for a story about Americans being receptive to the idea of a third party?

Oh sure, the story also mentioned Bob Barr and the Libertarian Party, and had a quote from political analyst John Avlon saying, "Voters are getting more and more frustrated with politics as usual," but that's a far cry from saying Americans are ready to cast off centuries of capitalist tradition and adopt the failed dogmas of Eastern Europe.

Yet CNN focused their story on the "little communist candidate who could," Rick Nagin. There was not even the hint of any skepticism from the CNN reporter about touting communism as a viable alternative to the Democrats and Republicans. Indeed, if you watched Costello's report, you got the idea that communism was as American as apple pie. Kind of like Nagin's concluding quote: "I consider myself to be a very patriotic American. I love this country."

That's nice. Swell. I bet Stalin liked his country too even though he killed 30 million of his fellow citizens. And I'm sure Chairman Mao was a big fan of China even though about 80 million Chinese are estimated to have perished "unexpectedly" during his reign.

But that could never happen here, right?

Well, probably not. At least, not as long as Americans continue to be told the truth, and can make informed decisions for themselves.

But what if we don't get the truth? What if we are fed an endless diet of anti-American propaganda from major news networks and major political parties? Isn't it possible then that we might fall prey to opportunistic charlatans who will pounce on the uninformed electorate like wolves in sheep's clothing?

The weird thing is that this Rick Nagin is indeed a serious candidate for the Cleveland City Council. That's certainly worth reporting. Flukes like this happen from time to time, such as socialist Bernie Sanders being elected to the Senate from Vermont.

And people ought to hear about Nagin. He is an intriguing candidate, who raises some interesting questions. According to Costello, he is both a registered Democrat AND a member of the Communist Party. He was quoted in the report on CNN's "American Morning" as saying, "I believe that corporate greed is the source of the problems in this country and we'd all be a lot better off if working people and their organizations were running things instead of big business."

Reporter Costello did not identify whether this quote was made by the "registered Democrat" side of Nagin, or the "member of the Communist Party," but the question is how many other Democrats, including elected officials, feel the same way about capitalism? Is disdain for free enterprise the "dirty little secret" of Democrats? I certainly hope not.

But when you read the glowing reviews for Michael Moore's latest film, you have to wonder. Moore, at least, comes right out and admits that he thinks the economic system that made our country great is "evil." In his new movie, "Capitalism: A Love Story," he blames people like you and me who value the American dream for the troubles of people who are struggling to make it in 21st-century America.

Oh sure, he singles out rich CEOs as the "great Satans" of America, but you know behind every "great Satan" with a Ferrari, there are a thousand "little Satans" driving Fords and thinking about Ferraris. Those wannabe CEOs are you and me, folks -- scrambling for our place on the ladder of success, trying to get ahead, and making Michael Moore see red as he thinks about how one man's success is another's "exploitation."

Heck, when you think about it, the problem all starts with the "teeny-tiny Satans" hawking lemonade from roadside stands to the "little Satans" driving by in their big bad Fords. Those kids are small-scale capitalists, and unless they are giving half their earnings to the kid down the street who didn't have the ambition to run a lemonade stand of his own but still wants to buy himself candy and a soda pop, they are also "evil." Share the wealth, dudes.

Of course, Michael Moore is smart enough not to attack your kids. If he did that, you wouldn't go see the capitalist-funded movies that have turned him into a multi-millionaire. Oh yeah, and did I say that I didn't know anyone who would vote for a communist for city council? I was wrong. I forgot about Michael Moore.

FAIRNESS AND FREE SPEECH: A MISMATCH?

November 8, 2009

"You cannot have an opposition movement without opposition media." —Van Jones, former Green Jobs Czar for President Obama.

Free speech and dictatorship don't mix.

Just think about it. If I were a Third World dictator and wanted to keep power indefinitely and still pretend to be legitimate, could I do so if the newspapers and television stations were all speaking out against me?

Heck no. Free speech is a powerful tool for democracy, as our Founding Fathers knew. That's why if I were a dictator, I might eventually take the step of shutting down the opposition newspapers and TV stations, like Hugo Chavez has done in Venezuela. But that has the disadvantage of confirming everyone's worst suspicions that I am indeed a ruthless dictator.

Dictators are cunning devils, however (which is probably how they got to be dictators in the first place), so they don't have to solve every problem with violence. Sometimes subterfuge can be just as effective.

Thus, if I were a subtle dictator, instead of using my police against the newspapers, I could use my legislature, or even my executive authority. It's not necessary to silence the opposition; it's just necessary to make them irrelevant. To do that, I would have to be able to make their words irrelevant, and to do that I would need to invent a "Fairness Doctrine."

What exactly is that, you ask?

Simply put, it is a policy that devalues free speech by requiring every argument put forth in public to have a mandatory counter-argument.

Sounds good in principle, I suppose, except when you value the voice of the people as a mechanism for putting a "governor" on the government. In a free society, if 80 percent of the people abhor their government, they can speak out loudly and insistently and overthrow their government peacefully.

But in a society where "Fairness" has been imposed, that is not possible. Instead, when the 80 percent speak out against my corrupt government, I would be able to demand equal time in the newspapers and radio and TV stations to tell the people why I am actually a kindly and benevolent dictator who should be thought of as the people's savior and advocate, not their enemy.

If there were a front-page article today saying my government was corrupt, I would demand a front-page article tomorrow saying my opponents were scurrilous liars who are paid propagandists for causes contrary to my lofty goals.

It couldn't happen in America, you say?

Hogwash. It already has happened in many small ways, and there is a movement afoot to reduce the opposition media in the United States to an irrelevant asterisk.

The Van Jones quote with which this column begins is merely the road sign pointing to the ultimate goal of total control of the media that some members of the ruling elite seem to have in mind as part of the "transformation" of America they envision.

Like all roads to hell, this one comes with the standard "good intentions."

The Fairness Doctrine was enacted by the Federal Communications Commission in 1949, and it was the rule of the land until it was abandoned in the mid-1980s. Its purpose was to ensure that various viewpoints would have access to the airwaves, and that no one used government-issued broadcast licenses to brainwash the public with a monolithic source of information.

That probably made sense in the 1940s when broadcasting was relatively new and diversity was relatively limited. But it became apparent in the ensuing years that the "Fairness Doctrine" could also be used as a cudgel to intimidate broadcasters from airing unpopular viewpoints or even as a way to punish those of an opposite political persuasion.

Thus, shortly after the Reuther Memorandum was sent to Attorney General Robert Kennedy advising him to use the FCC to crack down on the ability of the "radical right" to spread its message of "fear," the FCC issued a public notice in 1963 that did just that. (See last week's column to read more about the Reuther Memorandum.)

The FCC's notice advised broadcasters that they had an "affirmative obligation" to "afford reasonable opportunity for the presentation of contrasting viewpoints." It singled out programs that were "presented under the label of 'Americanism,' 'anti-communism,' or 'state's rights'" and told broadcasters that whenever such a viewpoint was aired, whether in a paid announcement or an editorial or even an official speech, the station was "obligated to make a reasonable effort to present the other opposing viewpoint."

You can imagine that this could create quite a problem. First of all, if you broadcast a program that was pro-American, could you really be forced by our own government to broadcast a program that was anti-American?

And the particulars were even more disturbing. If a program involved a "personal attack upon an individual or organization, the licensee must transmit the text of the broadcast to the person or group attacked, wherever located, either prior to or at the time of the broadcast, with a specific offer of his station's facilities for an adequate response."

Could you imagine if such a policy had been in effect after the attacks of Sept. 11? Whenever Osama bin Laden was denounced as a brutal killer, al-Qaida would be scoring more air time for their message of anti-Americanism! Of course, it might have helped the United States to track down Osama since all the news organizations in the country would have been investigating his whereabouts so that they could deliver their offer of an "adequate response."

Unbelievable, but this is actually the policy that was in place in our country for more than 35 years, and which numerous politicians and theoreticians of the left want to see reinstated.

Mark Lloyd, the FCC diversity czar, is on record as saying that "the Fairness Doctrine is not enough. Put some hard structural rules in place that are going to result in fairness."

Presumably that is fairness in the "Animal Farm" sense. Your remember George Orwell's "Animal Farm," right? In that book, the animals take over the farm with the best of intentions, but things go hideously wrong. Ultimately the high-minded principles of egalitarianism and opportunity turn into this simple rule of power politics: "All animals are equal, but some are more equal than others."

It's the same thing with fairness. If you are protecting the right of your own viewpoint to be heard, you are all in favor of fairness, but when the opposition wants to speak out against you, suddenly there are good and valid reasons to shut them up.

Mr. Jones, the avowed communist, said it best with his immortal words, "You cannot have an opposition movement without opposition media."

Over the next few months and years, we may get a chance to see that theory tested. The Obama administration has already started a full-frontal assault on Fox News and various conservative commentators. If Fox and Glenn Beck should thus suddenly disappear from the cable lineup sometime in the next few months, you will at least know what's to blame — good old "Fairness."

JOURNOLIST: A PEEK INSIDE THE MINISTRY OF PROPAGANDA

July 25, 2010

OK, so now we know that there is a liberal media conspiracy — as if we didn't already know that.

We also know that the liberal media will generate a massive drumbeat of propaganda to laughingly deride anyone who claims there is a "liberal media conspiracy."

And sadly, we also know that the liberal media will largely get away with it — again.

I am talking about the Journolist controversy, which confirms everyone's worst fears about how large elements of the media these days are nothing more than unofficial operatives for Democratic and left-wing politics.

But did you ever hear of Journolist? Or this controversy? Probably not. Because the gatekeepers of mainstream news are those very self-same liberal journalists who have been exposed as shills and hacks. They aren't likely to be playing up this story on the front page of the New York Times.

Here are the basic facts:

Journolist was an e-mail list-serv chat group that was supposed to provide a place for journalists and news-minded people to hash out the big stories of the day and put them in context. It was private, but like all list-servs generated a huge amount of e-mail that any individual member could store and reference later. Those e-mails, written casually between like-minded individuals, have now been leaked to the public at dailycaller.com, and expose a rat's nest of bias and collusion that would make any responsible journalist cringe.

The group was founded by Ezra Klein, who used to write for a left-wing publication, the American Prospect, but now writes for the purportedly mainstream Washington Post. Klein has confirmed that there were only a few rules for membership in

Journolist. "One is that you can't be working for the government. Another is that you're center to left of center..."

Within that private sanctuary therefore, journalists could let down their hair and relax, speaking freely of the political stories of the day such as the nomination of Sarah Palin as John McCain's running mate. The trouble is that reporters and opinion writers and left-wing bloggers were all sipping from the same cup, and the front-line reporters happily did the bidding of the left-wing bloggers.

Daniel Levy of the Century Foundation, a progressive think tank, made an intriguing comment about the role of the "non-official campaign" in destroying Palin's credibility:

"This seems to me like an occasion when the non-official campaign has a big role to play in defining Palin, shaping the terms of the conversation and saying things that the official campaign shouldn't say — very hard-hitting stuff, including some of the things that people have been noting here — scare people about having this woefully inexperienced, no foreign policy/national security/right-wing christia[n] wing-nut a heartbeat away... bang away at McCain's age making this unusually significant."

Considering the context, it is hard to see the "non-official campaign" cited by Levy as anything other than the liberal media, which so desperately wanted to replace the much-hated George W. Bush with a beloved progressive like Barack Obama.

The more you read from the now leaked e-mails the more apparent it becomes that these so-called journalists had an us vs. them mentality where "us" is "smart liberals" and "them" is "dangerous conservatives." That divide is apparent even when the writer is trying to persuade even more radical leftists to tone it down. For instance, when Chris Hayes, a writer for the Nation, pleaded with "mainstream" journalists to ignore the Jeremiah Wright story because it just hurt Obama, another blogger wrote back to deflect his argument partly with this line: "We make distinctions — they smear."

It is clear that the "we" is not journalists, but leftists. It is also clear throughout that the first allegiance of these so-called journalists is not to credibility and accuracy, but to a political cause. It is also clear that they DO smear.

It seems that some members of this group even went undercover as conservatives in an effort to spread left-wing propaganda more effectively. The Washington Post recently announced that it was firing its conservative news blogger David Weigel because, well, because he despised conservatives. His blog was called "Inside the conservative movement and the Republican Party with David Weigel." It should more accurately have been called "Infiltrating the conservative movement and the Republican Party with avowed leftist David Weigel."

A story by the Daily Caller exposed that Weigel was a member of Journolist and that he had used the list-serv as a forum to vent his hatred for conservatives. In one case, Weigel wrote that the problem with mainstream news is "this need to give equal/extra time to 'real American' views, no matter how f---ing moronic, which just so happen to be the views of the conglomerates that run the media and/or buy up ads."

Yep, much better to just tell "real Americans" what they should think, and "educate" them so they will realize how "evil" the Republicans really are. At least, that's the impression anyone will get who honestly looks at the "conversation" between liberal journalists that has now been exposed for all to see.

To the media elite, you and I are just morons.

That's why everything that happened to Sarah Palin in the 2008 campaign should be questioned. That's why all "mainstream" reporting about Barack Obama's progressive agenda should be doubted. That's why the campaign to smear Fox News should be seen for what it is — an effort to limit the information available to the public to what benefits the current administration.

The problem is, when the Fourth Estate works for the chief executive, not for the truth, then what we have is no longer a free press, but rather a Ministry of Propaganda.

WIKILEAKS CULPRITS MUST PAY A PRICE

August 8, 2010

It is being compared to the Pentagon Papers document dump of the Vietnam War era, but don't you believe it.

The WikiLeaks publication of thousands of pages of U.S. intelligence documents regarding the war in Afghanistan is much more devastating at a human level than the Pentagon Papers, and will no doubt result in many deaths than can never be justified or explained away.

The so-called Pentagon Papers project was a top-secret U.S. Department of Defense history of American political and military involvement in Vietnam from 1945 to 1967. It was leaked to the New York Times in 1971 by one of its authors, Daniel Ellsberg, and was a roadmap to the gargantuan lies told to the American public by our own government about how and why we were fighting the war in Southeast Asia.

Whether the Pentagon Papers leak was a violation of law or not may never be decided, but Arthur Ochs Sulzberger, president and publisher of The New York Times, probably was correct when he noted that the Pentagon Papers "were really a part of history that should have been made available, considerably longer ago. I ... didn't feel there was any breach of national security, in the sense that we were giving secrets to the enemy."

The Pentagon Papers were instead giving information to the American public about a war that was being fought in their name.

In the case of the WikiLeaks, something very different is happening. There is nothing, or very little, new about U.S. policy in the documents, as even President Obama has acknowledged, but there is a treasure trove of data about how the war is being fought on the ground in Afghanistan, which will very much aid and abet the enemy.

Secretary of Defense Robert Gates said, "The battlefield consequences of the release of these documents are potentially severe and dangerous for our troops, our allies and Afghan partners, and may well damage our relationships and reputation in that key part of the world. Intelligence sources and methods, as well as military tactics, techniques and procedures, will become known to our adversaries."

WikiLeaks founder Julian Assange has cavalierly dismissed the claim that innocent people or informants will likely be targeted as a result of the publication of the "Afghan War Diary" documents.

Admiral Mike Mullen, chairman of the Joint Chiefs of Staff, however, said this: "Mr. Assange can say whatever he likes about the greater good he thinks he and his source are doing, but the truth is they might already have on their hands the blood of some young soldier or that of an Afghan family. Disagree with the war all you want, take issue with the policy, challenge me or our ground commanders on the decisions we make to accomplish the mission we've been given, but don't put those who willingly go into harm's way even further in harm's way just to satisfy your need to make a point."

The possibility of revenge by the Taliban is not just hypothetical. Newsweek reports that, " A spokesman for the group quickly threatened to 'punish' any Afghan listed as having 'collaborated' with the U.S. and the Kabul authorities against the growing Taliban insurgency."

Indeed, "just four days after the documents were published, death threats began arriving at the homes of key tribal elders in southern Afghanistan. And over the weekend one tribal elder, Khalifa Abdullah, who the Taliban believed had been in close contact with the Americans, was taken from his home... and executed by insurgent gunmen."

Assange and anyone else who is found to be responsible for publishing this top-secret material should face prosecution to the fullest possible extent. War is a most serious business. Putting our soldiers' and allies' lives at risk should have the most serious consequences.

WHAT'S SO SCARY ABOUT SARAH?

January 23, 2011

Some people don't like Sarah Palin.

As an intellectual exercise, you might want to ask yourself why that is.

Is it because they don't like her personally or because they don't agree with her ideas?

I suppose some people might not like her because she speaks with a funny accent, or because she is from a rural state or because she likes to hunt and fish.

I think we can all agree that people who don't like her for any of those reasons, or because (shudder!) she goes to church, are narrow-minded and not really worthy of serious consideration. Besides, all of those characteristics could apply to Abe Lincoln just as easily, and from what we know he was considered quite likable personally.

But what if it is her ideas that people don't like? Isn't that fair?

Maybe so. Surely, there is room for disagreement on such significant policy issues as abortion or tax rates or immigration, but even if you support abortion or higher taxes or citizenship for illegal aliens, does that mean you have to dislike Palin as a human being? Do you have to belittle her? Do you have to distort her words?

Whatever happened to that civility we keep hearing about? It doesn't seem to apply when people talk about Sarah Palin. She has been vilified and smeared from the instant she arrived on the national scene as John McCain's vice-presidential pick. People have wished for her death. They have insulted her children. They have twisted her words. They have painted her as incoherent and illogical and finally — with the Tucson shooting — as an inspiration for killers.

And that's just what her fellow Republicans have said about her!

Here's a sampling at random:

Former Reagan speechwriter Peggy Noonan: "...there is little sign that she has the tools, the equipment, the knowledge or the philosophical grounding one hopes for, and expects, in a holder of high office."

Columnist Kathleen Parker: "Clearly Out Of Her League."

Former House Speaker Newt Gingrich: "I think that she's got to slow down and be more careful and think through what she's saying and how she's saying it."

Former George W. Bush speechwriter David Frum: Palin "should stop talking now."

Those last two comments seem to represent the mainstream Republican view of Palin — and certainly the mainstream Democratic view: SHE SHOULD JUST SHUT UP.

But why?

Well, let's face it, the usual reason people want to see someone else shut up is because they disagree with that person's point of view. It's not rocket science. The more your enemy talks, the more chance there is that someone will listen.

And what exactly is it that Palin is saying that mainstream Republicans are afraid of? What is she saying that scares all establishment politicians?

When you analyze her scary ideas, they usually come down to this — a belief in individual liberty and responsibility, a belief in limited government, a belief in American exceptionalism, and a belief in a Creator.

So what part of those things is offensive or stupid? What part of that "agenda" do mainstream Republicans want to run away from?

Individual liberty, responsibility, and limited government? Those ideas come from our Founding Fathers. American exceptionalism? That idea comes from a study of history. Belief in a Creator? That idea is the bedrock on which all our liberties are built. Look in the Declaration of Independence if you don't want to look in the Bible.

Just to make sure there was nothing scary about Sarah, I read the full text of Sarah Palin's Facebook statement about the Arizona shooting, which has been widely denounced as reprehensible, mostly by Democrats such as Chris Matthews and Jon Stewart. PoliticusUSA blogger Sarah Jones attacked the statement for its "volatile, incendiary rhetoric." Rep. Debbie Wasserman Schultz's spokesman said it showed "a complete ignorance of history — or blatant anti-Semitism."

I encourage you to read Palin's statement for yourself. Or watch it on Facebook. Just visit www.facebook.com/sarahpalin and look for the posting under the terrifying title, "America's Enduring Strength."

I can find nothing in it that any patriotic American — Republican, Democrat or independent — could possibly disagree with. It begins with a broken heart, mourning and "a healing process for the families touched by this tragedy and for our country." It ends with a prayer for the victims of the tragedy and a plea for "God's guidance and the peace He provides." In between, there is a lengthy meditation on the American spirit, the American political system, and American values.

It is a very thoughtful statement — filled with the kind of serious discourse we claim that we as Americans want our leaders to engage in — but because it was made by Sarah Palin, it was immediately dismissed as self-serving and sophomoric. Pundits pounced to persuade the consumers of cable news that Palin was once again fomenting hate. That Palin is not like the rest of America. That her ideas are somehow foreign and unattractive. That she is mean-spirited and downright stupid.

But listen to what she actually said about the shooting in Tucson and the debate that followed, and you will find out that she was just the opposite — kind-hearted, generous and thoughtful.

"Our exceptional nation, so vibrant with ideas and the passionate exchange and debate of ideas, is a light to the rest of the world," Palin said. "Congresswoman Giffords and her constituents were exercising their right to exchange ideas that day, to celebrate our Republic's core values and peacefully assemble to petition our government. It's inexcusable and incomprehensible why a single evil man took the lives of peaceful citizens that day..."

See anything you disagree with there?

How about this?

"The last election was all about taking responsibility for our country's future. President Obama and I may not agree on everything, but I know he would join me in affirming the health of our democratic process. Two years ago his party was victorious. Last November, the other party won. In both elections the will of the American people was heard, and the peaceful transition of power proved yet again the enduring strength of our Republic."

Not too radical, is it?

But what really bothered Palin haters is that she actually responded to their outrageous claims that she was somehow responsible for what the alleged pot-smoking, Bush-hating gunman did in Tucson. In other words, they were once again mad at her for daring to speak.

"Like many, I've spent the past few days reflecting on what happened and praying for guidance. After this shocking tragedy, I listened at first puzzled, then with concern, and now with sadness, to the irresponsible statements from people attempting to apportion blame for this terrible event," she said.

"Vigorous and spirited public debates during elections are among our most cherished traditions. And after the election, we shake hands and get back to work, and often both sides find common ground back in D.C. and elsewhere. If you don't like a person's vision for the country, you're free to debate that vision. If you don't like their ideas, you're free to propose better ideas. But, especially within hours of a tragedy unfolding, journalists and pundits should not manufacture a blood libel that serves only to incite the very hatred and violence they purport to condemn. That is reprehensible."

Well, it's easy to see why the irresponsible journalists and pundits who blamed Palin for the shooting deaths in Tucson would take offense at being chastised. But for the life of me I can't see why the American public would consider Sarah Palin dangerous because she told the truth. Lacking anything else to complain about, the pundits seized on Palin's use of the phrase "blood libel" to make the case that she was being "insensitive" to Jews in general or to Rep. Giffords, in particular, because she is Jewish.

Nothing could be further from the truth. The phrase "blood libel" refers to false allegations of responsibility for murders and death that were levied against the Jews in the Middle Ages and beyond by anti-Semites. The accusation of wrong-doing was supposed to be sufficient to prove guilt, and led to untold harm being done to innocent Jews through the years.

Palin likewise has been wrongfully accused, the blood in Tucson laid at her feet, and yet she was supposed to accede to this libel without protest for the sake of presumptive "civility." Again, the message to Sarah Palin both before and after her Facebook statement is the same: Shut up, Sarah!

But Sarah did not shut up, and her words — for those who can be bothered to study them — are thoughtful and profound.

"In an ideal world all discourse would be civil and all disagreements cordial. But our Founding Fathers knew they weren't designing a system for perfect men and women. If men and women were angels, there would be no need for government. Our Founders' genius was to design a system that helped settle the inevitable conflicts caused by our imperfect passions in civil ways. So, we must condemn violence if our Republic is to endure."

Nor does she leave it in the abstract. She provides evidence from nearly a year ago that she abhors political violence, and has said so publicly.

"As I said while campaigning for others last March in Arizona during a very heated primary race, "We know violence isn't the answer. When we 'take up our arms,' we're talking about our vote." Yes, our debates are full of passion, but we settle our political differences respectfully at the ballot box — as we did just two months ago, and as our Republic enables us to do again in the next election, and the next. That's who we are as Americans and how we were meant to be. Public discourse and debate isn't a sign of crisis, but of our enduring strength. It is part of why America is exceptional."

Please read the entire text of Palin's statement. Let me know if you are offended by any of her praise of American ideals. And as you meditate on the vast difference between what she said and what the mainstream media would have you believe she said, please pay close attention to the following words:

"No one should be deterred from speaking up and speaking out in peaceful dissent, and we certainly must not be deterred by those who embrace evil and call it good. And we will not be stopped from celebrating the greatness of our country and our foundational freedoms by those who mock its greatness by being intolerant of differing opinion and seeking to muzzle dissent with shrill cries of imagined insults."

If you don't like Sarah Palin, that's your business. But if you try to shut her up, that's everybody's business. She is the voice of liberty. Silence it, and we all suffer.

ANDERSON COOPER
AND THE 'BIG BAD BIRTHERS'

February 27, 2011

CNN's Anderson Cooper may actually think he is a fair-minded journalist. But probably someone in a mental institution somewhere thinks he is Anderson Cooper. Which just goes to prove that thinking something, doesn't make it so.

The problem, however, isn't what Anderson Cooper thinks about himself, but that other people actually take him seriously as a journalist and opinion maker, too.

I know, it's hard to believe. After all, Cooper is the guy who popularized calling Tea Party protesters "Teabaggers" even though he knew it was a derogatory term that referred to a sex act popular among homosexuals. He had to apologize for that, sort of, but what would be more appropriate would be an apology for pretending to be a fair journalist when he actually is a shill for left-wing causes.

But I should explain that the people who idolize Cooper —
and hold him up as a serious journalist — are none other than
the left-wing extremists who share his views.

Thus, after Cooper did an interview on Feb. 15 with
Montana Rep. Bob Wagner, R-Harrison, the so-called journalist
was being hailed as a hero on the left-wing blogosphere.
Headlines appeared on the Internet such as this:

"Anderson Cooper OWNS Montana 'Birther' Bob Wagner,"
"Montana Tea Party lawmaker schooled by Anderson Cooper"
and "Montana Birther Nut Lawmaker Becomes National Joke
on CNN."

And if you got all your news from what someone else tells
you, maybe that would be the end of the story. But I beg you to
watch the video for yourself, or better yet, read the transcript.
Bob Wagner was dignified, reasonable and polite — all the while
he was being ambushed by an agenda-driven Anderson Cooper.

So let's do to CNN and Cooper what Cooper claimed to be
doing in his interview with Wagner on Feb. 15 — "Keep them
honest."

First of all, let's provide something you didn't get in
Anderson Cooper's lengthy report — the facts about House Bill
205, which would require candidates for president and
Congress to provide Montana with proof that they meet the U.S.
Constitution's requirements for eligibility to hold those offices.

If the office sought is Congress, then the candidate would
have to provide proof of age since members of the House of
Representatives have to be 25 years old and senators have to be
30 years old to hold those offices.

If the office sought is president, then the candidate would
have to provide proof of age as well as proof that the candidate
was born "within a state or territory of the United States," since
the president must be 35 years old and a "natural born citizen"
of the United States.

Again, these requirements for federal office are established
in the U.S. Constitution. In addition to the age requirements for
serving in Congress, it should be noted that members of the
House must have been citizens for seven years prior to taking

office, and members of the Senate must have been citizens for at least nine years.

This is all quite plainly laid out as the law of the land. It is hoped that Congress demands proof of eligibility of its members before they are sworn in, but I have no reason to believe they do.

More to the point, however, we have all learned in the past two years that there is no procedure in place to establish the eligibility of a candidate to serve as president of the United States. Though the Constitution sets the rules; it provides no procedure through which the rules are to be applied.

The reason why this is currently relevant, of course, is because various U.S. citizens have questioned the eligibility, on various grounds, of President Barack Obama to hold the office in which he serves.

The matter of how that particular issue would be decided is irrelevant to a constitutionalist, however. What matters is that because the questions were raised, we have learned that there is no process, no procedure, no proof required to establish constitutional eligibility for a presidential candidate. Congress has refused to address the issue. Courts have avoided the issue. Citizens have been told they have no "standing" to raise the issue.

And so, it has become apparent that some kind of guideline needs to be established for enforcement of the constitutional provision on presidential eligibility. The only people who don't think so are people who think it is more important to protect Barack Obama than to protect the Constitution.

And into that category we can now safely assign Anderson Cooper. In his interview with Rep. Wagner, Cooper turned the proposed law into a vendetta against President Obama — when in fact the law would be applied equally to all candidates, and would neither target nor favor Obama.

Cooper, however, preceded the interview with Rep. Wagner by lumping him in with the so-called "birther movement," people who question the eligibility of President Obama to be president of the United States based on his birth status. Cooper then said it was pretty obvious that the "birthers" were wrong and, as I noted above, told us he was "keeping them honest."

The only problem is that Cooper wasn't providing useful background information for his interview with Rep. Wagner; he was "setting the stage" for an ambush.

Remember, Wagner's bill makes no reference to President Obama whatsoever. It is about a procedural matter for what you need to do to get on the ballot in Montana to run for federal office — namely that you have to establish your qualifications for the office.

But Anderson Cooper plainly wasn't interested in what was in the bill — he was interested in trying to paint Bob Wagner of Harrison, Montana, as one of those loco country folk who are not only racists and hate-mongers but also stupid.

Thus, after spending several minutes outlining why "birthers" are boobs, Cooper began his interview by asking Wagner whether he believed that Barack Obama is, in fact, a citizen of the United States.

Of course, Wagner is no expert on the president's citizenship status; nor is Cooper. The interview was supposed to be about HB 205, which makes no mention of President Obama. If Cooper were indeed a fair-minded journalist, he would have begun the interview by asking Wagner to explain the purpose of HB 205 and why he considers it an important change in Montana state law.

Wagner, needless to say, did not take the bait. He patiently explained to his interlocutor that he was "not really qualified" to pass judgment on President Obama's citizenship status. Moreover, he explained up front that "it's irrelevant."

Cooper pounced on Wagner, asking him, "What do you mean you're not qualified?"

Wagner, thinking perhaps that he really was dealing with a fair-minded journalist, tried to answer the question. He explained that he was not qualified because no one had offered him any proof on the matter, and thus he had no information to judge the matter, then went back to Cooper's original question and again said that his personal beliefs have no relevance to the law he had proposed.

Cooper no doubt felt like he had the poor, ill-prepared bumpkin legislator from Montana just where he wanted him. "How can you say there is no proof offered?" he taunted. "There's a certificate of live birth which was shown by his campaign in 2008 which has the seal of the — the raised seal of the state [of Hawaii], is signed off on."

Wagner tried to explain the difference between the "certificate of live birth" and a long-form birth certificate, but Cooper didn't seem interested. For the record, the certificate produced by President Obama's 2008 campaign is merely an acknowledgment that Barack Obama's birth was recorded by the state of Hawaii, but it provides no details as to where that birth took place. If you want to take the time to research this, you will see that there is considerable reason to believe that in 1961 it would have been possible to register the birth of a baby even if he was not born in Hawaii.

But, again, who cares? That is an issue specific to Hawaii, and not to the Constitution of the United States, and certainly not to the ongoing process to holding elections in the state of Montana. It would only be relevant if Rep. Wagner had said he was trying to prove that Barack Obama is not a natural-born citizen, but he never said that.

Nonetheless, Cooper drilled ahead with his attempt to make Wagner look stupid, and instead only made himself look uninformed.

Cooper thus pointed out to Rep. Wagner that "a certificate of live birth is good enough for the U.S. Passport Office to get a passport." Perhaps if Montana had been trying to tell the U.S. Passport Office how to do its job, that would have had some relevance, but it certainly had nothing to do with the question of a presidential candidate's ability to establish that he or she is a "natural-born citizen" and thus eligible to be president.

At this point, Cooper was throwing out various questions that were meant not to inform people about the bill, but to try to steer viewers into thinking Wagner was unreasonable. At one point Cooper even confused the issue of presidential eligibility with the 14th Amendment, which has absolutely no bearing on the citizenship qualifications of a president.

Moreover, he misstated the purpose of the 14th Amendment when he said, "Under U.S. law, anyone born in the United States, regardless of what their parents are, is considered a natural-born citizen."

But Wagner was having none of it.

"I don't believe that to be so," he correctly responded.

At one point, Cooper asked why the issue of presidential eligibility had never come up before in Montana — again trying to make it look like this proposal was all about Barack Obama. Cooper sneered at Wagner, "I mean, where was George Bush born?" as if the birthplace of George Bush was itself irrelevant.

But it is not.

If you are going to serve as president you should have to prove you are qualified to serve. Period. So instead of dismissing the mystery of where George Bush was born, Rep. Wagner rightly seized on it —

"That's exactly the problem," he told Cooper.

He then explained that up until 2008, people had assumed that there was a process for determining presidential eligibility, but that since then — because of the various court cases involving President Obama — it had been established that the only point where eligibility can be challenged is by the 50 states when they agree to place someone on the ballot.

"I guess it's back in our court, and we will take care of it," Wagner concluded.

I'm not sure whether or not Wagner is right about "taking care of it." Chances are that even if Montana's Legislature passes the bill, our Democratic governor will veto it.

But that's not the end of the story.

One thing Cooper did get right is that there are at least 10 other states also weighing bills that "in some form or other require presidential candidates to present proof of citizenship in a state to get on a ballot in that state."

Clearly, this is not just a crackpot idea that should be dismissed without serious examination. And if any one of those bills passes, then the public will be assured of more transparency in the process of electing presidents — something which all of us should support.

IT'S THE 'AP WORLD,' BUT NOT EVERYONE IS BUYING THEIR VISION

March 6, 2011

Matt Gouras of the Associated Press is apparently concerned that Montana is becoming a "laughingstock" because of conservative bills proposed by newly elected "Tea Party" legislators.

What he — and his bosses — ought to worry about is that the AP is becoming a "laughingstock" because of its biased reporting and blatant editorializing.

Case in point is Mr. Gouras' own story on the Montana Tea Party, which appeared in most Montana daily newspapers on Feb. 25. To anyone who is sensitive to the need for journalism to be fair and balanced, reading that story was the equivalent of being Tased. To say that I was stunned is an understatement.

Virtually the only fair writing in the entire lengthy story was the first paragraph:

"With each bill, newly elected tea party lawmakers are offering Montanans a vision of the future."

Gouras continued by invoking a litany of the supposed excesses of what he calls "Tea Party world":

"Their state would be a place where officials can ignore U.S. laws, force FBI agents to get a sheriff's OK before arresting anyone, ban abortions, limit sex education in schools and create armed citizen militias."

It's not really necessary to read any further to see what Mr. Gouras is up to. In the first three paragraphs, the bait has been laid. Then in the next paragraph, the bone-crunching trap closes shut as Mr. Gouras declares, "Not everyone is buying their vision. Some residents, Democratic Gov. Brian Schweitzer and even some Republican lawmakers say the bills are making Montana into a laughingstock. And, they say, the push to nullify federal laws could be dangerous."

"Some residents"? Is that the best he could do? I mean, don't "some residents" in Montana also believe that Republicans should be lined up against a wall and shot? Does that give them any kind of legitimacy? And as for the fact that there are Republican legislators in Montana who vote like Democrats — is that any different than in any other state in the Union?

At this point, Gouras prompts his one named expert — Gov. Schweitzer — to testify about just how "dangerous" these Tea Party folks could be:

"We are the United States of America," said Schweitzer. "This talk of nullifying is pretty toxic talk. That led to the Civil War."

Well, no it didn't. Not really. And having talked to the governor many times in the past 11 years, I am confident that he doesn't think it led to the Civil War either.

But more importantly, reporter Matt Gouras's primary witness against the "Tea Party world" — Gov. Schweitzer — is himself an occasional resident of that wacky world. In fact, he has signed at least two state laws — on Real ID and intrastate firearms possession — that directly challenged existing federal regulations and called them unconstitutional.

In discussing the states' rights movement with the Inter Lake editorial board just last year, Gov. Schweitzer emphasized state sovereignty and said, "I think people in Washington are getting nervous now that some of the states are getting kind of uppity."

Darn right.

So what has changed? Why was state sovereignty OK last year, but "pretty toxic" this year?

That would have been a reasonable question for Matt Gouras to have asked our governor, but he never got around to it. And even though Gouras includes a reference to the fight against Real ID later in the story, he fails to mention that Gov. Schweitzer was one of the dangerous Montana "wackos" who battled hardest to stop it.

I wish I could go through the entire story with you, and highlight all of the unfair reporting, but it would just take too long. One indication that this is a hatchet job, however, is that there is nary a quote from a conservative anywhere to be seen. Remember, this was supposed to be a news story, not an opinion column. You would think that a fair reporter who wanted to write a news story about the Tea Party agenda would have asked someone who supported the agenda to explain it to him. But in the nearly 1,000 words of this story, we get a total of just two quotes from supporters of the Tea Party.

In one, Rep. Derek Skees explains that nullification is not about creating a new Civil War. In the other, Rep. Cleve Loney is quoted as saying he doesn't intend for Montana to secede from the Union.

But even those two quotes exaggerate the amount of work that Mr. Gouras did to bring balance to his story. The quote from Mr. Loney wasn't the result of an interview at all, just a stray remark taken from floor debate in the House. And both quotes are reactions to spurious accusations. Nowhere in this story does Mr. Gouras allow a conservative to actually make the case why they believe the federal government has overstepped its bounds.

Indeed, there is absolutely no suggestion that Gouras intended to find out anything about the Tea Party agenda — he just wanted to write a story saying that some people don't like that agenda.

So what we get instead of fair and balanced reporting is the presumption that the Tea Party conservatives are extremists. Let's consider that list of "kooky" Tea Party ideas again, but this time let's not just take Mr. Gouras' word that they are somehow unique to the Tea Party movement or that these legislative proposals somehow relegate Montana to being a "laughingstock."

What is important to see is that Mr. Gouras is lumping in perfectly reasonable legislative solutions with some that are more extreme, and making no distinction between them. In other words, if you don't want to force the FBI to get a sheriff's approval to make an arrest, you also should be against banning abortion.

That is patently ridiculous. Forget about the sheriff issue. It may be novel — it may even be extreme — but that legislation was already dead by the time Gouras wrote his article. He knew that, but he wanted to try to make Montanans look kooky, so he threw the bill into his list — even though Montana had already rejected the bill. The point being that EVERYTHING the Tea Party movement — or, more to the point, any individual conservative legislator — wants to bring about must be equally kooky.

But consider this. State bans on abortion are not kooky. State bans or restrictions on abortion have existed since the nation was founded. It is not a state's right to ban abortion that is a novelty, but the notion that the federal government can prohibit states from doing so. Plainly, since 1973's Roe v. Wade ruling, the federal courts have not upheld state laws that are outright bans of abortion, but neither have they been presented with a state Legislature that defined life as beginning at conception. To mock the idea is to mock the very idea that states have rights.

Well, states do have rights — even though they have been chipped away by presidential ambition, federal court usurpation and congressional fiat over the past 200 years — and there is no reason why state legislators should automatically concede ground to the federal government.

Certainly, not everyone agrees that legal abortion is a good idea, and presumably if those abortion foes are also legislators, they have the right to try to craft a law that will pass constitutional muster, whether Mr. Gouras likes it or not.

And what about the last two items on the list of "kooky" Tea Party ideas? Schools and militias? Are these really crackpot ideas?

Since when doesn't the Montana Legislature have the right to address the curricula of our schools? If they don't have the right to do so, then how come they have mandated "Indian Education for All"? The state Constitution declares that Montana is "committed in its educational goals to the preservation of ... [American Indians'] cultural integrity." But it was the Legislature that decided how to press that agenda, resulting in the order that all schools across the state have to devote a portion of each year to integrating Native American history and culture into their curriculum.

If it is OK for the Legislature to encourage the teaching of American Indian education, then it is equally OK for the Legislature to discourage the teaching of sex education, isn't it? Anyone who has followed the case of what the Helena School District was encouraging elementary school students to learn will certainly understand why some legislators thought they had better speak up.

And as for the idea of an armed civilian militia, isn't that what we have now?

According to Article VI, Section 13 of the Montana Constitution, the "militia forces shall consist of all able-bodied citizens of the state except those exempted by law." So we already have a citizen militia, and since this is Montana it just goes to figure that we have a well-armed militia. Maybe some people call that a crackpot idea, but most of them live in New York or Massachusetts, not Montana.

This all comes under the general heading of caveat lector — "let the reader beware." Don't just assume that news articles are devoid of bias, opinion or misleading suppositions. Educate yourself first, and then be forearmed against all manner of "kooky" things — including reporters who try to pass opinion pieces off as objective news stories.

DON'T LET YOUR BIAS DO THE TALKING
(OR SEND E-MAILS)

March 13, 2011

While we are on the topic of bias, do I really need to point out that it's not exclusively a malady of the left?

A few people questioned my recent columns analyzing examples of left-wing bias on CNN and in Associated Press reporting, and thought they were themselves examples of biased reporting.

To which, I should respond first, that I am an opinion columnist and not a reporter. I write about topics that catch my attention, and try to write about them fairly. I always welcome criticism that shows me an error in my analysis, but more often than not just get attacked because people don't like my point of view.

Oh well, that's the nature of the business.

But whether we are columnists, reporters or just individual citizens, we all have a responsibility to be fair in our approach to facts. They should not be dismissed just because we don't like them, and they should not be considered gospel truth just because they tell us what we want to hear.

Unfortunately, it is all too easy for personal preferences to creep into reporting, as well as into reading — and we should all be on guard against that tendency. This is nothing new. Citizens have always had the ultimate responsibility for discernment between what is true and false, and it is they who must hold the press, as well as the politicians, accountable. Some such balance between the power of the people and the press is absolutely essential to the successful operation of our republic.

It was Thomas Jefferson who railed against "the falsehoods of a licentious press" while at the same time acknowledging that the free press is "the only safeguard of the public liberty."

Jefferson considered himself to be the target of biased reporting on numerous occasions, and said of his opponents the Federalists that, "They fill their newspapers with falsehoods, calumnies and audacities." Yet Jefferson thought that reason and humanity would prevail against any foolishness that appeared in the press, and he credited the common people with the ability to keep in check the excesses of bias that human nature creates in some journalists.

As Jefferson wrote in 1804, "The firmness with which the people have withstood the late abuses of the press, the discernment they have manifested between truth and falsehood shew that they may safely be trusted to hear everything true and false and form a correct judgment between them."

I would venture, however, that it is even harder for a modern citizen to "form a correct judgment" of truth and falsehood today than it was in Jefferson's time. That falls partly on the state of modern education, which we must leave for another column, and partly on the state of modern media.

Face it, information technology has grown exponentially since 1800, and with it has come a virtual flood of facts, fiction and fantasy. If Jefferson thought newspapers should be divided into four sections labeled "True, Probable, Wanting Confirmation and Lies," then what could he possibly think of the modern Internet, with its weird capacity for making everything seem true, leaving us with the necessary assumption that everything we are told may be a lie.

Almost every day, I receive some kind of e-mail that touts the remarkable, stupendous, unbelievable news that: a) Supreme Court justice Elena Kagan represented President Obama before the Supreme Court regarding his eligibility for office; b) Hillary Clinton and the U.N. are taking your guns away; c) President Obama is planning to tax all of your financial transactions by 1 percent; or d) it's already been proven that President Obama is a foreign national, but somehow the evidence is being covered up by the media.

Unfortunately, the people who send me these e-mails are so seduced by the "remarkable" and "stupendous" news that they forget it is also "unbelievable."

But a minimal amount of investigation — the simple steps of checking the facts for yourself and applying a small amount of brain power — quickly reveal that all those stories are totally false.

And guess what, they are false even if someone who invented the hoax includes a statement that the facts have all been verified by snopes.com, the website that is famous for exposing Internet hoaxes.

One of those stories above included a valid link to snopes.com in which a quick reading will reveal that Snopes totally contradicts the claims of the e-mailer. Here's the first paragraph of the e-mail, quoted verbatim:

"A one-percent transaction fee (TAX), proposed by President Obama's finance team, is recommending a transaction tax. His plan is to sneak it in after the November elections to keep it under the radar. This is a 1% tax on all transactions at any financial institution. Banks, Credit Unions, Savings and Loans, etc.."

Now, let's forget about the totally ungrammatical structure of the paragraph. The intent is clear — to link President Obama to a 1 percent tax. And the e-mail includes a link to http://www.snopes.com/politics/taxes/debtfree.asp where we are supposed to be assured of the truth of the claim.

But instead, we discover that the proposal is the brainchild of the little-known Democratic congressman, Rep. Chaka Fattah of Pennsylvania, who has been kicking the idea around since 2004. And yep, in 2010, he submitted the Debt Free America Act (HR 4646) that proposes to pay down the debt and eliminate the income tax with a 1 percent transaction tax. When checking on the status of that bill, I discovered that it was introduced on Feb. 23, 2010, and shuffled off to four committees the same day, never to be heard from again.

Back at Snopes, I was able to confirm the obvious: "President Obama's financial team" had nothing to do with the 1 percent transaction tax," nor did Nancy Pelosi — as another version of the e-mail hoax claimed. It was the work of one deluded, though perhaps well-intentioned, congressman.

The other phony e-mails are just as easily disproven. The one about Elena Kagan is particularly foolish. Someone tried to show that she would have a conflict of interest if the issue of

President Obama's eligibility were ever before the Supreme Court, and as evidence they presented a number of cases she had argued before the court in her role as solicitor general. The ultra-conservative website World Net Daily put out an article last August that claimed nine of these cases involved "Obama eligibility issues."

Unfortunately for World Net Daily, they provided links to the cases, and not one of them had anything to do with President Obama's birthplace or eligibility. They were simply cases that she had argued on behalf of the United States which included some mention — oftentimes very minor — of President Obama, who was technically her boss.

World Net Daily retracted their story, but unfortunately you cannot retract an e-mail, so this story has gone viral thanks to the proclivity of political junkies to forward junk mail to everyone they know — including newsroom editors.

One of the more boneheaded such e-mails is the one that claims that the group "Americans for Freedom of Information" has "released copies of President Obama's college transcripts from Occidental College," which indicate that "Obama, under the name of Barry Soetoro, received financial aid as a foreign student from Indonesia as an undergraduate." The e-mail then goes on to claim that Justice Antonin Scalia announced that the Supreme Court "agreed on Tuesday to hear arguments concerning Obama's legal eligibility to serve as President."

The truly funny thing about this e-mail is that it includes this howler — "Let other folks know this news, the media won't!"

I mean, what planet do you have to come from to believe that this news could ever be covered up — or even that the media would want to cover it up! Forget whether you are right wing or left wing for a minute. This would be the story of the century, if it were TRUE, but that little old four-letter word is a real stumbling block.

Oh, yeah, and if you bothered to check this Occidental College e-mail out on snopes.com, you would discover that the original e-mail was dated April 1, 2009. Can anyone say April Fool's?

Too bad there isn't a Truth Filter to stop idiotic outgoing e-mails to correspond with the Spam Filter we have to protect our in-box from obvious junk.

But in the absence of a gimmicky technical solution, a little common sense can go a long way in penetrating to the truth of these hyped-up partisan e-mails. I strongly encourage everyone to think twice before hitting the send button on any "too good to be true" e-mail "news story." But based on what hits my in-box everyday, I suspect the common sense approach may be in short supply.

Let us hope Jefferson is not turning over in his grave when he ponders whether citizens of the truly great nation he helped found still have the power to discern correctly between what is true and false.

IS A SLOW NEWS WEEK THE QUICK PATH TO ENLIGHTENMENT?

April 3, 2011

I spent the last week trying to pick a topic for this column, and finally decided to write about not picking a topic for this column.

As you know, I usually write about something in the national news — or try to shed some light on the news by providing perspective from the past — but that requires a willingness to sacrifice my characteristically cheerful disposition by sitting through endless dispatches from the war on sanity being waged in Washington, D.C.

And since for this past week, I have been on vacation with my family, I opted to hold onto the good cheer and jettison the bad news — you know, the endless bickering in Congress, the endless wars in the Middle East, the disasters both natural and unnatural which plague mankind. But before you think I am dumping on this newspaper, or any newspaper for that matter, let me hasten to explain.

Newspapers are just one part of the news business, and in my mind, the best part. But let's consider the huge difference between what a newspaper provides as food for thought and what the cable news industry force-feeds us 24 hours a day.

There is something almost calming about reading a daily newspaper, especially a local community newspaper such as the Daily Inter Lake. We have been telling the story of the Flathead Valley since 1889 — and for more than one-fifth of that time, I have been writing or editing for the Inter Lake. So let me be plain: I love newspapers in general, and this one in particular.

Sure, there's been bad news in the Inter Lake — plenty of it in 122 years. We've reported on too many wars and too many tragedies. Take your pick. For my part, I remember working that Fourth of July in 1987 when charismatic Terry Robinson and most of his fellow Montana Band members perished in a plane accident on Flathead Lake. I also still vividly recall working the wire shift one morning in 1994 and filling the last hole on Page 2 with what seemed like a relatively obscure story about the brutal murder of a woman who had been identified as O.J. Simpson's ex-wife. Little did I know how that story would end, and ultimately how it would radically change people's perspectives of the news.

And, of course, I remember the nation-changing cataclysm of Sept. 11, 2001 — when the Inter Lake put out what may have been the only "extra" edition in its history — a tear-filled catalog of horror.

So, yes, I've seen bad news in the 27 years I've worked here, and our longtime readers have seen even more of it, but reading a newspaper like the Inter Lake on a regular basis, you get more a sense of continuity than change, more a sense of connectedness than disruption, more a sense of pride than despair. You'll see bad news, but you have a choice whether to read it or not, and it's always balanced by the good news of accomplishment, charity and caring.

How different it is to watch cable news! With just a day's worth of viewing, you could not only lose confidence in your government, you could lose faith in God and see the worst in everything around you. And unlike a newspaper, which is a smorgasbord of information available to take or leave, watching cable news is like mainlining heroin. Once you tune in, you have no control over what kind of information is being channeled into you.

Bad news? You bet! On cable TV, even good news is bad news — as stories are manipulated and twisted for maximum effect to chew the very last bit of life out of them. Entering this alternate universe is like visiting a carnival funhouse — everything you see and experience is distorted and only vaguely related to reality. Every car on the freeway is potentially O.J. Simpson's white Bronco. Every new marriage is potentially a juicy divorce. And every hero is just 15 minutes away from being exposed as a fallible, foolish mortal.

If you are looking for enlightenment, then following the path of cable news is roughly the equivalent of walking over a bed of hot coals. If you persevere long enough, you might eventually reach that state of unholy enlightenment where Bill O'Reilly morphs into Rachel Maddow and Fox Knows becomes indistinguishable from MSNBC Knows Better. But before you experience that breakthrough to Buddhahood, you are probably going to get really burnt.

And not just because of the sad stories. Life — and therefore the news — is full of sadness. That's not a bulletin. I think you can find the same conclusion in Thoreau's "Walden," as well as in the aforementioned Buddha's First Noble Truth that there IS suffering. Nonetheless, I have to tell you that Buddha and Thoreau didn't know the half of it — because they did not have the parade of misery known as cable news and the fount of horrors known as the Internet constantly reinforcing their worst fears.

Nor do most of us who watch cable news stop long enough to really think about what we are filling our minds with. It's just information, right? The stuff of knowledge? But tell that to Adam and Eve. They discovered that "too much information" can lead to confusion and chaos, as well as knowledge.

And — as it turns out — less information can lead to peace. That, finally, is what I realized when I turned off CNN, Fox News and MSNBC for the week. Life is much closer to serene without the screaming and preening of Sean Hannity, Bill O'Reilly, Anderson Cooper, Chris Matthews and the other usual suspects.

Yes, the news remains just as bad as ever, but I don't need to be reminded of that 24 hours a day with the blaring, bleating blather of cable. So, while I have continued to read the Daily Inter Lake for news of the community and an overview of the world's sad state, I have steered clear of the grinding masticating maw of 24/7 cable news where every bit of gristle and gloom is regurgitated endlessly in an effort to sell us on the urgency of our own demise.

With just a newspaper in my hand instead of a remote control, I have lived life at a decent distance from the news, which means I have lived somewhat like my recent ancestors — one or two days removed from even the biggest catastrophe. It provides a buffer that may be vital to mental health in this world of woe.

I'm not sure I know what enlightenment is, but maybe it is something like this brief week of vacation that just ended — gathering up your loved ones, and letting go of your fears. Every once in a while, you just have to forget about the cable news and read the funny pages — even if you can't get a column out of it.

COMMUNITY NEWSPAPERS: THE HEART OF AMERICA

December 25, 2011

Christmas is a time to remember our blessings, and for me, having the opportunity to work at the Daily Inter Lake since 1984 counts as one of the best in a life full of them.

Come Jan. 24, I will have worked at this paper for 28 years, which will be exactly half my life. Considering that I never planned to be a journalist, never expected to live in Montana, and had virtually never heard of Kalispell until the week before I moved here, that's not too bad. And considering that I had lived in six different cities in the preceding seven years, it is nothing short of a miracle that I actually put down roots and called someplace home.

"Someplace" turned out to be the best place of all — Kalispell, Montana — and I never seriously considering moving anywhere else again after my first few weeks here.

Nor, for that matter, did I ever seriously think of finding a new employer. The Inter Lake has long since been part of my family, and I am part of it. As they say, ink runs in my veins.

But when I thought about it recently, I realized that ink runs in all our veins. In a very real way, the community newspaper is the lifeblood of America. Reaching back to the days of Ben Franklin, we Americans have always counted on our local newspaper to inform us, intrigue us and infuriate us. Indeed, as in all love affairs, there have been many fits of pique along with moments of passion in our journey together. You might say that for most of us, newspapers not only stir the blood, but sometimes make it boil.

Indeed, the more I study the history of newspapers, including the Daily Inter Lake, the more surprised I am that some people think the local newspaper (and its editors) should be the equivalent of an obedient child — seen but not heard. That is anything but the norm.

Instead, local newspapers have more often been brash, bold and beautifully independent — clamoring for what they thought was right, laboring to fix what they saw as wrongs, proud to lead their communities and not remain in the background.

Certainly, the Inter Lake has been a part of everyday life in the Flathead for many years — even before it was published every day. Started as a weekly in 1889 in the town of Demersville, the paper moved a few miles north with almost all the other businesses in that town when Kalispell was founded in 1891. The original editor, C.O. Ingalls, was by all accounts a feisty gentleman who did not hesitate to call 'em like he saw 'em — and for that matter so was his wife and reporter, Emma, who famously took on a corrupt judge in Demersville and won.

She wrote in one news story, "His court is famous at the Supreme Court of Montana because of his arbitrary decisions which were always in favor of the last drink of whisky."

C.O. Ingalls was publisher of the paper, with a brief gap, until 1894, when it was sold to R.M. Goshorn, who also never shied away from a fight. He continued the Inter Lake as a weekly until 1908. Then, after his son's untimely death, Goshorn decided to turn the paper into a daily to keep his mind off his troubles. Finally, in 1913, he sold the paper to the only group that has ever owned it as a strictly partisan publication. As reported by the Inter Lake in 1919, "following the presidential campaign of 1912, a large number of progressives in the county formed a company... and bought the paper from Mr. Goshorn."

Indeed, progressivism in the wake of Teddy Roosevelt's Bull Moose run for president in 1912 was so popular in Kalispell that former Sen. Joseph M. Dixon, owner of the Missoulian and campaign manager for TR, launched his own failed bid for a progressive third party from Kalispell in 1913.

Those old-time stories from yellowed and brittle newspapers tell the history of America better than any historian could ever do. Reading through the archives of the Inter Lake or any other newspaper that has lasted more than 100 years will take you on a journey that is vivid and diverse. If the past is prologue, it is also much more. The further we get from it, the more it seems like a strange new world altogether. Indeed, it is hard to follow the currents of history and linger in the backwaters of forgotten lore without feeling somewhat like the explorers Lewis & Clark pressing into the unknown.

At the same time, the newspaper is itself a journal of discovery — recounting the highs and lows of a community that is inventing itself over time. We've discovered some good things about ourselves, and some horrible things — and we've held an ongoing debate about how to get better.

In fact, if you had to summarize the role of community newspapers, it would be just that — to hold a conversation. And it's not a conversation between the newspaper and the community, but rather an invitation for the community to have a conversation with itself.

These columns I write are one small part of that, geared toward my personal interests in American history and national politics, but the paper is so much more than one person's opinion. That's why I labeled my column as the "Editor's 2 cents." You can take or leave my opinion, but you can't do without the newspaper because the newspaper is all of us — our past, our present and our future.

A community paper that is worthy of the name is filled with the hopes and dreams of thousands of people. When you open up these pages, you are literally taking the pulse of Kalispell, of Whitefish, Columbia Falls and Flathead County. And you'll have your hands full with everything that makes a community — pet peeves and philosophy, kids and old people, county fairs and local colleges, planning and zoning, businesses and charities, holiday greetings, letters from readers, government for good and for bad, plenty of pictures with lots of local faces, schools and churches, fund-raisers and festivals, crime and justice, comics and puzzles, and all the sports that you can possibly fit. Plus all that beautiful advertising that make it all possible in the first place.

That, of course, is just the start — the raw material that makes the community newspaper take on its most important role — as the glue that holds a community together, the common identity that is reflected back to each one of us — the conscience, the history and the future of our hometowns.

So, on this Christmas holiday, when you are counting your blessings, I hope you will agree with me that no matter how much you may not like one story or one reporter or even one editor, you see the value of having a newspaper that tells the story of you, your kids and your neighbors — tells what makes us live and breathe, work and play. Tells what inspires us and what we fear. Tells the truth about our strengths and our troubles.

Community newspapers cannot die — because if they do, then America will have lost its heart.

PENETRATING THE ILLUSION OF TOLERANCE AND DIVERSITY

January 15, 2012

Cue the theme music.

"You're traveling through another dimension, a dimension not only of sight and sound but of mind; a journey into a wondrous land whose boundaries are that of imagination. That's the signpost up ahead..."

Yep, it's "The Twilight Zone" — or is it MSNBC?

Sometimes, it's hard to tell the difference.

Take the case of Patrick J. Buchanan, who went from being the highly paid token conservative at the far-left news network to being the scapegoat for liberal rage when his bosses found out he had written a book that paints liberalism as a clear and present danger to the future of America.

The rise and fall of Buchanan at MSNBC reads like a final irony-laden episode of "The Twilight Zone." But what happens on MSNBC is black-and-white fantasy nearly every day of the week, not just when Buchanan is being thrown under the bus. The truth of the matter is that every show on MSNBC is identical — the liberal hosts asks their guest or panel of guests whether Republicans are scary, racist or just plain stupid, and then the guest or panel smirks, says "good question," and confidently answers, "All of the above," as the host chortles.

Except Buchanan, of course, did not play along. He was there as the token conservative in order to provide proof that liberals really do respect diversity of opinion — except when they don't.

Liberals love tolerance for gays, Muslims and potty talk, but it turns out they are not too much in favor of people who think differently than they do. Diversity is cool if it entails people of a variety of skin colors spouting the same mix of tired slogans and Obama worship, but not so cool if it involves people actually questioning liberal shibboleths no matter what their skin color is (check out Herman Cain and Allen West for more details).

Rod Serling, the creator of "Twilight Zone," was a master of skewering this kind of hypocrisy, and though you can't pigeonhole the genius of Serling and his co-creators, it is safe to say that the show was a weekly chronicle of the dubious fate of small minds and big egos. More often than not, there was a recurring theme of how fear can shape and distort people's lives, and sometimes even their faces.

In the wake of the McCarthy era, Serling was sensitive to any attempt to put people into cookie cutters and try to make them come out looking alike. He warned that sometimes the cookie cutter approach works only if you are willing to sacrifice individuality — and maybe a few fingers and toes.

One memorable episode of "The Twilight Zone" tells the story of a young woman who is hideously disfigured, but is being provided by the State with one last chance to become "normal." Doctors perform surgery on her in an effort to transfigure her into someone who can live among other people without shame. When the bandages come off, she is revealed to be a stunning beauty — who elicits gasps from the surrounding nurses and doctors NOT because of their surgical success, but because they had failed to transform her into what they are — piggishly ugly trolls from another planet. The title of the episode says it all — "Eye of the Beholder."

I imagine that Pat Buchanan must feel a bit like that lovely lady when he considers his ill-fitting tenure at MSNBC, where he was the lone redoubt of traditional American values amid dozens of smugly sincere liberals who practiced a form of tolerance by agreeing to sit next to Buchanan without picking up rocks and stoning him on camera.

Tsk-tsk, his fellow MSNBC'ers probably muttered. Poor Buchanan! So different. So handicapped. But we really must try to overlook how hideously conservative he is, and pretend that nothing is wrong! After all, we are liberals and therefore respect diversity and practice tolerance — no matter how painful it is to do so.

Except one day, Pat Buchanan wasn't there any more. He had been diversified into the literal "Twilight Zone" of unofficial, unannounced suspension from the channel. Not for moral turpitude. Not because he had violated a code of ethics. Not for conflict of interest. But because he wrote a book.

Yep, the purveyors of "diversity for all" had just met their match — a book called "Suicide of a Superpower: Will America Survive to 2025?"

MSNBC President Phil Griffin probably got a phone call from someone pretty high up in the chain of command — maybe even someone in the White House, who knows? — and pronounced thumbs down not just on the book, but on Buchanan.

"The ideas he put forth aren't really appropriate for national dialogue, much less the dialogue on MSNBC," Griffin said.

Say what? Arguing about the survival of our country is not "appropriate" for the national dialogue? Then what is? Just ordering flowers for the funeral?

What's classy is that no one from the network even bothered to tell Buchanan he was suspended. He was quite sick in December, and maybe the network execs just hoped he would do the right thing and die to spare the nation any further distasteful discussion of national suicide.

But, alas, he got better, leaving his bosses in an uncomfortable position or either being loyal to their longtime employee or just pandering to their viewers and pretending they were "shocked" by Buchanan's book.

This is too cute by half. It's not like MSNBC could have been surprised to find out what Buchanan thinks. After all, they have been paying him to be an expert commentator on politics for most of the past decade — and Buchanan is nothing if not outspoken.

Having someone as high profile and as conservative as Buchanan on the channel allowed MSNBC to pass itself off as supremely tolerant. After all, Buchanan had run for president as a Republican and even worked for Ronald Reagan. But when push came to shove, the illusion of tolerance and diversity was less important to MSNBC than the certainty of liberal hegemony on the channel's endless panels.

Why did his bosses finally silence him? We may never know exactly, but clearly tolerance has its limits when it comes to white males over the age of 50 who profess their Christian faith, lament the decline of American values and mock the Obama White House.

Come to think of it, maybe that's why some local liberals squirm every Sunday morning when another of my columns shows up with the same unrepentant conservative viewpoint. Some of them may even be hoping for the day when I will star in that "Twilight Zone" episode where I have to go in for my "adjustment" and get straightened out — not in my spine but in my thinking.

It's not surprising though, is it? In an entitlement society, lots of people think that every community is entitled to its very own liberal newspaper editor. After all, why should any of us be deprived of the illusion of tolerance?

Celebrate diversity — by thanking God that you have a token conservative at the helm of the local newspaper. And if you ever wake up and find me missing one Sunday morning, don't panic, don't fret ... You'll find me hosting a new show with Patrick Buchanan debating the true meaning of tolerance in ... (cue ending music) ... "The Twilight Zone."

ORWELL, THE 'TRUTH' AND A TROUBLING TREND

March 25, 2012

Ronald Reagan famously joked that "the trouble with our liberal friends is not that they're ignorant; it's just that they know so much that isn't so."

Unfortunately, these days the joke is starting to sound like a broken record — and it doesn't just apply to "our liberal friends" either. More and more, we ALL know (or repeat as if we know) so much that isn't so that I have to wonder whether many of us haven't fallen victim to what George Orwell called "doublethink," the ability to substitute one reality for another because it is politically expedient to do so.

As described by Orwell in his famous novel "1984," the Ministry of Truth works constantly to update the past to bring it into alignment with the ruling party's current propaganda. They do this through a massive campaign to falsify public records and to delete opposing ideas.

Anything that no longer corresponded with the official version of reality was discarded by employees of the Ministry of Truth by sending it down a chute to "enormous furnaces which were hidden somewhere in the recesses of the building." These chutes that led to collective amnesia were known as "memory holes," and if you are starting to have the feeling that what you read and hear in the news no longer corresponds to what you remember, it may be because your old truths have gone down Orwell's Memory Hole.

Winston Smith, the hero of "1984," works at the Ministry of Truth, editing newspaper articles so they conform with the needs of the Party. Mind you, he does not work on the articles that will appear in tomorrow's paper, but the ones that appeared in yesterday's paper, or last year's. It is his job to tidy up the past to make the world look like a place where nothing would work without the absolute control of Big Brother to guide us and protect us. And as a faithful apparatchik, Winston Smith is expected to edit history and then promptly forget that he has done so because to recognize his own deceit would mean disloyalty to the Party.

As Orwell explains, "Doublethink lies at the very heart of the Party, since the essential act of the Party is to use conscious deception while retaining the firmness of purpose that goes with complete honesty. To tell deliberate lies while genuinely believing them and to forget any fact that has become inconvenient, and then, when it becomes necessary again, to draw it back from oblivion for just so long as it is needed, to deny the existence of objective reality and all the while to take account of the reality which one denies — all this is indispensably necessary. Even in using the word doublethink it is necessary to exercise doublethink. For by using the word one admits that one is tampering with reality; by a fresh act of doublethink one erases this knowledge; and so on indefinitely, with the lie always one leap ahead of the truth."

If that doesn't describe the state of modern political discourse, I don't know what does.

It is virtually impossible that educated people could sincerely believe some of the things they routinely say, but they sincerely believe they believe it. A case in point from recent history is the lead-up to the Iraq War.

After the Ministry of Truth also known as the Democratic Party got through with it, there has been a common acceptance of the "fact" that President Bush claimed Iraq was responsible for the 9/11 attacks and used that as a justification for war. He didn't, and yet almost no one bothers to go back and examine the printed record to verify what really happened. Instead, we just listen to the repeated mantra of the major media that "Bush lied and people died," and start to assume it is true.

This is an ominous national occurrence of doublethink. Millions of people who lived through the same traumatic experience were somehow convinced to shed their collective memory of what happened, and substitute a plausible, yet totally manufactured narrative that better fitted the needs of a political agenda.

In the world of "1984," such a massive manipulation of reality involved a dedicated bureaucracy in the Ministry of Truth, where workers like Winston Smith located "embarrassing" realities and changed them into "encouraging" falsities. It also had to be understood by the reader to be metaphoric only. There was no way to completely "alter, or, as the official phrase had it, to rectify" everything in print. Yet that was what Orwell, through the genius of his paranoia, was able to convince us took place in the fictional nation-state of Oceania.

"This process of continuous alteration was applied not only to newspapers, but to books, periodicals, pamphlets, posters, leaflets, films, sound-tracks, cartoons, photographs — to every kind of literature or documentation which might conceivably hold any political or ideological significance. Day by day and almost minute by minute the past was brought up to date. In this way every prediction made by the Party could be shown by documentary evidence to have been correct, nor was any item of news, or any expression of opinion, which conflicted with the needs of the moment, ever allowed to remain on record."

In other words, the Ministry of Truth was a fictional version of the Internet, or more specifically, of "Wikipedia" — that ever-changing truth machine that has conveniently replaced the bulky multi-volume "Encyclopedia Britannica" as everyman's source of established knowledge. And because Wikipedia is entirely digital it actually allows Orwell's worst nightmare of total information control to come true.

Wikipedia has already insinuated itself into our lives as the main source of information for schoolchildren, casual searchers and yes even newspeople. An instance of a journalist using doublethink can be seen with Soledad O'Brien's infamous CNN interview with breitbart.com editor Joel Pollak about the critical race theory, Professor Derrick Bell and Harvard Law student Barack Obama.

O'Brien said Obama's championing of Bell was no big deal because Bell's critical race theory was just a harmless academic theory about the "intersection of race and politics and the law." She also denied adamantly that the theory had anything to do with "white supremacy," as Pollak insisted.

It's suspected now that her producer was whispering in her ear with the definition she rattled off after Pollak had challenged her. The actual entry at Wikipedia says that critical race theory "is an academic discipline focused upon the intersection of race, law and power." Not an exact match to O'Brien's words, but close enough to raise suspicion.

More interestingly, soon after the interview took place, the Wikipedia article on critical race theory was edited to remove a reference to white supremacy and thus to conform with the claims of O'Brien, the media champion of President Obama. It was an interesting example of the "intersection" of media, politics and propaganda, and should make everyone wary of everything they hear reported on CNN, at the very least

Meanwhile, because of the vigilance of conservatives who are wary of Wikipedia, the transparent attempt to alter or "rectify" the Critical Race Theory entry was quickly spotted. The entry was later frozen back to its original content, but how many other transformations of reality on Wikipedia go unnoticed, unacknowledged, and unsuspected?

Frankly, this is a problem that is only going to get worse.

As long as there are "paper" newspapers in hand, someone like me can fact-check the false assertions of the national propaganda machine that George Bush had linked Saddam Hussein to the attacks of 9/11. But once information goes entirely digital, then there is almost no way to assure that the "facts" there today will still be there tomorrow, nor that the yesterday you read about today resembles the yesterday that you yourself lived. Doublethink is about to become doublelife. Everything can be re-invented, and everything inconvenient can be deleted.

Maybe it already has. As I was researching this column by studying digitized microfilm images of newspapers at www.newspaperarchive.com in search of any claims of "links between Iraq and al-Qaida," I noticed that I often got the following message:

"We apologize for the inconvenience but the page you are trying to view is not available. When possible, missing or corrupted page files will be replaced as resources allow. Unfortunately we are not able to give a timeframe regarding individual page replacements."

Could that page have disappeared down the Memory Hole? Only Big Brother knows for sure, and he isn't talking.

LINCOLN, COMPROMISE
AND THE PRICE TO PAY

December 2, 2012

This just in — compromise to a liberal really does mean compromising your principles, and you don't have to believe me. Just read what liberal columnist David Brooks had to say about the new film "Lincoln":

"We live in an anti-political moment, when many people — young people especially — think politics is a low, nasty, corrupt and usually fruitless business. It's much nobler to do community service or just avoid all that putrid noise.

"I hope everybody who shares this anti-political mood will go out to see 'Lincoln,'" wrote Brooks. "The movie portrays the nobility of politics in exactly the right way."

Note the phrase: "Nobility of politics" — and then watch what follows from the pen of this award-winning New York Times columnist:

"[The film] shows that you can do more good in politics than in any other sphere. You can end slavery, open opportunity and fight poverty. But you can achieve these things only if you are willing to stain your own character in order to serve others — if you are willing to bamboozle, trim, compromise and be slippery and hypocritical..."

Say what?

Did Brooks really slip "compromise" in there between "bamboozle" and "hypocritical" with nary a wink or a nod? Are we supposed to thus see compromise in a better light? Or is it really hypocrisy that Brooks is trying to elevate?

He finishes up his paean to "Lincoln" by painting a portrait of the 16th president as a precursor to the Chicago ward heelers who never let principle stand in the way of winning:

"To lead his country through a war, to finagle his ideas through Congress, Lincoln feels compelled to ignore court decisions, dole out patronage, play legalistic games, deceive his supporters and accept the fact that every time he addresses one problem he ends up creating others down the road."

And then Brooks concludes with his warm and fuzzy bromide of the week:

"Politics is noble because it involves personal compromise for the public good."

Ah yes, the noble politics of patronage and bamboozling. Those were sure the good old days, weren't they?

But more importantly than Brooks' near beatific ability to overlook human frailties in Lincoln is his own gargantuan ability to completely miss the point.

The film "Lincoln" depicts the absolute opposite of real compromise. Lincoln does not give an inch in his negotiations with slavery supporters. He has a principle that he is committed to, and he crushes his opposition both with his skillful maneuvering AND his refusal to succumb to arguments about why he should meet in the middle.

Very clearly, "Lincoln" is not about a compromise of ideas, where you give up something and I give up something in order to reach a middle ground. It is rather about compromising one's own moral standards in order to do — in one case — what is right (Lincoln using bribery to win votes to end slavery) and in the other case to do what is wrong (sell your vote to the highest bidder).

The people who sold their votes to Lincoln certainly compromised their principles — however much we in retrospect disagree with them and find them morally repugnant — but what about this does David Brooks find laudable? Victory at any cost? The ends justify the means?

Is that really the role model we wish to use in our modern politics? If so, we don't have to go all the way back to Lincoln to get the lesson; we could just go back 50 years. Ultimately, as envisioned by David Brooks (and some extent Steven Spielberg) Lincoln turns out to just be LBJ without the Texas accent.

But if we do venture all the way back to the 19th century, maybe we should do so with our eyes open. There is a lot of history back there, and not all of it is in Technicolor.

Compromise, you see, is what created all the problems that culminated in the Civil War and its half a million dead Americans. It was constitutional compromise back in 1787 that gave us the provision that slaves should count as three-fifths of a person for purposes of divvying up legislative districts. It was a noble compromise aimed at preventing the slave states from gaining too much power, but nonetheless it carries that same stench which inevitably follows all horse-trading.

Nor was it the last compromise that led inevitably to war by treating principle as something that could be squeezed into geographic boundaries.

The Missouri Compromise of 1820 banned slavery in the northern parts of the Louisiana Purchase, but allowed it in Missouri, Oklahoma, New Mexico, Arizona, most of southern California, and the southern tip of Nevada. That compromise probably sounded good if you were a black in the northern territories; not so good if you lived in New Mexico or Missouri.

Then there was the Kansas-Nebraska Act of 1854, which repealed the Missouri Compromise and declared that the new territories of Kansas and Nebraska could decide for themselves whether they would have slavery. This proves two things — 1) that a compromise is only as good as what the NEXT Congress decides, and 2) that compromise can be a bloody mess:

The Kansas-Nebraska Act, formulated by Lincoln's arch-nemesis, Democratic Sen. Steven Douglas of Illinois, encouraged pro- and anti-slavery forces to converge in the Kansas Territory for the purpose of swaying the vote on slavery. The result was anarchy as the opposing sides waged a virtual civil war for four long years in what became known as "Bleeding Kansas."

Another result of this "compromise" was the creation of the Republican Party, as abolitionist forces joined together to fight the spread of slavery. Their rapid rise resulted in the election of Lincoln as president just six years later, thus ensuring a war between the states as first South Carolina and then other Southern slave states declared their intent to secede from the Union.

It was only Lincoln's refusal to compromise on the matter of slavery which finally forced the country to deal with its tarnished concepts of liberty and equality. And when the phony compromises of 75 years collapsed, they collapsed hard. Yes, more than half a million dead in the Civil War, and yet the price had to be paid. For principle.

So, too, it always must be. Principles can be compromised for 10 years or a hundred years, but eventually they rise up again with a vengeance. Spending human capital in the form of slavery took a horrible toll on our country, which could not be disguised by the bloody bandages of periodic compromise.

In the same way, for the past 100 years, our nation has been spending the proceeds generated by its productive capitalist economy in order to fund ever more expensive social programs and benefits. Endless compromises have ensured that this redistribution of wealth would continue — no matter how much it has drained our economy and our moral fiber of their sustenance.

Whether principle will prevail in the current debate over government spending for programs it cannot afford, I do not know. But I do know one thing — compromise is not an answer; it is just a guarantee that when we hit the wall of truth later, when principle finally collects its price, there will be hell to pay.

THE TWO ALS AND A NATIONAL SHAME

January 20, 2013

If you needed more evidence that the United States is in full self-destruct mode, you got it last week when it was announced that former Vice President Al Gore had sold his failed cable talk network Current TV to Al Jazeera for $500 million.

Gore wasn't the only partner in Current TV, so he is expected to reap only about $70 million, but that's a pretty hefty haul for a guy who was worth under $2 million when he ran for president in the year 2000. Nor can you attribute the big cash infusion to his brilliance as an entrepreneur. Current TV was a dismal failure in all regards, and has practically no market value as an economic engine.

However, as a propaganda outlet for the Muslim Brotherhood, al-Qaida and extreme Islam, it is priceless. The name Al Jazeera literally means The Peninsula in Arabic, and it is a reference to the Arabian Peninsula, where it is based in Qatar. But Al Jazeera America, as Current TV will be renamed when it begins programming from its New York headquarters, should really be nicknamed "The Beachhead" because it is a bold incursion of anti-U.S. propaganda directly into the homes of millions of Americans.

Of course, "progressives" like Al Gore don't recognize any distinction between the United States and the rest of the world. They believe that truth is "relative" and that it will be a good thing when ultimately a global "brotherhood of man" replaces nations and, as John Lennon wrote, "the world will live as one."

This notion of one-world government has been tried before. Hitler was a big proponent of it, as was Stalin, but not surprisingly the unification that they attempted did not have anything to do with brotherhood. It was all about manipulation, oppression and prevarication. But though their propaganda worked to persuade some people that they were only interested in "living life in peace," very few Americans were ever fooled by them. There was a nearly united front against the forces of anti-Americanism. Indeed, strange as it sounds today, we even had representatives in Congress who investigated un-American activities in order to keep us safe.

No, that could never happen nowadays.. If you are anti-American, well, that is your right. As a result of the "anything goes" Sixties and the "me, my, mine" Seventies, we have been indoctrinated to believe that as an American, you should be able to believe whatever you want. And maybe there is some truth to that, but the difference between America 50, 60 and 70 years ago, and the America of today is that in those days there was actually a sense of shame. You might not go to jail because you wanted to overthrow our Constitution, but you certainly wouldn't be welcome at the church social, and you sure as heck wouldn't be elected to office.

Nowadays, being anti-American is cool. Just bring some potato salad for the pot luck and all is forgiven. Or, if you are Al "Inconvenient Truth" Gore, just spend enough of your ill-gotten loot on progressive causes, and no one will even think to ask why you sold your cable network to oil-rich, repressive Qatar.

Which brings us back to Al Jazeera. No way, no how such an organization could have ever gotten a foothold in the United States 50 years ago. It would be the equivalent of FDR allowing the Japanese to broadcast Tokyo Rose's WWII propaganda direct from Los Angeles. National security wouldn't stand for it, and neither would the American people.

But now, a radical group like the Muslim Brotherhood — which wields huge influence over Al Jazeera — can purchase its way into the American mainstream with no comment by the American government and barely any notice by the American people. And if that doesn't scare you, nothing will.

ONE GOOD REASON NOT TO TRUST FOX NEWS

February 24, 2013

What's good for the goose is good for the gander, and the same thing goes for Al Gore and Rupert Murdoch, right?

I wrote a column recently excoriating Al Gore for selling his Current TV cable channel to Al Jazeera, the Arabic news broadcast company based in Qatar. It isn't just that Al Jazeera is Arabic, but rather that it is a mouthpiece for the Muslim Brotherhood and other Islamist causes.

Turns out that the new Al Jazeera America may not be the only problem, however. An interview with columnist Diana West on the website www.radicalislam.org has pointed to Rupert Murdoch's Fox News as another unlikely point of origin for Islamic propaganda in the United States.

Before we consider the particulars, let's look at the larger picture.

Does American freedom of the press mean that our country is obligated to provide a forum for those who would destroy us? That is the central philosophical question on which hinges our cultural survival — for if we cannot ban anti-American propaganda within our own borders, then the Constitution is indeed a suicide pact, as a Supreme Court justice once famously assured us it wasn't.

Yes, I know we are a diverse society, and we welcome all opinions, but nonetheless it is insane to allow foreign agents to promote anti-American viewpoints from within our very own shores. That's why I wrote a column last month that blasted Gore for selling his company to Al Jazeera and its Muslim Brotherhood backers.

But this isn't just a problem created by liberal Democrats. It is a social problem, and it reaches so deep that it avoids any partisan label. There was plenty of evidence of American subservience to Islamic sensitivities during the Bush administration. President Bush was famous for calling Islam a "religion of peace" at the same time when its clerics were calling for his head on a platter.

More recently, a perfect example is the failure of the Army to declare the attack at Fort Hood either a military attack or terrorism. Nope, just a plain old psycho who coincidentally happened to be a Muslim in communication with Islamic terror leader Anwar al-Awlaki.

And one more example: The U.S. military has responded to attacks on our soldiers by their Afghan trainees not by halting the training programs, but by implementing "Islamic sensitivity" sessions so that our GIs know why they annoy the Afghans so much.

Which brings us back to Fox News and Rupert Murdoch. I'd been vaguely aware that a minority shareholder in Fox News was Saudi Prince Alwaleed bin Talal, but the interview with Diana West showed just how much concern that should cause. Not only does bin Talal own 7 percent of Murdoch's News Corp, but Murdoch also owns 19 percent of Rotana, which is bin Talal's Arabic media group. These two are intimately involved in each other's profit motives, and West makes a convincing case that Fox News has avoided controversial topics involving Islam ever since bin Talal made his first investment in news Corp in 2005.

Indeed, bin Talal bragged publicly that year about complaining to Murdoch that Fox News was characterizing street violence in Paris as "Muslim riots." A short while later, Fox joined the rest of the mainstream media in referring to the "civil riots" in Paris without reference to the Islamic origin of the unrest.

It appears that Alwaleed's investment in Fox News, as well as Al Jazeera's purchase of Current TV, both represent the culmination of a plan which Alwaleed himself expressed in a 2002 interview with his own Arab News:

"Arab countries can influence U.S. decision making "if they unite through economic interests, not political... We have to be logical and understand that the U.S. administration is subject to U.S. public opinion. ... And to bring the decision-maker on your side, you not only have to be active in the U.S. Congress or the administration, but also inside U.S. society."

That is an absolutely transparent confession of what is going on, and yet Congress, the news media and the American public just act as though it doesn't matter. They apparently believe that the United States is invulnerable to any threat — foreign or domestic — and that we really ought to just welcome our Muslim brothers to our shore as part of the great American melting pot that is now so diluted that there is virtually nothing American left about it.

Ask yourself: How exactly does the United States benefit by having the propaganda arm of the Muslim Brotherhood and the worldwide Islamic revolution being welcomed into millions of homes across the country?

I guess there's nothing like humanizing the face of jihad so that Mr. and Mrs America can start to feel better about submitting to sharia (Islamic law) and dhimmitude (subservience by non-Muslims to their Islamic betters). Not much chance we will be watching programming on the "Real Oppressed Wives of The Casbah" or "My Big Fat Obnoxious Terrorist." Instead, it will be a steady stream of how reasonable, rational and peaceful everyone is in the Middle East when they are not throwing together a "spontaneous demonstration" outside the U.S. mission in Benghazi, sentencing rape victims to death for provoking men by not wearing a burka, or stoning Christians for... well... for being Christians.

Oh, wait, I remember now. As I have been informed by my liberal betters, there is no reason to fear Islam. It is just right-wing hate speech to point out the historical basis of that fear. It is bug-eyed McCarthyism to suggest that foreign elements might not have America's best interests at heart (even though history has proven that McCarthy was right about the Soviet Union's spy network operating throughout the U.S. government in the 1950s).

Muslims, we are told, are not our enemy until they do something to prove they are an enemy. But tell that to journalist Danny Pearl, who was kidnapped in Pakistan in 2001 by Islamic fundamentalists who later cut his head off. Tell it to Nick Berg, a Jewish American businessman who was executed in Iraq by the terrorist Abu Musab al-Zarqawi in 2004. Tell it to Eugene Armstrong or Jack Hensley, American contractors who were also decapitated after being captured in Iraq in 2004. These are but the tiniest indicators of the nature of Islam, but like the arrow of a compass aiming infallibly toward the magnetic field at the North Pole, these murders point inexorably toward the gathering force that confronts Western civilization.

But, of course, we need to all try to get along — so the less said about those brutal murders the better. We don't want to insult our Muslim brothers by making them feel unwelcome. Remember, our self-interest as a free society should always come second if there is the slightest chance that our honesty might offend someone from a more oppressive, less tolerant culture. Otherwise we are being selfish, and that is politically incorrect.

Which is why, I suppose, there is absolutely no way for our country to stop our enemies from taking over our media centers, our digital networks, our manufacturing facilities, probably even our military and our government eventually. We are just too darn polite to ever say anything about how much our institutions and traditions mean to us. We used to fight to the death to preserve our culture, but now we are way TOO cultured to presume that the American way of life is in any way better than any other.

Hey, maybe that anti-American propaganda is working! Just a thought.

REWRITING HISTORY
AND 'LOOKING BACKWARD'

June 23, 2013

One thing that's incredibly tiresome about being a conservative is how people rewrite history so that they can pigeonhole you as a racist, a fascist or a dangerous radical.

The most common tactic is to claim that Republicans were the party of slavery and that they had opposed equal rights for blacks. This is, of course, untrue, but in a culture that devalues history and inflates the value of punditry, truth is whatever is repeated often enough in a chain e-mail.

An example of this kind of distortion occurred last week in response to Louisiana state Sen. Elbert Guillory's announcement that he was switching from the Democratic to Republican party. He pointed out that, "It was the Republican President Dwight Eisenhower who championed the Civil Rights Act of 1957, but it was Democrats in the Senate who filibustered the bill."

This outraged many liberals, including blogger Sean McElwee, who writes for a website called "The Moderate Voice." In his column, "Elbert Guillory's Confused History," he calls out the newly declared Republican for stopping his historical review with Eisenhower.

"After all," he says, "it was Democrats that pushed the Civil Rights Act of 1964 and Voting Rights Act of 1965 through Congress..."

And thus, once again, the conservative voice is silenced — or at least slandered (I don't think Sen. Guillory has any intention of keeping quiet!) — by distortions and outright lies.

Let's revisit the historical record on those two landmark pieces of legislation that were supposedly pushed through Congress by Democrats. It's not that hard to find out the truth — but sometimes it's hard for "moderate" writers like McElwee to tell it.

A quick Internet search reveals the following: 69 percent of Senate Democrats supported the Civil Rights Act of 1964, but that margin of support was far surpassed by the Republican Party — where the bill had 82 percent support!

It was virtually the same story in the House, where only 63 percent of Democrats supported the end of Jim Crow laws, but fully 80 percent of Republicans did! Makes sense considering that Republicans were the party of Lincoln, abolition and emancipation!

By the following year, Democrats were starting to come along, and a larger proportion of them supported the Voting Rights Act of 1965, but they still trailed behind Republicans. In the Senate, particularly, Republican support (94 percent) far outweighed Democratic support (73 percent).

You could make the case that McElwee made an honest error, but maybe he was intentionally misleading his readers the same way he does by putting his column on a website called The Moderate Voice. His "moderate" voice in the last month has blasted Tea Party advocate Michele Bachman, touted the usefulness of gun-control laws, lamented the "manufactured Benghazi scandal," and praised "affirmative action."

Besides, no matter how many people point out his error, it is very likely no correction will be forthcoming because McElwee — like so many progressive authors — is writing about the world he wants to exist, not the one that does exist.

Maybe what really outraged McElwee is the fact that Sen. Guillory is not just conservative, not just Republican, but also a black conservative and that he is speaking out against what he calls "the illusion that ... [Democratic] policies are what's best for black people."

Guillory's message continues:

"You see, at the heart of liberalism is the idea that only a great and powerful big government can be the benefactor of social justice for all Americans. But the left is only concerned with one thing: control. And they disguise this control as charity."

You can find evidence of this throughout the progressive movement — from Margaret Sanger, the founder of Planned Parenthood who was an avowed racist and a proponent of eugenics "to assist the race toward the elimination of the unfit" — to Occupy Wall Street, which wants to create a benevolent society based on two concepts — redistribution of wealth and reinvention of human nature.

If you sense a disconnect between the two strains of progressivism — taking care of everyone's needs on the one hand and eliminating the unfit on the other — then you are close to penetrating the legerdemain of misdirection that has kept so many enthralled to progressive rhetoric for so long.

Back in the early 1890s, the socialist Edward Bellamy was seeking to fundamentally transform the country into a place where "the economic equality of all the citizens [would be] the guarantee of individual liberty and dignity."

That quote is from an 1894 interview with The Galveston News that makes for fascinating reading today because of its hints about the progressive world view that has come to dominate Washington, D.C., in recent years.

Bellamy's utopian novel "Looking Backward" engendered a cadre of like-minded socialists who envisioned "the abolition of private capitalism and the substitution of some form of co-operative industry" run by the state. The collapse of his Nationalist movement, coincidentally, is dated to have occurred in 1894, although it is certainly arguable that much of what Bellamy fancied has ultimately come to pass — namely, Dictatorship by Benevolent Big Government.

As Bellamy told the Galveston News reporter in 1894: "The only hope for the laboring classes is the collective or public conduct of industry by the people through their governmental agencies for the common interest. More and more, the working masses are beginning to see that this is for them the only way out."

In other words, Bellamy foresaw a world where Big Government would be the champion of the working people, and the workers would accept the heavy hand of the government gladly because it provided for their needs, if not always their wants.

Of course, the right hand did not always know what the left hand was doing. Bellamy argued that the people would rise up in revolution in order to better themselves, but as in Orwell's "Animal Farm," some of the people were more equal than others.

Good progressive that he was, Bellamy looked forward to a world where people could be socially engineered from their backwards state into good Americans. Sen. Guillory might be worried that Bellamy was talking about the black population, but no, his disdain was directed toward the Slavs — the people of Eastern Europe, who at that time were immigrating to America in great numbers.

Asked by the reporter whether he was worried "that the immigration of large masses of ignorant people, especially the Slavs, has anything more than a temporary effect on the general intelligence," Bellamy coolly replied, "This is bad of course," but he generously opined that even the Slavs "have as much right to come here as my forefathers had."

But would they help the peaceful revolution that Bellamy anticipated?

"You must not imagine... that these people are Socialists or Nationalists. They have no idea whatever. They are not intelligent enough."

You would not expect a progressive to say such a nasty thing, mostly because we have been taught for the past 20 years or so that only conservatives say frightful things about classes of people. But there it is. In black and white. A progressive who is a racist — or at least a bigot. Imagine that.

Bellamy went on to explain why massive immigration was not going to be stopped anytime soon by "legal legislative check," and perhaps that explanation is worth considering today as we are on the eve of so-called "comprehensive immigration reform."

"The labor organizations are not likely to succeed in this [effort to restrict immigration], because the capitalist interests desire that this immigration shall continue and that it shall be from the poorest classes of Europeans, because they desire cheap labor and the presence of these poorer classes of European immigrants enables them to reduce the wages of the American working man more successfully than they otherwise would be enabled to do."

Substitute "Latin Americans" for "Europeans," and you begin to sense a common thread between today's immigration fight and the one of 1894. And while I disagree heartily with Bellamy's disdain for the Slavs, I have to agree with him that immigration policy is set not for the benefit of the worker, but for the benefit of the employer. If we are really going to empower the working people, we should start with our own — and not just import millions of foreign workers for the convenience (connivance?) of Big Business.

Now that is a progressive idea I can get behind.

AL JAZEERA AND THE SOFT UNDERBELLY OF AMERICA

September 1, 2013

Can you imagine Adolf Hitler owning a TV news network that spewed his hateful rhetoric across the United States either before or during World War II?

Certainly not, but let's be more creative. Imagine a German citizen, maybe a Nazi Party member or maybe not, who talked about free exchange of ideas and a balanced approach that would find common ground between the Germans and the Americans.

Sounds more inviting, doesn't it? You could air the Nazi point-of-view as a "counterpoint" to anti-Nazi "propaganda" in order to make sure that Americans were able to make an "informed decision" about their supposed "enemies."

But yet, one can't imagine the America of Franklin Roosevelt tolerating or even contemplating the possibility of a beachhead of foreign Nazi rhetoric on our shores, even though plenty of homegrown sympathizers certainly had a large bullhorn prior to Pearl Harbor.

That model should still be in place. Let Americans say what they want, no matter how horrible, because of the First Amendment, but don't allow foreigners to gain constitutional protections for their attempts to undermine our government, our way of life, or our vital national interests.

This principle doesn't have anything to do with the First Amendment or tolerance of other people's ideas. It has to do with self-preservation. If you are engaged in a war for cultural survival, you don't just turn a blind eye to a foreign effort to subvert your nation from within.

Unfortunately, that instinct for survival no longer exists in modern America — which, like it or not, is engaged in a long-term battle of wills with Islamism, the movement to impose the political and cultural version of Islam known across the globe in a worldwide caliphate dedicated to the implementation of sharia (Islamic law).

Consider the little-heralded arrival on Aug. 20 of Al Jazeera America, an English language version of the worldwide Al Jazeera network owned by the royal family of Qatar and which has well-documented ties to the Muslim Brotherhood and the Hamas terrorist organization.

With such innocuous slogans as "Shouldn't news just give the facts?" and "Change the way you look at news," Al Jazeera America hopes to paint itself as just one more news network, only better. And they have spared no expense in working to look like just that.

Well-known news personalities such as John Siegenthaler of NBC, Soledad O'Brien and Ali Velshi of CNN, and David Shuster, who worked at both Fox News and MSNBC, are among the many familiar faces on the new channel. Shuster most recently had a gig on Current TV, the left-wing cable channel that Al Gore and his cronies sold to Al Jazeera in January for a tidy profit of filthy petro-dollars.

With all that high-paid window dressing, Al Jazeera America is well-positioned to claim that it is just one more channel trying to make a buck by serving its viewers with interesting and entertaining news coverage.

And from the response so far, Al Jazeera doesn't even really have to make a case to justify its existence. In the America of 2013, hardly anyone cares that this foreign source of propaganda has taken its place at the table with NBC, CBS, CNN and Fox News. (And, yes, I know that Fox News has a major Arab investor, and I don't like that either, but there is a difference between investing and having a controlling interest.)

This is where the true danger arises. Forget about the foreign propaganda element, and think about how dangerous it is to give a foreign national interest which harbors anti-American sentiments full access to the protections of the First Amendment's press guarantees.

Just last week, Al Jazeera America's website ran a story headlined, "Snowden leaks intelligence 'black budget' to Washington Post." This story should never have been printed in the first place as its reveals classified information provided to the Post by national-security thief Edward Snowden and only serves the purpose of weakening our government's efforts to keep us safe from foreign enemies across the globe.

We can debate for years whether or not the First Amendment should protect a domestic newspaper such as the Washington Post that publishes top-secret information. It is easy to make the case that the newspaper is working against America's interest, but we do have to have at least some confidence that the owners of the Washington Post are not anti-American.

It is noteworthy that the Post published the following disclaimer in its story: "The Post only revealed select portions of the U.S. intelligence budget to prevent opposing intelligence agencies from apprehending Washington's priorities and modes of operation."

I would argue that what the Post did publish has already aided and abetted "opposing intelligence agencies" from Korea, Russia, China, Iran and elsewhere, but more importantly the Post is providing cover for the inevitable day when Al Jazeera America gets classified national-security data leaked to it and decides to publish ALL of it — or, God forbid, to send it directly to Saudi Arabia, Yemen, Syria or Iran. Just another milestone of investigative reporting, right? And all protected by the First Amendment!

Is the world really that different today than it was in 1940? Are we so utterly naive these days that we no longer believe foreign agents want to corrupt and destroy our American institutions? Or are we just so afraid of being called politically incorrect that we will no longer rise up to defend our own interests?

Unfortunately the answers to those questions redound to our approaching doom. No... the world is not different than it was in 1940 when it comes to global ambitions, but YES we are increasingly naive and fearful about how to respond to global threats. That combination leaves us at the mercy of our enemies, and I suspect they will show no mercy at all.

WHEN DOES 2 PLUS 2 EQUAL XX?

October 13, 2013

"How many fingers am I holding up, Winston?"

With those words, the enigmatic agent of the Thought Police known as O'Brien begins his education of Winston Smith, the doomed hero of George Orwell's "1984."

O'Brien is holding up four fingers, as Winston correctly reports during his interrogation. But this is not the answer which Big Brother is looking for, so O'Brien asks Winston, "And if the party says that it is not four but five — then how many?"

Winston still says four, and thus gets his first blast of pain from the torture device in the interrogation room — Room 101 — the room of lies and of nightmares.

Several blasts of pain later, and still clinging to his knowledge that O'Brien is holding up four fingers — no more and no less — Winston asks pleadingly "What else can I say?"

At this point, Winston still believes in objective truth, but O'Brien and his pain machine still have a lot to teach him — even though O'Brien laments that Winston is a "slow learner."

"How can I help it?" Winston asks. "How can I help seeing what is in front of my eyes? Two and two are four."

O'Brien is bemused by Winston's innocence. "Sometimes, Winston" he replies to him. "Sometimes they are five. Sometimes they are three. Sometimes they are all of them at once. You must try harder. It is not easy to become sane."

Not too much longer, after numerous shuddering bouts of pain, Winston confirms what he has been told to think — four fingers is actually five. Under duress, he has given up the evidence of his own eyes. Objective reality has been replaced with political reality, or as we call it today, political correctness. This is the state whereby reality is adjusted to fit the politically convenient "truth," rather than the truth reflecting what is objectively called reality.

George Orwell, of course, was writing a novel. So far as we know, the Western democratic republics are not inflicting pain on their own citizens in order to extract politically correct slogans out of them. Nonetheless, Orwell was a prophet whose Thought Police actually prefigure the modern media as a force used to condition the citizenry to reject objective truth (singular) and accept multiple convenient truths in its place.

A remarkable example of this came to my attention last week when I was scanning the Associated Press news wire and read a story about the indictment of 13 members of the Internet hacking group called Anonymous.

Zipping along to see how the government was handling these cyber-terrorists, I stumbled over the following paragraph:

"In December 2010, the conspirators discussed possible targets related to WikiLeaks, which received more than 700,000 documents and some battlefield video from Army Pvt. Chelsea Manning, the largest-volume leak of classified material in U.S. history."

Being relatively well-informed about the WikiLeaks case, I was surprised I had never heard of Chelsea Manning. Yet there was something troublingly familiar about the name. Then I remembered that the main leaker in the WikiLeaks case was named Bradley Manning. Could there be a connection? Sure enough, a quick Google search turned up an entry for Chelsea Manning in Wikipedia, and when I clicked on it, I came to this description:

"Chelsea Elizabeth Manning (born Bradley Edward Manning, December 17, 1987) is a United States Army soldier who was convicted in July 2013 of violations of the Espionage Act and other offenses, after releasing the largest set of classified documents ever leaked to the public. Manning was sentenced to confinement for 35 years and to be dishonorably discharged from the Army... In a statement the day after sentencing, Manning said she had felt female since childhood, asked to be known as Chelsea, and expressed a desire to undergo hormone replacement therapy."

OK, so Chelsea Manning was really Bradley Manning. Whether Bradley wanted to be known as Chelsea was of no importance to me whatsoever, but what astounded me is that the AP had not only granted Manning's wish to call him Chelsea, but had also done so without any kind of notice to the public that Chelsea was the faux name of the well-known convicted spy. It was as though Bradley Manning had never existed, just as in O'Brien's world of "1984," two plus two had never equaled four if Big Brother said so.

The more I read, the more I was befuddled by how easily the AP and Wikipedia were able to alter reality and turn a man into a woman. The Wikipedia story referred to Manning with female pronouns throughout the story, even in reference to activities that had clearly taken place when he was indisputably a "he" and not a "she."

Was there some political agenda at work? The AP would never admit to such a scenario, but isn't calling a man a woman a huge political statement? What concerns me is that massive amounts of people will see nothing wrong with the Associated

Press and other news organizations calling a man a woman, because, after all, he asked for it!

As for me, I am asking the same question Winston Smith asked, "How can I help seeing what is in front of my eyes? Two and two are four." Likewise a man is a man, a woman is a woman, and a traitor is a traitor — by any name.

Of course, I haven't visited Room 101 yet, but until then I am sticking with this formula that I learned back in grade school: XX equals female and XY equals male. No matter how much a doctor's scalpel and hormones can reshape the exterior of a man, there is one thing that doesn't change — and never will. That little old Y chromosome that made Bradley Manning a man is an inconvenient truth that can't be denied, no matter how much the Associated Press insists that it can.

MAN-GIVEN RIGHTS
AND GOVERNMENT GONE WILD

February 16, 2014

Just what we needed — another item to add to the ever burgeoning file labeled "Things that can't possibly be true in America, but are anyway." Consider this monstrosity:

Our formerly constitutional government, in the form of the Federal Communications Commission, has developed a plan to put observers in the nation's newsrooms in order to better understand "the process by which stories are selected."

Of course, they won't just "understand" the process; they will most assuredly and dangerously alter it, merely by the implied threat of their presence in the formerly sacrosanct newsroom. Just ask anyone who ever worked for a newspaper in Soviet Russia or Hitler's Germany or even Chavez's Venezuela.

There is a very good reason why we have a First Amendment to the Constitution. The Founding Fathers had experienced directly the chilling effect of a capricious and imperious government on the free exchange of ideas, so they prohibited Congress from making any law "abridging the freedom of speech, or of the press." Through the years, this prohibition has been widened by the courts to protect the press from interference by virtually any unit of government, and so it has stood until now — a bedrock principle that has generally come to be known as "freedom of the press."

But that has given way to "freedom of the government" to do whatever it wants to do. You heard in this column, and in many other forums, the warning that if the federal bureaucracy could force you to buy health insurance today, then there was no longer any meaningful limit on government power. But even I never imagined how quickly the Constitution would erode, nor how little outcry there would be when the president arrogated to himself the power to write and rewrite laws, nor how quickly forgotten would be the abuse of the taxing power of the federal government through the IRS to punish enemies and shape political debate.

Oh yes, I am aware that a dedicated band of big-government disciples will deny, deflect and disclaim any allegation of a continuous concerted effort to subvert our rights. They will try to paint me as an extremist or a racist or a raving lunatic. It's OK. I've been called worse. And more importantly, calling me names does not make the abuses of power disappear. They are plainly there for anyone to see. Just do a Google search for IRS abuses or Benghazi coverup or Obamacare mandate delays.

Or look up Ajit Pai. He's the member of the Federal Communications Commission who blew the whistle last week with an op-ed in the Wall Street Journal about the agency's initiative to get to the bottom of the mystery of why television and radio broadcasters are not telling the story the federal government wants them to tell.

That's a scary proposition on a lot of levels. Not just because the government is shoving its nose where it doesn't belong, but because most of us who don't work for the federal government are asking just the opposite question: Why is the national media so compliant and virtually complicit in pushing big government's agenda of radical environmentalism, economic justice, and social change?

Well, maybe now we will get the answers! The FCC is about to launch a program they call a "Multi-Market Study of Critical Information Needs," which according to Pai will "send researchers to grill reporters, editors and station owners about how they decide which stories to run." They are scheduled to start the shenanigans with a "field test" in Columbia, S.C., but it shouldn't be long before FCC goons are setting up shop in TV stations and radio studios across the nation. Heck, they are even going to be "interviewing" newspaper editors and reporters, but it's all voluntary, mind you, so there's no "real" violation of freedom of the press, is there?

Or maybe I should say there's no real "freedom of the press," is there?

Apparently, the underlying purpose of this whole charade is to declare yet another of the new "man-given rights" (like the right to affordable health care) which expand the power of government to interfere in our lives and private decisions. The report that promoted the idea of "critical information needs" came out of USC's Annenberg School of Communications in 2012. Read the executive summary at http://transition.fcc.gov/ocbo/Executive_Summary.pdf and you will discover the following conclusions:

"(1) There is an identifiable set of basic information needs that individuals need met to navigate everyday life, and that communities need to have met in order to thrive; (2) Low income and some minority and marginalized communities within metropolitan and rural areas and areas that are "lower-information" areas are likely to be systematically disadvantaged in both personal and community opportunities when information needs lag or go unmet; and (3) Information goods are public goods; the failure to provide them is, in part, a market failure.")

If you don't recognize the language, this is the beginning of an effort to declare a new "right" to "information goods" that will be provided, if necessary, by government fiat to "systematically disadvantaged" low-income and minority communities in order to make sure that they have access to "forms of information that are necessary for citizens and community members to live safe and healthy lives."

And why shouldn't the government think it can force broadcasters and newspapers to carry the kind of information that is deemed "necessary" for a safe and healthy life? Hasn't the government already taken over health care — an industry that comprises one-sixth of the entire national economy? And didn't the Supreme Court confirm the appropriateness of this extra-constitutional power grab? So why would government stop declaring new man-given rights that extend the power of the government in all directions in order to protect us from ourselves?

In case, you were wondering, here are the "critical information needs" which the government want to ensure by eliminating the free press: emergencies and risks, health and welfare, education, transportation, economic opportunities, the environment, civic information and political information.

If you don't recognize the danger of government dictating to the press how to cover these topics, then you have helped me answer an age-old question asked whenever innocence is abused in the name of the people: "Just how could that happen?"

Now we know.

DESPITE SETBACK, THE FCC'S SNOUT IS UNDER THE TENT

February 23, 2014

Chalk one up for the good guys — well, sort of.

After a week of mockery, derision, and disdain, the Federal Communications Commission has announced that it won't put observers in newsrooms after all.

FCC Commissioner Ajit Pai's op-ed in the Wall Street Journal on Feb. 10 had alerted the public to the dangers of having government representatives querying news bosses about how they decide what stories to cover — and which ones not to cover.

The implicit threat of such heavy-handed research is that the government could be on the verge of announcing that IT will decide what stories are important to cover, just as it has decided what kind of cars you should buy (no "clunkers"!), what kind of health insurance you should have (Obamacare!) and what kind of dust is the right kind (whatever kind the EPA says!).

I wrote about that threat in this column last week, just ahead of an avalanche of coverage everywhere except on the major mainstream networks, which may have viewed the proposal as just a new phase of their "partnership" with the government to promote social justice and class warfare.

The academic study which led to the FCC plan to infiltrate the nation's newsrooms, was conducted by the Annenberg School of Communications at USC. It posited the existence of "critical information needs" and concluded that the mass media was failing to meet those needs, thus leaving "low income and some minority and marginalized communities" ... "systematically disadvantaged in both personal and community opportunities."

When you sorted out the gobbledygook (or what Orwell called "sheer cloudy vagueness") you can only be left with the impression that some pointy heads at the FCC felt it was their obligation to massage the message coming out of newsrooms so that these so-called "critical needs" were being met. In other words, the most overt move toward government control of the media since the Sedition Act of 1918.

But, hey, relax. Uncle Sam has thrown up his hands and surrendered. FCC Spokesperson Shannon Gilson "set the record straight" in a statement released Friday.

"To be clear," Gilson said, "media owners and journalists will no longer be asked to participate in the Columbia, S.C., pilot study. The pilot will not be undertaken until a new study design is final. Any subsequent market studies conducted by the FCC, if determined necessary, will not seek participation from or include questions for media owners, news directors or reporters.

"Any suggestion that the FCC intends to regulate the speech of news media or plans to put monitors in America's newsrooms is false."

Well, thanks, Shannon. I feel a lot better now.

At least I did until remembered how many times advocates of unlimited government tried and failed to pass universal health insurance, going back to the drawing board each time. They tweaked their proposals and shot them out again, never able to overcome the underlying argument against government intrusion, but instead increasing their efforts to "educate" the public on how poverty wickedly leaves "critical health needs" unmet.

Eventually having the government tell you what doctor to see seems like a small price to pay in order to ensure that your neighbor has health care. (Well, you are paying your neighbor's premium, too, but even that seems like a small price to pay, doesn't it? After all, you wouldn't really want to see you neighbor get sick and die, would you, you heartless bastard?)

So don't expect this issue to go away. The camel's nose is already under the tent, and when the sultans of the news media fall fast asleep after getting drunk on their own self-importance, you can bet the camel is coming inside.

Or is a pig's snout the better metaphor? Read George Orwell's "Animal Farm" for a lesson in just how easy it is for the pigs to gull the rest of the animals into going along to get along. That works out just fine as long as you mind your own business or until it is your turn to be sent to the knacker. Look it up, and then consider whether you really want to trust your god-given rights over to the FCC or any other government agency.

The most critical of all our "information needs" is to keep the government out of the information business — period.

A STAR — NO, AN AMERICAN
HERO —IS BORN!

March 9, 2014

The best show on TV last week wasn't "The Walking Dead." It wasn't "Downton Abbey." And it sure wasn't "The Academy Awards."

As a matter of fact, the best show on television last week was on an obscure video channel that airs in a few key Time Warner Cable markets such as New York and San Francisco; Comcast markets throughout California and Chicago; and Dish-TV in D.C.

You've probably never heard of it. RT-America was founded in 2005, but made the mistake of first operating under its real name "Russia Today," which probably complicated its efforts to subvert American institutions by spreading anti-capitalist, anti-American, pro-Russian propaganda in our homeland. MSNBC and CNN have certainly demonstrated that it is much easier to go the anti-America route if you don't have Russia in your name.

So once the Kremlin wised up (oh yeah, did I mention that RT-America is owned by the Russian government?), Russia Today was glammed up as RT-America and thus became a true threat to our nation.

Of course, I know that the good old progressives among us are harumphing and throwing up their hands at this point, pointing to the good old First Amendment and saying that the Constitution protects Russians, too, or else what good is it? I know they are going to laugh at me and derisively insist that some two-bit TV channel with a handful of viewers is much less of a threat to the country than the Koch Brothers or the Tea Party or Ted Cruz or Rush Limbaugh (you know, those people who actually wave the Grand Old Flag and want to restore "the republic for which it stands" to its former greatness. I know those angry progs don't get the old-fashioned bit about patriotism and national security, and if you dare to bring up "the communist threat," they will throw around the specter of Sen. Joe McCarthy like it was some of that slimy ectoplasm from "Ghostbusters." Man, if they nail you with that stuff, you will be radioactive! Say goodbye to all your fair-weather friends!

But I don't care what they throw at me. I am still on the side of Harry Truman, John Kennedy and J. Edgar Hoover when it comes to those sneaky Russians. I just find it hard to trust them after the whole "enslaving Eastern Europe" thing.

Which brings us back around to the best show on TV last week, heck maybe the best show on TV this year, when a new American hero was born. No matter what else she has done before, or does after, former RT-America anchorwoman Liz Wahl should always be remembered and thanked for telling the truth about "the enemy within."

Wahl had spent the last two weeks feeding the Kremlin's propaganda to her gullible American TV audience about the Ukrainian uprising and the Russian occupation of Crimea. But finally, she couldn't ignore her conscience any longer, so she looked straight into the camera and told her Russian bosses to take her job and shove it. It was only 75 seconds, but it was the best 75 seconds on TV in a long time, and no doubt the most-watched clip ever produced by RT-America. You can watch the full clip on YouTube, but here is the bulk of it:

"...[A]s a reporter on this network I face many ethical and moral challenges, especially me personally, coming from my family whose grandparents... came here as refugees during the Hungarian revolution, ironically to escape Soviet forces. I have family... on my mother's side that sees the daily grind of poverty, and I'm very lucky to have grown up here in the United States. I'm the daughter of a veteran. My partner is a physician at a military base where he sees every day the first-hand accounts of the ultimate prices that people pay for this country. And that is why personally, I cannot be part of a network funded by the Russian government that whitewashes the actions of [Russian President Vladimir] Putin. I'm proud to be an American, and believe in disseminating the truth. And that is why, after this newscast, I'm resigning."

You go, Liz!

Nor did she shut up after that. In an interview with James Kirchick at the Daily Beast, she gave an analysis of how the Kremlin influences the on-air content at RT-America:

"I think management is able to manipulate the very young and naive employees. They will find ways to punish you covertly and reward those that do go along with their narrative.

"It's interesting that our motto is 'Question More' [because] in order to succeed there, you don't question... In a way you kind of suppress any concerns that you have and play the game."

Nor does the presence of born-in-the-USA hosts like Wahl and good old Larry King (yep, he didn't retire when CNN dumped him; he just moved further left!) make RT-America any less dangerous. Of course, the opposite is true; those infectious on-air personalities are the agent of infection by which the Kremlin can corrupt our American values and attack our institutions.

"They're definitely at the top, the Russians, they're kind of able to pull the strings," Wahl told Kirchick. "I just think it's absurd that we're just a few blocks away from the White House and this is all able to go along... It actually makes me feel sick that I worked there. It's not a sound news organization, not when your agenda is making America look bad."

But it's a great strategy for chipping away at America's already tarnished luster. As Wahl said about the target audience of young Americans, "I think some of them are kind of like this hipster generation, they just kind of think it's cool to question authority."

Yeah, question American "authority," and bow to Russian "authoritarianism."

Why, the only thing smarter than using trendy talk-show hosts to spread your anti-American agenda would be to recruit beautiful Hollywood actors and actresses to speak on behalf of the progressive leftist agenda. But, hey, maybe that is next!

THE FREEDOM NOT TO QUESTION CLIMATE CHANGE

April 6, 2014

The campaign to marginalize conservatives and their traditional values has many facets. Last week, we talked about the efforts in academia to restrict access to people whose beliefs are not in tune with modern liberalism, but that is just one small component of an ongoing multi-front war.

Today, let's focus on climate change and the effort by the left to lull you into peaceful acquiescence of a world view that will allow "people smarter than you" to make massive changes in our economy in order to protect you from an impending crisis.

I know, I know, it sounds a lot like Obamacare, but the "climate change" campaign is even more insidious, dangerous and potentially world-altering. The goal of eliminating fossil fuels would inevitably reduce civilization to a thin veneer of culture over a primitive hunting-gathering society (Think "The Hunger Games"). So with such huge consequences, it would seem a reasonable request to have a debate about the validity of the science which demands such earth-shattering changes from society.

But free debate is the last thing that climate-change proponents want. Instead, they want everyone to accept "settled science" and move on to the "solution."

Settled or not, by now everyone has their own either well-informed or less-informed opinions about climate change (formerly known as global warming until the earth stopped warming appreciably), but anyone who is being serious about the discussion has to admit two things — 1) the earth's climate is certainly changing, and 2) we don't know why.

The first point is a truism. The earth's climate is changing now, in 2014, just like it has always been changing. Climate is a dynamic, not a static system. Ergo, climate change in itself does not prove anything.

The second dictum seems to be the sticking point: We don't know why. True science should begin with an acknowledgment that all knowledge is amorphous and subject to change for reasons that may evade detection by us mere mortals, rather than solid and settled. Yes, we humans have devised very canny systems to describe approximations of the truth, but we do not know and are not capable of knowing THE truth.

Unfortunately, when science is viewed as a tool not for advancement of knowledge, but for the reform of human behavior, it is useful for certain scientists and their allies to promote the idea of solid-state, settled science in order to nudge people to adopt what they consider to be socially desirable behavior. It's really not much different from the use of religion in primitive societies to scare people into toeing the line. If you question the "settled science" or "settled religion," you run the risk of being called, in one case, a "denier," and in the other case, a heretic.

Now, I imagine many reasonable people among my readers are, at this point, saying that surely I am exaggerating. After all, even though there is some controversy over global warming or climate change, surely there is room for both sides in the debate.

Not so quick, Copernicus! Just like there wasn't room for both sides in the Middle Ages when we were debating whether the sun revolved around the earth or not, there is an ever-constricting circle of silent hell for so-called climate change "deniers" in our society. Don't take it from me; consider the policy of the Los Angeles Times, which recently announced that it won't publish letters that challenge the scientific orthodoxy that humans are causing climate change.

The argument by the Times' opinion page editor, Paul Thornton, is that "these letters don't make it into our pages" because "saying 'there's no sign humans have caused climate change' is not stating an opinion, it's asserting a factual inaccuracy."

That's the beauty of orthodoxy. You don't have to allow any competing points of view to interfere with what you already know to be true. Thornton said he didn't even need to think for himself; all he had to do was "rely on the experts." Maybe not the same experts as those papists who lit Giordano Bruno at the stake and came perilously close to doing the same thing to Galileo Galilei, but experts who are just as afraid of dissent and debate.

Not surprisingly the condemnation of unorthodox points of view has a chilling effect on debate, scientific or otherwise. The church burned Bruno for just that purpose — to make of him an example, so that fellow scientists like Galileo would step back into line and say what everybody already knew was true — the earth is the center of the universe. Thank God that some people challenge the "experts" or else we would still be living in the Middle Ages today.

Or maybe we are. Lawrence Torcello, an assistant professor of philosophy at Rochester Institute of Technology, recently wrote an article at theconversation.com where he asked, "Is misinformation about the climate criminally negligent?"

You already know the answer. If a conservative speaks out in opposition to liberal orthodoxy, he or she is immediately branded as foolish, corrupt or criminal. Neither truth nor untainted motives are mitigating factors. As Torcello sees it, being part of a well-funded campaign to explain the flaws of prevailing climate-change theory means you are criminally negligent because you are impeding the public's ability to resist the allegedly horrific and deadly effects of climate change. Apparently, the freedom to resist a prevailing orthodoxy diminishes inversely to the level of risk imputed by the theory in dispute. Who knows, maybe the climate change theorists are right? Maybe there will be more deaths in coming years, but wouldn't it be funny if the increased deaths were caused by burning at the stake all those climate deniers who are so dangerous?

Panic is the last refuge of an orthodoxy under attack. Adam Weinstein of Gawker.com took up Torcello's torch, and carried it down the road apiece.

"Man-made climate change happens," Weinstein insists. "Man-made climate change kills a lot of people. It's going to kill a lot more. We have laws on the books to punish anyone whose lies contribute to people's deaths. It's time to punish the climate-change liars."

He goes on with a genuine passion for chaos that is almost hypnotic:

"Attempts to deceive the public on climate change, and to consequently block any public policy to tackle it, contribute to roughly 150,000 deaths a year already," Weinstein claims. "Those denialists should face jail. They should face fines. They should face lawsuits from the classes of people whose lives and livelihoods are most threatened by denialist tactics."

Of course, both Weinstein and Torcello almost apologetically explain that they don't want to lock up "the man on the street" who is just spouting "a socialist United Nations conspiracy" he read somewhere on the Internet. Weinstein dismisses that man — the man on the street — you and your neighbor — as "an idiot" not worth worrying about.

But, of course, they do worry. They worry enough to threaten to arrest you, or if not you, then the people who you rely on for an alternative viewpoint to the prevailing orthodoxy of climate doom. They worry enough to keep you out of the Los Angeles Times, and no doubt other liberal newspapers. They are worried, or they wouldn't be trying to scare you with intimidation and insults.

Would they?

'BE ON GUARD': DEMAND TRUTH ABOUT BENGHAZI

September 7, 2014

Are you tired of being lied to yet?

My guess is no... because Americans seem to have developed an infinite capacity for patience with a federal government that is increasingly mettlesome, mendacious and menacing.

Don't care about the IRS being used to target and silence people because of their political persuasion? Unconcerned about a president who chooses to ignore laws he doesn't like and who illegally invents laws that are convenient to his agenda? Slept through the invasion of illegal aliens that was sponsored and funded by the Border Patrol and Justice Department? Can't be bothered to ask why carriers of the dreadful Ebola virus are being transported from Africa to various hospitals across the United States?

You are not alone. Literally millions of American citizens just like you have decided that as long as they have the necessities of life — good football on Sunday afternoons, Facebook (or Snapchat, Instagram, Twitter) on their cellphones, and an Obamacare ID card in their pocketbooks — they don't need to take an active interest in something as remote and monolithic as the federal bureaucracy. That's someone else's job, isn't it?

Well, no. It's not. It's actually the duty of any citizen. As Thomas Jefferson wrote in 1800, "It behooves our citizens to be on their guard, to be firm in their principles, and full of confidence in themselves. We are able to preserve our self-government if we will but think so."

And we will lose our self-government if we think someone else will do it for us — which is why, on this September morning, four days before the second anniversary of the attack on the U.S. mission in Benghazi that occurred on Sept. 11, 2012, I am writing once again to encourage my fellow citizens "to be on their guard, to be firm in their principles" and to be "full of confidence in themselves" but not in their government.

This last Friday night, an interview was aired which should convince American citizens once and for all that their government is not telling the truth about what happened in Libya two years ago. That's been obvious to many of us for months, but despite the naming of a select committee by the U.S. House of Representatives to investigate what could have happened, what should have happened, and what really did happen in Benghazi, we still know precious little.

But as of Friday, we know a little more — and it's not good. Thanks to a special report on Fox News by Bret Baier, we now have the inside story of the security team based at the secret

CIA annex in Benghazi, about a mile from the U.S. mission where Islamic terrorists attacked and killed U.S. Ambassador Chris Stevens and Foreign Service officer Sean Smith. It was on the roof of that annex where, in the early morning hours of Sept. 12, CIA contractors Tyrone Woods and Glen Doherty were later killed by mortar fire.

Now, three security officers stationed at that annex have come forward to tell their story. Not to a government panel. Not to the president. Not to Congress. But on their own, as the authors of a book and as guests on a television show.

Don't you think we should have heard their story before? It is one of the most mystifying elements of the lethargy of the American people that they have not demanded with one loud voice to know why these and other survivors of the attack have not been publicly questioned. Because questions, despite the assurances of the White House and the State Department, have certainly remained unanswered.

It doesn't matter how many kangaroo courts of inquiry are convened, the elephant in the room is still the lack of response by the United States to a clear and present danger.

So now, at last, we get part of the answer from Kris Paronto, Mark Geist and John Tiegen, who were in the CIA annex on Sept. 11, 2012, and have collaborated with author Mitchell Zuckoff on a book entitled "13 Hours: The Inside Account of What Really Happened in Benghazi."

The security officers confirm that they got word of the attack on the mission compound almost immediately when it began at 9:40 p.m. local time, but what has never been known before is that their response to the mission was intentionally delayed.

Paronto told Baier: "Five minutes, we're ready. It was thumbs up, thumbs up, we're ready to go."

Only they were told not to go. The top CIA officer in Benghazi, whom the three security officers refer to as "Bob," delayed the team's response by nearly half an hour.

Tiegen continued the story: "It had probably been 15 minutes I think, and... I just said, 'Hey, you know, we gotta — we need to get over there, we're losing the initiative'... And Bob just looks straight at me and said, 'Stand down, you need to wait.'"

Paronto says they were getting calls from the State Department personnel at the mission, saying, "Hey, we're taking fire, we need you guys here, we need help."

The order from "Bob" to respond to the crisis never came, so Paronto, Tiegen and Geist headed to the mission on their own, without orders. They also asked their CIA bosses to request armed air support, but it never came.

The 25- to 30-minute delay in responding may have been the difference between life and death for Stevens and Smith, the contractors agreed.

"Ambassador Stevens and Sean [Smith], yeah, they would still be alive, my gut is yes," Paronto said. And Tiegen added, "I strongly believe if we'd left immediately, they'd still be alive today."

There is also every reason to expect that an early response would have resulted in a far different outcome for Ty Woods and Glen Doherty as well. The CIA annex might well have been evacuated long before the assault began if the ambassador and his aides had been rescued from the mission compound at the start of the crisis.

Unfortunately, based on everything we know about the American public, there is also every reason to believe that this new information will fall on deaf ears. Demanding accountability seems to be less important than protecting the political flank, no matter how many lives have been lost.

Got lies? The American public is buying.

But if you are ready to look for the truth, if you are ready to do your duty as a citizen of the country that Thomas Jefferson co-founded, then "be on guard" and "be firm in your principles." Just maybe, you can make a difference.

The Fox News special featuring Paronto, Geist and Tiegen will air again today at 6 and 9 p.m. Mountain Time. Please watch it, and don't look for excuses why it isn't true; look for reasons why you had to wait so long to hear the truth.

IT'S TIME TO STOP THE LYNG!

December 14, 2014

Divide and conquer.

That's the old reliable formula for defeating your enemy, and unfortunately it's being used with absolute effectiveness by the power elites in our national media and government. Just as immoral regimes of the past have lied to their people in order to generate division and hatred among races, religions and cultures, so too does it seem that America has been beset with poisonous lies whose only aim is to tear us asunder.

You certainly can see the template for that vicious strategy employed in the last few months in the race war that many have tried to foment in the wake of isolated incidents involving black men killed in confrontations with white police. It's as though these young protesters have never heard of a white man being killed by a white policeman, a black man killed by a black policeman, or even a white man killed by a black policeman. And far be it from them to ever consider the many cases where white policeman have been killed by young black men.

Let's assume that the rioters, protesters and demonstrators don't know any better. Shouldn't their leaders? Shouldn't congressmen? Shouldn't the attorney general? Shouldn't the president?

But it seems that for many so-called leaders all that matters is the chaos and confusion that can be caused by channeling the anger of the mob against the status quo, against the government, against social norms. The race baiters who engage in this kind of behavior are just as conscious of the blood that will be spilled by their rhetoric as the men and women who condition pit bulls to rip each other apart with predictable ferocious suicidal rage.

Thinking about the ease with which so many supposedly educated Americans were manipulated into blood-curdling fury by the grand-jury decisions in the Michael Brown and Eric

Garner cases made me realize that most of the problems in our country are caused by people who lie brazenly in order to pit one segment of society against another.

So my new battle cry is: Stop lying!

—Stop Lying About Racial Inequality. Yes, it exists, but it does not exist at this point because white people are trying to crush black people. Most white people want black people to have great lives, happy lives, fulfilled lives. To think otherwise is absurd. If most white people were truly racist idiots, they would not have created all the civil-rights protections, affirmative-action programs and anti-poverty programs that they have tried in the last 50 years. And while we are on the topic, most of those anti-poverty programs have done nothing more than institutionalize poverty in black communities. If we want to change black lives for the better, we need to try something new. I'm open to suggestions, but a good starting place would be to ban Al Sharpton.

—Stop Lying About Economic Inequality: Does an income gap exist between the rich and poor? You bet. Is there any way for that gap not to exist? Not unless Congress decides to pass a law against reality. (Note to self: Congress cannot legislate reality any more than it can endow people with unalienable rights.)

Instead of complaining about income inequality, or legislating against it, people who don't like it should be examining the roots causes of it. That would do a lot more to help poor people in our society than implementing Marxist redistribution of wealth schemes such as the Affordable Care Act. The one thing we know about Marxism from experience is that it doesn't work unless propped up by a military dictatorship (Russia) or by massive foreign aid (Cuba). And if you think China is a Marxist success story, you either don't know anything about Marxism or you don't know anything about China.

There are many root causes of income inequality and of the growing gap between the rich and poor in the United States, but for now let's just consider one. We are importing millions of impoverished people into our country as illegal aliens. Obviously that has to increase income inequality. It is also an inconvenient truth that the same people who are the loudest critics of income inequality are the largest supporters of importing poverty. Do you think there might be an underlying agenda?

Stop Lying about the Gender Wage Gap: This one is so blatantly false that it merits its own heading in the Diagnostic and Statistical Manual of Mental Disorders, used by psychiatrists to categorize the varieties of delusional experience. In the old days, the Gender Wage Gap would have been a subcategory of "mass hysteria."

Thousands, perhaps millions, of Americans have mindlessly repeated the mantra that women are paid 77 percent of what men are paid for the same work. Outrageous! Except it is simply not true. In fact, women in the aggregate are paid 77 percent of what men in the aggregate are paid for completely different types of work, different levels of experience, and with different goals.

Of course, there are already laws that forbid pay discrimination against women, but perhaps the best one of all is the law of supply and demand. If women were in fact paid 77 percent of what men make for the same job with the same level of experience and the same abilities, then all employers would try to hire women in order to enjoy the salary savings, and in short order the law of supply and demand would push women's wages to the same as men's — if not higher. Or has the law of supply and demand been rescinded by Congress along with reality?

Stop Lying about the College Campus Rape Epidemic: The Rolling Stone rape story retraction/apology brings into focus the so-called college rape epidemic. We are led to believe that women on college campuses are in greater danger than women elsewhere, thus impugning the character of male college students everywhere. But before we jump to conclusions, let's think about the underlying facts.

First of all, the number of women on college campuses has increased dramatically over the past 20 years. That means the number of actual sex assaults against women will increase statistically even if the rate of assault has remained the same. In addition, the willingness of women to report being sexually assaulted has also dramatically increased, which might lead a casual observer to assume that the number of assaults has increased. That assumption may or may not be true.

But even more important from a sociological point of view is that society has deemed it entirely appropriate for men and women to live together not just in the same college dorms, but on the same floors of the same college dorms, and sometimes side by side in college dormitory rooms. Now, unless some liberal professor somewhere has figured out a way to neuter college-age men, the expectation that there will not be inappropriate and even criminal sexual behavior in that setting is absurd.

Stop lying to yourself about human behavior. Having men and women live together in close quarters will always result in an increase in sexual activity, both voluntary and forcible. Because there are bad people, rape will always exist. If you truly want to lessen sexual assaults on campus, then bring back men's and women's separate dorms.

Stop Lying About the Republican War on Women: What exactly is this anyway? From what I can tell it consists of three parts. The phony gender pay gap; allowing employers to make their own decisions about what kind of health insurance coverage to provide for their employees, in particular contraception and abortion; and seeking restrictions on abortion.

As noted above, the gender pay gap is a chimera that has as much chance of being proven as the tooth fairy. The matter of health insurance is not an attack on women, but a defense of free enterprise and religious conscience. To see it otherwise is to turn truth on its head.

And finally, most particularly, the abortion issue is not a war on women; it is a war on children. After all, to be a real war, there have to be deaths, don't there? And there have been more than 55 million deaths of American babies caused by abortion since the procedure was legalized by the Supreme Court in 1973.

Stop lying about the war on women, and start worrying about the war on children! Don't care about children? Then say so, but don't blame Republicans because they do!

These are a few examples grabbed from today's headlines almost at random. The list of such fakery and foolishness in our current political climate is almost infinite. You can throw the Republican lies about opposing Obamacare, illegal immigration and endless government borrowing onto the pile. It's not just a Democrat problem. It's a national problem. And the worst part of it is that tens of millions of Americans know the truth and remain silent.

Well, as Edmund Burke is reputed to have said, "All that is necessary for the triumph of evil is that good men do nothing." Speak up, America, or there won't be any America left. Silence is a vote for the lie.

WHY IS CONGRESS ALL TALK, NO ACTION?

February 22, 2015

Lately I've been wondering when Congress ceased to be a functional unit of government.

Oh, I know that Congress still exists and still passes laws, but forget about that old "checks and balances" thing. Congress doesn't take itself seriously anymore, and based on its average approval rating of about 10 percent, neither does the American public.

Congress as a deliberative body, and as the instrument of the people's power, has for all intents and purposes ceased to exist. The true function of the Congress today is that of the Lord High Treasurer, and Congress has turned spending money into an art form. In other sectors this is known by names such as bribery or payoffs, but in Congress it is known as appropriations.

But other than spending money, what is Congress most known for?

In a word, talking!

In fact, you could say that Congress is all talk and no action. There doesn't seem to be any real intention among our senators and representatives to uphold their oath of office and to "defend the Constitution of the United States against all enemies, foreign and domestic."

Otherwise, they would need to put a halt to massive amounts of unconstitutional lawmaking in their own body, unconstitutional executive overreach by the president, and unconstitutional judicial overreach by the Supreme Court.

So what exactly — and this is a question I have been pondering for quite some time — turned the Congress into so much window dressing? And when did it happen?

Let's start with the second question first. I grew up in the 1950s and '60s and would argue that from my youthful perspective it did seem that the Congress was engaged in serious debates about policy. The Civil Rights Act, the Voting Rights Act, the Wilderness Act, the Clean Water Act — you could put together quite a significant list of accomplishments, but even if you disagree with any of the particular bills that were passed by Congress, you can certainly concur that the august body was getting something done.

Even through the 1970s, one could make the case that Congress was engaged in a great debate about the future of the nation, but something happened in the past 30 or 40 years that has sapped the energy out of the institution, and one morning not too long ago while preparing breakfast I think I figured out what it was — television.

It was in 1979 when the House inaugurated the first live televised proceedings from the House floor, probably inspired by the success of the live Watergate hearings — not so much at rooting out evil, but at turning senators into celebrities. Forebodingly, the first member of Congress to speak before the cameras on March 19, 1979, was Rep. Al Gore Jr., who parlayed his youthful good looks and Southern charm into a successful Senate election in 1984 and then the vice presidency in 1992. Does anyone better define the empty suit of modern American politicians than Gore?

But this is an indictment not of individuals of either party, but of an institution that has been corrupted by fame. Television, in short, has sucked the soul out of the Congress. Nothing demonstrates that better than the so-called "special order" speeches in which House members rise on the floor of the House to make impassioned pleas for their pet causes before an empty House chamber but potentially an audience of millions of TV and Internet viewers.

The premise of televising House and Senate proceedings is that members of Congress are doing the people's business, and ought to be doing so under the spotlight. In fact, the result of these televised speeches is that our elected officials are doing their own business — getting themselves re-elected — on our time and our dime.

I can't prove it, but I suspect that if we removed those TV cameras from Congress, we would see a nearly immediate resurgence of collegiality in the Senate and House — with an accompanying jump in productivity and approval ratings.

Heck, maybe we could even step back from the brink of bankruptcy and convince our legislators to do the right thing — put their interest in getting re-elected behind them and tell the ugly truth to the voters:

"Sorry, folks. We can't keep spending money we don't have on programs the Constitution doesn't permit us to create in the first place! From now on, you'll have to rely on American ingenuity instead of congressional handouts, and if anyone doesn't like it, let us remind you that the porous border is a two-way street!"

FRAMEWORK 'DEAL' MORE LIKE NUCLEAR RORSCHACH TEST

April 12, 2015

Something unusual happened last week: President Obama told the truth. But don't worry, the State Department quickly told a lie to cover it up.

The short version is this: The president said that in the 13th year after the nuclear "deal" with Iran, the Islamic republic will be able to build a nuclear bomb virtually on demand.

Wow! Scary! You might almost question whether the United States has any idea what it is doing in the nuclear negotiations with Iran if that is the expected outcome.

In fact, a reporter did question just that on Tuesday, and was told by State Department spokeswoman Marie Harf that the president never said what he plainly had said on video.

"I think his words were a little mixed up there... but what he was referring to was a scenario in which there was no deal. If you go back and look at the transcript, I know it's a little confusing... it's my understanding that he was referring to — even though it was a little muddled in the words, too — a scenario in which there was no deal... It was more of a hypothetical... He was NOT indicating what would happen under an agreement in those years..."

Well, let's roll the tape. Or "go back and look at the transcript." I did, and oops the president DID SO indicate what would happen "under an agreement" in those years.

In the interview with Steve Inskeep on National Public Radio, Obama didn't leave any room for interpretation. Inskeep was questioning the president about the proposed Iranian deal, and pointed out that "People are asking, 'What will happen in 10 or 15 years as the deal starts to expire?'"

Inskeep then specifically asked President Obama about the deal's apparent intention to leave enriched uranium inside Iran rather than moving it to a neutral country where it could be monitored closely.

The president dismisses Inskeep's concern, and then says, "What is a more relevant fear [than Iran holding on to its current stockpiles] would be that in year 13, 14, 15, they have advanced centrifuges that enrich uranium fairly rapidly, and at that point the breakout times would have shrunk almost down to zero."

Breakout time is "nuke negotiator" lingo for the time it would take to create an atomic bomb starting from today.

The president went on to explain that, "currently, the breakout times are only about two to three months by our intelligence estimates. So essentially, we're purchasing for 13, 14, 15 years assurances that the breakout is at least a year... — that if they decided to break the deal, kick out all the inspectors, break the seals and go for a bomb, we'd have over a year to respond. And we have those assurances for at least well over a decade."

It's of course no accident that the president is referring to "year 13, 14 and 15." That is clearly "year 13" of the deal. It is meaningless otherwise to use the phrase.

And despite Marie Harf's best straight-faced lie, the president's truth is there for all to see. You just have to think for yourself instead of being told by Marie that the so-called "muddled" words don't mean what they plainly say.

Again, let President Obama tell it for himself:

"...In years 13 and 14, it is possible that those breakout times would have been much shorter, but at that point we have much better ideas about what it is that their program involves. We have much more insight into their capabilities. And the option of a future president to take action if in fact they try to obtain a nuclear weapon is undiminished."

Clearly, Obama is acknowledging that in years 13 and 14 of the treaty, the breakout times may be a month or less if Iran backs out of the treaty. We know that he is talking about the treaty because he points out that as a result of the treaty we now "have much better ideas about what it is that their program involves. We have much more insight into their capabilities."

That insight exists because of the weapons inspections that the United States and its partners would have been carrying out for 10 or more years.

Much more concerning even than the president's inability to communicate clearly with his own State Department is the complete breakdown in communications between the United States and Iran over just what the nuclear "deal" consists of. How you can even call it a "deal" is a mystery when the two sides seem to be looking at two completely different, contradictory and mutually exclusive documents.

Heck, within hours of the framework "deal" being announced on April 2, both sides were calling each other liars. Virtually no significant point of the deal was seen the same way by both the Iranians and the United States.

We said the sanctions would be gradually lifted based on Iran's performance in allowing inspections and taking other treaty-mandated actions. Iran said the sanctions would be lifted immediately without Iran performing any task.

We said Iran was going to allow inspections at its secret military facilities. They said no inspections would be allowed at any military facilities, secret or otherwise.

We said Iran has agreed to stop using advanced centrifuges. They said "work on advanced centrifuges shall continue on the basis of a 10-year plan."

We said Iran had agreed to dismantle the core of the heavy water plutonium plant in Arak. They said, "No way!"

It is hard to know how to assess a deal that is put together like a Rorschach test. You know, the psychological test that features an ink blot that could be interpreted as anything from a sexy woman to a hedgehog, depending on the predilections of the observer.

What is apparent to any observer, however, is that the American negotiators are either the worst negotiators of all time or outright liars. The deal they got in their own minds justifies President Obama's Nobel Peace Prize, but the deal they really got apparently justifies locking them up as the biggest con men since Bernie Madoff.

One person who thinks so is the Supreme leader of Iran, the Ayatollah Khamenei, who broke his silence this week to categorize the Obama administration as "lying," "deceptive" and "devilish."

Well, we know one thing for sure: One of them has to be lying — President Obama or the Ayatollah Khamenei. So let's look at the record.

This is not the first time that the veracity of the president has been questioned. Consider Benghazi, Bowe Bergdahl, Fort Hood, Libya, Obamacare, Fast and Furious. And remember when President Obama drew a "red line" in Syria and said that if Assad used chemical weapons against his own people, he would pay a terrible price? Assad used the weapons, and Obama's word proved to be good for — nothing.

On the other hand, the ayatollah has declared "death to America" and vowed to see the annihilation of Israel. Step by step, year by year, he moves toward those goals.

So who ya gonna trust? The ayatollah may be on to something.

FREE SPEECH ON A LEASH IS A DEAD DOG

May 10, 2015

If you needed any evidence that Bizarro World is populated by both Democrats and Republicans last week offered plenty.

To review, Bizarro World is the comic-book world where everything is proudly backwards, and sadly its confines extend well beyond the borders of Washington, D.C., although that place may be considered its honorary capital.

If you need an example of how Bizarro World works, consider the miraculous reversal of right and wrong (or is that "write and wrong"?) that took place when two wannabe jihadis drove a thousand miles to massacre participants in a "Draw the Prophet" contest in Garland, Texas.

Normally, we consider cartoonists, authors, and social activists good citizens, and we view people who enter public places with the intention of slaughtering innocent civilians to be somewhere between psychopathic and just plain evil. But not in Bizarro World.

An event that should have united the nation in revulsion for the Islamic terrorists who intended to impose a sharia-compliant death penalty on event organizer Pam Geller has instead become a cause celebre for appeasement.

Yes, Pam Geller provoked the attack by doing something on American soil that is strictly prohibited by the Qu'ran, the holy book of Islam (namely, encouraging people to make an artistic representation of the prophet Muhammad), but Geller did so in sympathy with the martyrs of free speech who have perished previously because they have offended Islam.

In particular, she conceived of the "Draw the Prophet" contest in January after a Muslim group sponsored a "Stand With the Prophet" event to express solidarity with the terrorists who carried out the Charlie Hebdo massacre in Paris. Her idea was to send a message that Americans would never bow to threats of violence and sacrifice their First Amendment right to free speech.

Unfortunately, it turned out other Americans — for all I know, a majority of Americans — disagree with her and have shamed her in the public square as a provocateur who more or less deserves to die for her brazen slap in the face to Islamic law.

"It's her own fault," we hear. "Why draw Muhammad when you know Muslims consider it blasphemy? We ought to be more civil and respectful..."

You could almost imagine the shrines being erected across America to honor the memories of terrorist Elton Simpson and his roommate Nadir Soofi for their sacrifice in defending the prophet.

I wish I could lambaste MSNBC, Rachel Maddow and the New York Times for spearheading a liberal attack on conservative firebrand Pam Geller, and conclude that it was just an overdose of diversity-fortified Kool-Aid that had led to the retreat from free speech. But, sadly, some of the loudest critics of Geller were bastions of the conservative media and establishment such as Donald Trump and Catholic League spokesman Bill Donahue.

Fox News was just as much at fault as MSNBC, with Martha MacCallum naively advising Geller that the best way for her to exercise free speech would have been to keep quiet.

"If you want to make a difference, you do it in a Christian way; you don't do it in a crass, crude way by insulting someone's religion. You do it by rising above that and saying we are not like you."

No, that's how you sink into the shadows like a coward.

Geller wisely called MacCallum's apologist rhetoric "the language of the conquered," and tried to caution the TV host that this is not a religious issue but a political issue, but it was hopeless. So far as MacCallum was concerned, Geller had caused the shooting in Texas, and ought to hang her head in shame.

"Political cartoons is political opinion," Geller explained, "and when you seek to impose the sharia restrictions of Islam on free speech, that is a political move."

Considering the importation of hundreds of thousands of Islamic refugees into the country, and the growing impact that Muslim ideology is having in our country, it is a warning that ought to be heeded now, before it is too late. Theo Van Gogh was murdered for exposing the intolerance of Islam; the Charlie Hebdo cartoonists were murdered for drawing cartoons of Muhammad; if Geller is next, will she just be considered an acceptable loss by the apologists for diversity?

One thing is for certain. The world has not seen the end of martyrs who will die at the hand of Islam. Whether it is Egyptian Coptics who are beheaded, Somali Christians who are shot, Iraqi Yazidis who are crucified, or American businessmen and women who are burned alive and crushed in New York skyscrapers, martyrs to Islam will continue to multiply — not because of what they say, but because of what the Qu'ran says.

Shutting up is not an option.

As Geller told Martha MacCallum, "I will not abridge my freedom so as not to offend savages."

BENGHAZI: A SMOKING GUN AND THE RUSH TO AVOID JUDGMENT

May 31, 2015

Four months ago, I lamented the lackadaisical approach of Congress to ferreting out the truth about the murder of four Americans in Benghazi, Libya, on Sept. 11, 2012.

Today, I lament the lackadaisical approach of the mainstream media and the American public. How much more evidence do you need that we were lied to by the Obama administration in their rush to avoid judgment by the voting public and by history for the death of a U.S. ambassador and three of his aides and defenders.

In case you missed it — and I know that 90 percent of you did — the smoking gun surfaced this month that proved once and for all that the "cover story" about the attack being a "spontaneous" mob action was just what many of us have been saying all along — nonsense.

Why am I so confident? Because on May 18, the organization Judicial Watch released dozens of official documents it obtained through the Freedom of Information process.

In particular, a Defense Intelligence Agency report dated Sept. 12, 2012, the day after the Benghazi attack, stated categorically (although not definitively) "The attack on the American consulate in Benghazi was planned and executed by the Brigades of the Captive Omar Abdul Rahman (BCOAR). BCOAR is also responsible for past attacks on the Red Cross in Benghazi and the attack on the British ambassador...

"The attack was planned ten or more days prior on approximately 01 September 2012. The intention was to attack the consulate and kill as many Americans as possible to seek revenge for U.S. killing of Aboyahiye (ALALIBY) in Pakistan and in memorial of the 11 September 2001 attacks on the World Trade Center buildings."

Enough said. End of story. The execrable falsehoods mouthed by UN Ambassador Susan Rice, Secretary of State Hillary Clinton and President Barack Obama about a YouTube video spurring a "spontaneous" mob attack have been revealed in all their ignominy.

Four months ago, I affirmed that "the massacre at Benghazi is not going away." I wrote about the work of brave private citizens who formed the Citizens Commission on Benghazi and collaborated with journalist Jerome Corsi to bring forth the real record of what had taken place before, during and after the attack that killed Ambassador Chris Stevens, Foreign Service Officer Sean Smith and CIA contractors Tyrone S. Woods and Glen Doherty.

I stated, "I know that no matter how inconvenient, unpleasant or downright threatening the truth is, it will eventually come out, thanks to patriotic Americans who are willing to dodge unfriendly fire from the U.S. media and political hacks in order to honor the principle that you never leave a fellow soldier behind."

Today, I must also acknowledge the work of Judicial Watch in relentlessly pursuing the truth. No one can once again say that Susan Rice or Hillary Clinton didn't knowingly mislead the public when they sought to deflect attention away from the terrorists who carried out the attack.

But are you not outraged that no one in Washington cares — that the mainstream media don't think it is important enough to tell you? I searched daily for an Associated Press story trumpeting the truth about Benghazi, but entirely in vain. The mainstream media can bury a story just as deep as a cautious mass murderer can bury a body.

Of course the story has been there in plain sight all along for anyone who really cared to question authority — who didn't just parrot the official story that somehow the attack on the mission in Benghazi had been inspired by the mob's anger over that obscure YouTube video called "The Innocence of Muslims."

Unfortunately, most people did go along with the "official story." Both Democrats and Republicans provided cover for the administration officials who allowed the attack to happen and then covered up their own mistakes. Yes, there have been congressional hearings that have "vindicated" Clinton, Rice and Obama, but they were in large measure a whitewash, and an embarrassingly obvious one at that.

Those who said the whole truth came out as a result of those hearings have since then conveniently shut their eyes, their ears and their minds, and called the rest of us "conspiracy theorists" — a charge which is supposed to reduce you to irrelevance.

Well, the facts are not irrelevant, and if American politicians, journalists and voters do not care enough about the truth to pursue it relentlessly, then it is they who are irrelevant.

BOEHNER, MCCARTHY AND THE BIG BAD MEDIA

October 11, 2015

Learning the news through the prism of the 24-hour cable news channels is rapidly becoming an exercise in futility. For the most part, you are neither learning, nor getting the news.

I'm actually starting to yearn for the good old days when Dan Rather only had 24 minutes a night to try to push his agenda on the nation rather than the 24 hours a day that are granted to CNN, MSNBC and Fox News.

Case in point was last week's collapse of the "smooth transition" of power in the House of Representatives from the widely despised John Boehner to his second-in-command Kevin McCarthy. According to the news brokers at the Big Three cable outlets, government business in Washington, D.C., had ground to an absolute halt as a result of McCarthy announcing he didn't want to be speaker after all. This was painted as the biggest crisis in the federal government since the assassination of JFK, if not Lincoln!

It was almost as if some of these "news" people had gotten a memo saying, "McCarthy is our guy. Life is going to be good going forward." Then when McCarthy was out, they panicked. Shepard Smith on Fox was absolutely dumbfounded, if not just dumb, in his repeated assertion that the crisis could not get any worse. Megyn Kelly, Donald Trump's favorite provocateur interlocutor at Fox was no better, although she looked more able to weather the collapse of Western civilization than poor Shep. Of course, CNN and MSNBC were just as worried about how the poor muddled Republicans could possibly put Humpty-Dumpty together again. Crocodile tears were spewed liberally as commentators bemoaned how "right wing nut jobs" had sabotaged the candidacy of the anointed one.

As for McCarthy, he looked happy as a clam. He didn't feel he owed an explanation to the pack of journalists baying at his heels. He said he didn't think he would be able to put together the votes to win, which is probably true. He said he thought the House could be better served by a "fresh face," which is definitely true. But the capital press gang wouldn't take no for an answer. They were convinced that McCarthy was Boehner's divine choice to ascend to power. Or maybe they just thought McCarthy would be a disaster in the role of House speaker, and they couldn't believe such a prime GOP catastrophe had been narrowly averted.

Face it, McCarthy, having accomplished virtually nothing, and having done it extremely well, was the perfect shadow to step in and do the bidding of the establishment power brokers. At least he was perfect until he opened his mouth and said one of the stupidest things any politician has ever uttered. I'm sure you heard of this one! In an interview with Sean Hannity on Fox News, McCarthy described how he would be different than Boehner:

"What you're going to see is a conservative speaker that takes a conservative congress that puts a strategy to fight and win. And let me give you one example. Everybody thought Hillary Clinton was unbeatable, right? But we put together a Benghazi special committee, a select committee. What are her numbers today? Her numbers are dropping. Why? Because she's un-trustable. But no one would have known any of that had happened —"

Hannity stopped McCarthy at that point and changed the subject, but the damage was already done and totally self-inflicted. In less than 30 seconds, McCarthy had accomplished what no Democrat had been able to do for the last three years — pin the blame for politicizing the murder of four Americans in Benghazi on the Republicans who have been trying to get to the bottom of what really happened before and after the attack in Libya.

McCarthy had single-handedly handed former Secretary of State Hillary Clinton a "get out of jail free" card as she prepared for her appearance before the House Select Committee on Benghazi later this month. Committee chairman Trey Gowdy had bent over backwards for the last 18 months to avoid any taint of partisanship. The committee has mostly done its work behind the scenes, far away from the 24/7 headline-making machinery of the cable-news outlets. In fact, Gowdy has been so conscientiously considerate of appearances that he has angered conservatives such as myself for seeming to be dragging his feet instead of doggedly pursuing the truth.

No wonder the opinion makers at CNN, Fox and MSNBC were sorry to see McCarthy go. This guy promised to make Boehner look like a true statesman, and would have turned the GOP base even more apoplectic than it has been. In other words, a win-win for the media pundits and the D.C. plutocracy. This weekend, the same power brokers who gave us Boehner and tried to give us McCarthy are hard at work trying to convince Paul Ryan he is the only possible savior of the GOP establishment. The only problem being that trying to save the moribund GOP establishment could very well mean his own political death sentence. Rest in peace, Eric Cantor. Rest in peace, John Boehner. Rest in peace, Jeb Bush? We shall see.

A DEBATE THAT WILL LIVE IN INFAMY

November 1, 2015

As I write this, it's approximately 48 hours since CNBC launched a sneak attack on the Republican presidential candidates in Boulder, Colorado, and the political battle lines are still being drawn, but one things is certain: War has been declared.

Another thing is almost certain as well: Just as with Pearl Harbor, when the Japanese drew first blood, they had no idea what kind of massive response they were about to see leveled back at them.

The three stooges, er, moderators who set out to do battle with the top 10 candidates in the Wednesday evening debate are either as out of touch with reality as Jeb Bush, or they went into the debate like wannabe martyr jihadis who gladly strap on a stick-dynamite bomb for the sheer pleasure of taking out the enemy.

The first question was no doubt meant to distract the candidates. First of all, the candidates had been promised an opening statement, which didn't materialize. (John Kasich, to his credit — and this is the only thing I will give him credit for — pretended he didn't hear the question and gave his prepared opening statement anyway.) Second of all, the question was so inane ("name your biggest weakness"!) that some of the candidates may have worried they were being lured into a deadly "battle of wits" with a Sicilian (see "The Princess Bride" for more details!).

But it was with the second question that the scales started to fall away from everyone's eyes as it became obvious that the questioners were not wits, but world-class buffoons who considered themselves the arbiters of intelligence and good taste (once again, check out that Sicilian in "The Princess Bride").

John Harwood, the lead buffoon — whose name will live in infamy as long as there are debates — tried to humiliate Donald

Trump by mocking several key planks of his very popular platform, and then asking "Is this a comic book version of a presidential campaign?"

Trump, who by now is used to pretentious journalists trying to ambush him (pace Megyn Kelly), politely pointed out to Harwood that it was "not a very nicely asked question the way you say that."

After that, Harwood's co-inquisitor Becky Quick went after Ben Carson, the top dog among Republican candidates for the past week or two, and told him his flat tax plan doesn't make any sense. Now, she may be right, but the proper way to run a debate is to give the candidate enough rope to hang himself, with the able assistance of his opponents, not to garrote the poor man while he is belly up to a podium. Quick not only asked the question, she then told Carson he was either a liar or stupid (OK, not in so many words) for failing to agree with her that his tax plan was a great big poopie diaper (OK, not in so many words).

After Harwood tried unsuccessfully to get Gov. Kasich to repeat some inflammatory comments he had made the previous day about Trump and Carson, the conversation moved on to some other candidates.

The last moderator, Carl Quintanilla, managed to anger the entire population of the United States by defending the IRS from Carly Fiorina's plan to reduce the federal tax code from 73,000 pages down to three. "Is that using really small type?" Quintanilla chimed in (twice actually, probably because he couldn't understand why he didn't get a laugh the first time) sounding for all the world like a snarky seventh-grader who has no idea why he can't get a date.

The next question, also by Quintanilla, tried to body check Marco Rubio into the wall and make him cry. Calling Rubio "a young man in a hurry" (for the record, he's 44), Quintanilla told the U.S. senator he should "slow down, get a few more things done" before running for president, and show up for more votes in the do-nothing Senate.

Naturally, this made Marco mad, but he didn't fight back. He got even by knocking Quintanilla's curveball out of the park:

"That's exactly what the Republican establishment says too. Why don't you wait in line? Wait for what? This country is running out of time. We can't afford to have another four years like the last eight years."

Quintanilla didn't know he had been flanked, so he continued to press forward with his failed line of attack. "The Sun-Sentinel [says] you act like you hate your job. Do you?"

Rubio suddenly sounded more like President Reagan than the dopey kid wet behind the ears that Quintanilla painted him to be: "I read that editorial today with a great amusement. It's actually evidence of the bias that exists in the American media today." Rubio pointed out the hypocrisy of a newspaper that endorsed John Kerry and Barack Obama when they missed multiple votes as U.S. senators while running for president, but is morally offended by his own necessity of doing the same.

It was at this point when Jeb Bush decided to commit ritual harakiri by hitching his wagon to the moderators' flailing fortunes. For a second, it appeared that Bush would come to the defense of his former apprentice Rubio. If he had done so, with passion and righteous anger, he might have saved his campaign. Instead he pointed the wrong end of his dull blade at Rubio and impaled himself on a foolish demand that Rubio should resign from the Senate. If absence from one's job were enough to necessitate resignation, then Gov. Bush would have resigned from the presidential race long ago because he certainly hasn't been present and accounted for in this primary campaign!

Rubio quickly dispatched Bush by noting the self-evident truth that the reason his former mentor was criticizing his Senate record was because "someone has convinced you that attacking me is going to help you."

Fittingly, John Harwood circled around the already savaged Gov. Bush and asked him to explain why he was such an abject failure, but with a brilliant stroke of liberal bias, Harwood encouraged Bush to blame the dopey Republicans who aren't smart enough to vote for him.

"Ben Bernanke, who was appointed Fed chairman by your brother, recently wrote a book in which he said he no longer considers himself a Republican because the Republican Party has given in to Know-Nothingism. Is that why you're having a difficult time in this race?"

You have to hand it to Harwood. By working in the Bernanke quote about Know-Nothingism, he appealed to both the ill-informed majority of Democrat voters who would assume it simply meant Republicans are stupid, and also to the better-informed voters who knew it referred to a 19th century movement opposed to unrestricted immigration because they feared it would alter the character of our nation.

Harwood may have even been hoping he could coax Bush into saying something stupid about illegal immigration such as his classic description of crossing the border illegally as "an act of love." Bush didn't take the bait, possibly because he was still weakened by being worked over by Rubio a minute before.

Becky Quick came back into the fray to taunt Carly Fiorina with a familiar jab at her record as the CEO of Hewlett Packard, a position from which she was fired. Fiorina gave her usual, well-rehearsed response to the attack, and then it was Sen. Ted Cruz's turn.

Carl Quintanilla thought he would taunt Cruz, a dedicated opponent of more government spending while the national debt is $19 trillion and rising: "Doesn't your opposition show that you're not the kind of problem solver American voters want?"

Well, Boy Howdy! There's no getting anything past these moderators. For sure, the American voters want someone who will send them and their children deeper into debt. No doubt, they oppose principled leadership that tells the truth about our inability to maintain our welfare state into the far-distant future (let's say about 2030). And so, of course, Ted Cruz is anathema to the bought-and-paid-for American voter.

But just a minute. Ted Cruz is having none of it. Suddenly, he rises up like a Shakespearean hero and fights back. He's mad as hell, and he's not going to take it any more, and the American public watches enamored as someone finally speaks blistering truth to the bullies.

"The questions that have been asked so far in this debate illustrate why the American people don't trust the media. This is not a cage match. And, you look at the questions — 'Donald Trump, are you a comic-book villain?' 'Ben Carson, can you do math?' 'John Kasich, will you insult two people over here?' 'Marco Rubio, why don't you resign?' 'Jeb Bush, why have your numbers fallen?' How about talking about the substantive issues the people care about?"

All across America people stood cheering in their living rooms. "You go Ted. You tell 'em."

The sneak attack had been effectively countered, and from that point forward, most of the candidates joined forces against the slippery sloppy questions. The entire nation rose up to ask, "Could those moderators possibly have not known how foolish they were? And what does that say about the mainstream media?"

Watch the tape, or read the transcript of the debate online. You owe it to yourself to see the blatant attempt to manipulate public opinion by insulting the standard-bearers of the Republican Party. There is no reasonable, responsible Democrat anywhere who could defend the behavior of the three intemperate moderators.

You could almost say there was "blood coming out of [their] eyes; blood coming out of [their] wherever..." except we now know you can't say that. Oh wait, it was the now totally discredited mainstream media that told us you can't say it, so maybe Trump was right when he said it after all.

WILL TRUMP SURVIVE ABORTION MINEFIELD?

April 3, 2016

There are some things you just don't say.

At least, there are some things you don't say if you are a conservative. That goes for both candidates and columnists. You learn to tiptoe around controversy in order to avoid losing voters, friends, readers, supporters, whatever it happens to be.

This is the America we live in now.

So when Donald Trump said he thought women who have abortions should be punished, it came as no surprise that he was blasted to kingdom come.

You just don't say that kind of thing any more. Even if you believe it, you don't say it — because you don't want to offend the millions of women who have had abortions. The art of politics, after all, is not offending a majority of voters so that you can be elected in order to not offend a majority of legislators so that you can pass legislation that will not offend a majority of lobbyists, special interests and media personalities so that you can be re-elected on a platform of being inoffensive.

Or you could be Donald Trump, and try to speak from your heart rather than from what is convenient or politically correct.

Of course, with his latest comments on abortion, Trump may have gone too far to ever be elected. He may have gone from being politically incorrect to being politically unviable.

We shall see. Trump is certainly unpredictable, but the machinations of the political world are not. The establishment has been gunning for Trump since day one, and they may finally have nailed him.

When I heard Trump was doing a town hall meeting with Chris Matthews on MSNBC, I thought, uh oh, that's a huge mistake. Oil and water. Or more to the point, fire and gasoline.

Sure enough, Matthews loaded up on Trump with one of his patented questions, which he has asked numerous times before to see if he can get a reaction. Matthews, an avowed Catholic, said he has "never understood the pro-life position" and then asked Trump of abortion, "What crime is it?"

Trump pointed out that it is "a human life," meaning the end result of abortion is the taking of a human life.

At this juncture, Matthews asked Trump his million-dollar question — the one which every politician is smart enough not to answer, or to answer in a politically correct manner, but which Trump in his untrained, off-the-cuff manner, tried to respond to with an honest and common-sense answer.

"Should the woman be punished for having an abortion?"

There are lots of politically correct answers possible:

— "The woman is being punished enough by being deprived of her child, and will be wracked with guilt for what she has done."

— "The woman is a victim as much as her child."

— "If Roe v. Wade is overturned, that's going to have to be decided by individual states. It's unlikely that any state will punish a woman for having an abortion, but we will have to wait and see."

Then when Chris Matthews comes back and says "This is not something you can dodge," you dodge again and say something like, "The first thing we have to do is stop — as a society — sanctioning the killing of unborn babies. Where we go from there, it's unclear, but we as a society will be better off as soon as we restore the sanctity of innocent human life."

If you know how the game is played, you don't answer the question. You sidestep. You tiptoe. You play politics.

But Trump doesn't do what he is supposed to do. In Trump's mind, the world is black and white. That's probably why he appeals to blue-collar voters and infuriates ivory-tower elites.

But when you come right down to it — if abortion is made illegal (which is the premise of Matthews' question) then there has to be culpability on the part of the willing woman as well as on the person performing the abortion, doesn't there?

Isn't that the premise of charging a prostitute with a crime? Or a drug user? What makes it such a stretch to charge a woman with having an illegal abortion? What makes it "politically incorrect" to talk about punishment for a crime?

Only one thing — the belief that there is no God, and therefore no absolute right and wrong. That's why drug users are now seen as victims instead of criminals. That's why prostitution is largely viewed as a victimless crime. And, yes, that's why women think they should have a right to end their pregnancy whether or not it also means ending a human life.

But even my 5-year-old is smart enough to see the evasion of responsibility implicit in that point of view. We were watching Hillary Clinton defend abortion and vilify Trump on the news, and my son Huzhao asked me what it was about.

I told him that Trump had made the case for punishment for women who have an abortion and that some women did not like that idea.

Huzhao's response? "Then why do they get pregnant in the first place?"

I guess to a 5-year-old, morality is also black and white. If it's wrong, why do it?

Say what you like about Trump (or what you don't like!) but he has generated more honest discussion of big issues in the past nine months than any other candidate: Nations need borders ... Nations don't need to import terrorists ... War is not always the answer ... Free trade is not always fair trade ... World security is expensive and the United States can't pay for all of it ... And yeah, actions have consequences.

Trump never said what he thought the punishment should be for a woman who has an abortion. Maybe it will just be a guilty conscience after all, but in a world of good and evil acts, the consequences of evil must be acknowledged somehow. It's not politically correct, but it just makes sense.

MORE THAN MEETS THE EYE (OR EAR): PUTTING THE MEDIA 'UNDER THE GUN'

June 5, 2016

Did you hear Katie Couric got exposed for touting her left-wing anti-gun agenda in a new TV documentary called "Under the Gun"? Big surprise, huh?

Oh please, it's no shock to anyone who has been paying attention. The mainstream media and the left-wing political establishment have been playing footsie for longer than anyone remembers.

Just last week, in addition to the misleading editing in Couric's documentary, it was revealed that the U.S. State Department had intentionally edited out a question and answer from the online archive of a press conference from 2013.

Fox News reporter James Rosen had asked State Department spokeswoman Jen Psaki whether her predecessor had lied when she told Rosen there had been no "direct secret bilateral talks" between the United States and Iran.

Psaki didn't confirm that anyone from the State Department had lied, but she noted in classic doublespeak that "there are times where diplomacy needs privacy in order to progress."

So what did the "most transparent administration in history" do about it when they realized the Q&A session was "politically inconvenient" if not incorrect? Why, easy! They sent it down George Orwell's "memory hole," the final resting place in "Nineteen Eighty Four" for all such "inconvenient" facts. The video was edited, and the exchange magically disappeared due to what the State Department first called a "glitch" and last week confirmed was instead political manipulation by some unnamed bureaucrat who ordered another unnamed bureaucrat to "excise the video." Oops, but no harm, no foul, right?

Interestingly, the reason this unethical edit was discovered is because Rosen was following up on a New York Times article that revealed that the Obama administration had manipulated reporters in order to pursue their agenda of getting the public behind the Iran nuclear deal. As described by Abigail Williams on the nbcnews.com website, the New York Times article "portrayed White House Deputy National Security Adviser Ben Rhodes as bragging that his war room had created an 'echo-chamber' for hundreds of often clueless reporters covering the [Iran deal] negotiations."

It's hard to know what is worse: "clueless reporters" being manipulated by government officials to spread propaganda, or deceptive reporters manipulating video to spread their own propaganda?

In the latter category, we have the aforementioned Katie Couric documentary which infamously tried to make gun-rights advocates look like they were totally stumped by Couric's "hard-line" questioning.

Couric asks, "If there are no background checks for gun purchasers, how do you prevent felons or terrorists from purchasing a gun?" Then, for eight long seconds the camera pans over several members of the Virginia Citizens Defense League as they appear to be at a total loss for words. If the documentary had aired on Comedy Central instead of Epix, the soundtrack would have added the disconcerting chirping of crickets to emphasize the silence in the room.

Fortunately, audio of the actual interview exists — and reveals that there was no pause at all as the Second Amendment supporters immediately point out first that many felons have their gun rights restored after serving their sentence, and second that in other cases laws exist to prevent certain "classes of people from being in possession of firearms."

The goal of the editing by director Stephanie Soechtig was, plain and simple, to make it look like Second Amendment supporters don't know what they are talking about, and in particular don't have any viable answers to serious questions.

This kind of spin has been going on for a long time, which is why the trust level for journalists is unfortunately low. I wrote about Couric's dishonesty way back in 2008 after her famous interview with Alaska Gov. Sarah Palin, then running for vice president. In that interview, Couric made up a statement and attributed it to Palin and then challenged her to defend it.

That was all part of the famous false narrative that Palin had said she could see Russia from her house. She didn't. Comedian Tina Fey did. But it all started because Charlie Gibson of ABC News produced a deceptively edited interview with Palin in which she gave quite a thorough analysis of U.S.-Russian relations. Asked about her statement that the Russians are "next door neighbors" of Alaska, she noted, "I'm giving you that perspective of how small our world is and how important it is that we work with our allies to keep good relations with all of these countries, especially Russia."

That entire (and entirely reasonable) response was edited out of the interview, along with about half of her concerns about Russia. Why? Because it sounded too coherent, too intelligent and too (yeah) reasonable for a Republican ... Palin had to be put in her place.

Then when Couric did her interview with Palin a few weeks later, she said to the governor, "You've cited Alaska's proximity to Russia as part of your foreign policy experience. What did you mean by that?"

Of course, Palin never said any such thing, but what she did say only saw the light of day in a transcript released by ABC News, but read by only a fraction of the people who saw the original faked interview. As always (until Donald Trump) the media controlled the narrative.

So, whether the government is faking history or the press is faking interviews, the losers are everyday Americans. Do you agree? Millions of people do.

I'm a member of the press, and have been for many years. I recognize that a free press is vital to our continued freedom, but I'm not sure that what we have at the national level is a free press any longer so much as a "bought and paid for" press. Trump says the "political press is among the most dishonest people" he has ever met. I don't know about that, but it's plain that a lot of them are either "dishonest" or "clueless." Take your pick.

And if you want to consider yourself truly informed, do yourself a favor: Dig deeper. There's more there than meets the eye (or the ear).

'MEDIAGATE': THE SCANDAL YOU WON'T HEAR ABOUT ON CABLE NEWS

August 7, 2016

In the last two weeks, it has become obvious that a political scandal is unfolding which exceeds in scope anything seen previously in our country's 240-year history.

What could that be? Is it the fact that leaked emails proved that the Democratic Party rigged the election cycle to ensure that Hillary Clinton would be nominated for president instead of her grassroots opponent, Bernie Sanders? Or the fact that it became firmly established that the Obama administration had essentially agreed to pay ransom to Iran for the release of our hostages? How about the fact that President Obama — acting more like Hugo Chavez than George Washington — announced from the White House that one of the two people who have a chance to be the next president of the United States is "unfit to serve" in that office?

All of those were bad enough, but they don't come close to the importance of the political scandal that you will never hear reported on cable news or in the pages of the New York Times. I'm talking about "Mediagate" — the attempted coup d'etat by the talking heads at CNN, Fox News, and MSNBC, who aimed salvo after salvo of Trumped-up stories at the GOP nominee as soon as he appeared to be closing in on Hillary Clinton following the Republican National Convention.

What a disastrous week for Donald Trump, but more importantly what a disastrous week for the nation — which has proven to be in thrall to the steady, hypnotic drumbeat of lies and distortions from the national media. "Trump hates babies."

"Trump's wife violated immigration rules." "Trump says Ivanka won't let herself be sexually harassed." (What's wrong with that?) Look past the talking heads on each of these supposed stories, and there is nothing there but another attempt to discredit Trump by people who don't like Trump.

The biggest example of that was the non-story about Trump supposedly attacking the Khans, the Gold Star family who denounced him at the Democratic convention. If you actually look at what Trump said in response, the worst he ever did was ask why Mrs. Khan did not speak even though she appeared on the stage alongside her husband. Mr. Khan on the other hand questioned Trump's patriotism, his knowledge of the Constitution and essentially called him a bigot. In the real world, Trump showed admirable restraint in the face of this attack, especially when it was eventually discovered that Mr. Khan is an advocate of the primacy of Islamic sharia law over all other law, including the Constitution.

But the Khan-troversy was just one of many hyped-up stories rolled out over two weeks by the national media so they could ask the one over-riding important question over and over: "When will Donald Trump withdraw as the GOP nominee?" To anyone who was watching with an open mind, it was obvious that the media was creating the story, not reporting it.

Let's go back to the beginning. The countdown of lies, innuendoes and slander against Trump all started immediately after the July 27 press conference held by Trump at his resort in Doral, Florida. This was the point where polls were showing Trump leading or tied in several key swing states and ahead in several national polls. Panic was setting in among Democrats and their allies in the media.

It was also a few days after Wikileaks had published those thousands of emails and voicemails that had been hacked from the Democratic National Committee. This was no coincidence, but rather was the beginning of a concerted effort by the media to rehabilitate Hillary Clinton as the historic first woman presidential nominee in U.S. history.

The emails made it plain that Bernie Sanders had been dead right when he claimed that the DNC had rigged the election to ensure a positive outcome for Clinton. In the leaked emails, Democrat officials had questioned Sanders' faith as a Jew; they tag-teamed with journalists to sabotage him; and they kowtowed to the Clinton campaign, all the while pretending to be neutral players. This was a disaster for the Democratic Party — a huge story that made it clear that Clinton was not just an establishment hack, but a dishonest one at that. Democratic Party Chair Debbie Wasserman Schultz resigned in "disgrace" (and then was hired the same week by Clinton as a campaign adviser!) but the story just wouldn't go away.

People were actually starting to ask questions about Clinton's dubious moral character and her role in the scandal, but since Clinton didn't have any answers, she did what she does best and deflected the story. Instead of explaining why she had lied for months about collaborating with the DNC to steal the election, she and her surrogates led the lapdog media to instead question whether or not the supposed Russian hackers had leaked the damaging evidence against Hillary in order to boost Trump's chances in the election.

This was a ridiculous allegation, which didn't do justice to a former member of the "most transparent administration in history," but that aside, it served its purpose. The bloodhounds of the cable news factory were off the scent of the real story and barking up the wrong tree in no time. It was all about how the evil leader of the bad Russians, Vladimir Putin, loves Donald Trump, the evil leader of the bad Republicans.

So come that Wednesday, Trump held a press conference to respond to the Clinton email scandal (I mean the NEW email scandal, not the private insecure Clinton email server scandal which FBI director James Comey called an example of gross negligence by the former secretary of state!) and the allegations that he and Putin were secret lovers.

Trump answered questions for more than an hour, lots of questions, including several about the DNC email breach. Trump gave one funny response, in particular, where he did a jazzy riff on the idea that the Russians, who supposedly had hacked into the DNC server, might have also hacked into the soft target of Hillary's private server when she was secretary of state and therefore might have copies of the thousands of "private" emails which she and her lawyers had deleted from the public record shortly before telling the public that the server existed in the first place back in March 2015. In a poke at Clinton, Trump joked that if the Russians had the deleted emails, they would be doing the media and the nation a service if they turned them over.

Innocent enough, right?

Not hardly. As soon as the press conference was over, I heard a news anchor on one of the cable channels announce that the major news coming out of the session was that Trump had recklessly invited the Russians to hack Hillary Clinton's emails as secretary of state and thus put national security at risk!

Say what!

First of all, it was a joke, people! Secondly, there is nothing to hack! The server doesn't exist anymore. Do the folks at MSNBC really think that after the FBI got through looking the email server over, that they plugged it back into the Internet? Third, the emails that were deleted by Clinton's lawyers were supposedly all private and personal and had nothing to do with national security in the first place!

But most importantly, Trump never said anything remotely like what the cable channels and internet news outlets started chanting in unison — "Reckless Trump asks evil Russians to hack Honest Hillary Clinton's emails!"

So let's look at the actual "incriminating" statement by Trump:

"[I]f it is Russia — which it's probably not, nobody knows who it is — but if it is Russia, it's really bad for a different reason, because it shows how little respect they have for our country, when they would hack into a major party and get everything. But it would be interesting to see — I will tell you this: Russia, if you're listening, I hope you're able to find the 30,000 e-mails that are missing. I think you will probably be rewarded mightily by our press. Let's see if that happens. That'll be next."

So, first of all, Trump says he doesn't think the Russians have the emails. (Recent speculation by a former National Security Agency official named William Binney is that it was the U.S.'s own security apparatus that hacked and released the DNC treasure trove, but who knows?) Trump then says that if it is the Russians who did it, we have a serious problem because they have shown disrespect for us. And finally, he pivots from the DNC hack to the deleted Clinton emails, and makes the JOKE that he hopes Russia is "able to find the 30,000 emails that are missing." Notice, he does not say HACK, but rather FIND, as in, "If you already hacked that INSECURE server in Hillary Clinton's basement, it would be kind of cool if you could share the thousands of emails that Hillary Clinton didn't think the public should see."

It was actually quite funny, but unfortunately Trump always forgets that what he calls the "dishonest media" are going to take his words and twist them seven ways from Sunday in order to paint him as "unfit to serve" and to ensure the election of their preferred candidate — Hillary Clinton.

Hopefully, the average American will not forget. Let the voter beware.

WHO'S SCARIER? REPUBLICANS OR REFUGEES?

August 29, 2016

A family of six Congolese refugees arrived in Missoula, Montana, last week to begin their new life far from the Tanzanian refugee camp where they had lived for many years.

Good for them. May they be blessed with a better life in our great state and country. We all should wish them well.

Our nation has always welcomed newcomers, including refugees from war-torn countries, to join us in pursuit of the American dream. We will continue to do so, but that does not mean we should ever violate our own best interests. Our welcome mat should never be an excuse to treat average Americans like a doormat.

Unfortunately, too many voices, including two Montana newspapers, have tried to vilify everyday Americans who insist that our own safety and well-being must come first — yes, even before the interests of refugees.

Both the Missoulian and the Bozeman Chronicle ran editorials last week that chastised GOP gubernatorial candidate Greg Gianforte for sending out a campaign mailer that proclaims "Montana security first" and chides Gov. Steve Bullock for refusing to challenge federal programs that are bringing thousands of Syrian refugees to small towns across the United States.

The Chronicle declared that "this kind of rhetoric has thoroughly polluted our national political dialogue," and the Missoulian condemns it as "fear-mongering."

Both editorials imply that Gianforte was being "insensitive" because his flier was released about the same time the African family moved to Missoula, as if concerns about the safety of American citizens should go on hiatus whenever someone's feelings might be hurt.

How absurd. If we do not want the American dream to turn into the American nightmare, we cannot pretend that our good will can protect us from other people's bad intentions. And for the record, there are millions of people in the world who have evil intentions when it comes to the United States.

Of course, the lucky family from the Congo could be made up of marvelous people who will do very well here. Again, we all hope so, but do not be so naive as to think that all the refugees who will be coming to Montana in the coming years will be fine and upstanding people.

Safe Landing, the local organization that invited the International Rescue Committee to Missoula, is no doubt well-meaning, but by appealing to emotion rather than logic in making the case for refugee resettlement, the organization could well be a Dangerous Launch for terrorism instead of a Safe Landing for refugees.

How many Americans have to be killed by refugees or Mideastern immigrants such as the Tsarnaev brothers (Boston Marathon bombing), Omar Mateen (Pulse nightclub massacre), Syed Farook and Tashfeen Malik (San Bernardino massacre) or Muhammad Youssef Abdulazeez (Chattanooga military recruiter shootings) before the Missoulian and the Bozeman Chronicle recognize there is a real problem? Are we supposed to be OK with a couple dozen murders of Americans per year in exchange for feeling good about helping refugees escape their own countries? It's not fear-mongering when you can point to dead bodies, is it?

The International Rescue Committee has a well-documented agenda of seeding a community like Missoula with non-threatening refugees like the Congolese family, but then later switching to bringing in refugees who could themselves be Muslim extremists or might easily provide cover for Mideastern terrorists. If we ignore that history, then shame on us.

Safe Landing, and apologists like the Missoulian editorial board, find no cause for concern. They say that Syrian refugees who might ultimately be transplanted into Western Montana will be thoroughly vetted before they arrive. But that flies in the face of statements by FBI director James Comey and others responsible for national security who have confirmed that there is no way possible to "vet" refugees from places like Syria where there are no government records, no infrastructure, and no shortage of enemies of the United States.

Defenders of Safe Landing also reject the evidence of other communities that have previously imported refugees into their mix with oftentimes disastrous results. You only need read about the case of the 5-year-old girl who was reportedly sexually assaulted by two or three young Muslim migrant boys in Twin Falls, Idaho, to understand what could be at risk. The worst part of that story was that public officials and the media tried to make the girl and her family the villains instead of the victims.

It is literally too heart-breaking for me to even write about the facts of the rape case, but I encourage you to do a web search for "Twin Falls refugee rape" and read about it for yourself. Lots of stories online make excuses for the accused assailants, but ask yourself whether the parents of the little girl and the neighbor who witnessed her being assaulted have any reason to make up the story?

If you are not made sick to your stomach by the self-serving politicians, prosecutors and media experts who tried to cover up or excuse the incident, then you no doubt will already be calling me a fear-monger for taking the side of a 5-year-old girl who has been scarred for life.

That little girl is now a refugee, too. She and her family had to flee from their home because of harassment from her attackers and their relatives. How many more Americans should be made to fear for their lives, their safety and their well-being in order to make foreigners feel welcome among us?

Something is rotten in the state of Idaho, and if Greg Gianforte wants to protect Montana families from having to suffer like this Twin Falls family, then I don't see why he should be ashamed about it, and I am sure he is not.

Can Montana's governor take on the federal government over the refugee issue, and win? I'm not sure, but I do remember Gov. Brian Schweitzer taking on the president over a much less important issue like Real ID, and at least making a stand for the rights of Montana citizens. I would love to see Gov. Bullock do the same when it comes to protecting not just the rights, but the very lives, of Montanans.

It wouldn't hurt if the newspapers of Montana encouraged him, too, instead of pretending that we have more to fear from Republicans than refugees.

GOP SUICIDE AND OTHER LIBERAL LEAPS

September 4, 2016

Longtime Clinton operative James Carville said last week that the Republican Party is committing suicide by supporting Donald Trump.

But if there is a realistic chance of a GOP suicide happening, it will probably be from standing too close to Democrats when their heads explode on election night after Trump is named the next president.

Amazingly, the Democratic brain trust (which includes official members like Carville and honorary members like members of the left-wing media) continue to be proudly wrong about everything Trump.

Wednesday was one of Trump's finest days, and one of the worst for the mainstream media. First, the GOP candidate scored his private meeting with Enrique Peña Nieto, the president of Mexico, then acted graciously and humbly in a joint press conference with Peña Nieto. When asked by a reporter about the issue of who was going to pay for Trump's proposed border wall, the candidate said, "We did not discuss that."

CNN's Paul Begala, also a longtime operative of the Clinton clan, seized on that as if Trump had somehow betrayed his loyal followers. He said Trump "wimped out" and suggested that Trump's remarkable visit to Mexico City was now to be counted as a dismal failure.

Say what? First of all, no one cares who is going to pay for the wall except Trump. He added that flourish about Mexico paying for the wall midway through the primary campaign, and it's a good line to get a rally excited, but honestly after waiting for more than 10 years for a wall to be built, most supporters of border security would be willing to kick in a hundred bucks each to make sure it happens. Anything other than waiting for a Washington, D.C., politician to deliver what was promised so long ago!

Of course, later that day, when President Peña Nieto took a page from Trump's playbook and Tweeted that he had told Trump that Mexico would not pay for the wall, the new "scandal" of the hour was that Trump had lied when he said, "We did not discuss that." On CNN, MSNBC and Fox News, there was a palpable sense of relief as commentators felt it was safe to stop having to say that Trump had looked "presidential" and could pivot to the more familiar "Trump screwed up." In the hours of coverage I watched, I only heard one commentator point out the obvious: The statements by Peña Nieto and Trump were not mutually exclusive.

Finally, two days later, confirmation came in a story from the Wall Street Journal:

"A person close to Mr. Peña Nieto said that 'since there was such a clear disagreement in preparatory conversations over issues about the wall and its payment, both parties agreed not to discuss them at the meeting, and instead talk about other topics, such as the great contribution that the Mexican community makes in the U.S., illegal drugs and weapons trafficking, bilateral trade, within North America and the rest of the world.' The person added: "Before the conversation began, Mr. Peña Nieto reiterated to Mr. Trump that Mexico won't pay for any wall, and as agreed, they discussed other topics."

Imagine that! They agreed to hold substantive discussions about topics where they could find agreement instead of fighting over matters where they had little common ground. And yet, to this day, liberal Democrats are whining that Trump betrayed his cause by not attempting to browbeat the Mexican president into submission. Unbelievable!

The liberal media also tried to shame Trump because his Wednesday night speech on immigration took a different tone than his earlier session with the president of Mexico. At that important policy address, Trump did indeed emphasize that Mexico would be paying for the wall, but that same Wall Street Journal article revealed that Trump's speech as originally scripted would have omitted the line. It was only after Peña Nieto went public with his private declaration that Trump inserted the new sentence about Mexico: "They don't know it yet, but they're going to pay for the wall."

As he told the Wall Street Journal, "I had no choice."

The line gave the chattering heads on cable news something to pick over, but the American public was focused instead on Trump's comprehensive 10-point immigration plan. It scared liberals, who forgot that it mirrored much of what President Bill Clinton proposed back in 1996. They characterized it as being like a "Hitler speech" or a "Klan rally,"even taking offense at Trump highlighting the plight of families whose loved ones were killed by illegal aliens.

As journalist Mark McKinnon said on Twitter, "Trump surrounded on Phoenix stage by 'Angel Moms' who say their kids were murdered by illegal immigrants. This is pretty much a hate rally."

No, the only hate is directed toward Donald Trump and his declared love of America. That's what seems to rattle liberals the most, whether it's about immigration or about anything else.

As Trump said Wednesday, "We need a system that serves our needs, not the needs of others. Remember, under a Trump administration it's called America first."

So scary for the mainstream media! Heads will definitely explode should Trump be elected Nov. 8.

'DISHONEST MEDIA' RATCHET UP
THE ATTACKS

October 9, 2016

Some of the loudest cheers Donald Trump gets when he's holding a rally is when he blasts the "dishonest media."

It doesn't take a genius to figure out why.

Regular people, it turns out, are smarter than the journalists, talk-show hosts and pundits who make up stories on a regular basis to promote their own point of view. People object to being treated like morons, and they resent the media for thinking they can say anything and get away with it no matter how blatantly false.

One of the best of those fake stories made the rounds last week, when the Associated Press published a story headlined, "Giuliani says Trump is better for the U.S. 'than a woman.'"

Whoa! You would think even the most deplorable of Trump's supporters would know better than to make such an idiotic statement! So when I saw the headline, I eagerly read the story to find out just why Mayor Rudy Giuliani had made such a stupid comment.

But wait! He never said that at all! And even the unnamed author of the story must have known it wasn't true because he began his story with the following:

"Did Rudy Giuliani really mean to say Donald Trump would make a better president than Hillary Clinton because he's a man?"

Everyone reading the story with a scintilla of common sense would have been shouting, "OF COURSE NOT" — especially if they kept reading to find out what Giuliani really said.

So here it is. In response to a question on ABC's "This Week" about Trump's tax forms that were published by the New York Times, Giuliani compared Trump's business acumen to Hillary Clinton's and asked the following question:

"Don't you think a man who has this kind of economic genius is a lot better for the United States than a woman, and the only thing she's ever produced is a lot of work for the FBI checking out her emails?"

Yep, there it is ... the incriminating statement ... in plain English ... if you slice it and dice it ... and throw out the last half of the sentence!

Giuliani's real meaning was self-evident: "Don't you think a man who has this kind of economic genius is a lot better for the United States than a woman who has never produced anything except a lot of work for the FBI checking out her emails?"

A fifth-grader could have figured it out, so at least now we know that the Associated Press is not smarter than a fifth-grader. Nor are the folks at the New York Times, the Washington Post, Politico or dozens of other news organizations that published the phony story and headline online or in print.

The object of the distorted story, in case you hadn't figured it out, was not to make Rudy Giuliani look like a chump, but to make women angry at Donald Trump.

There's nothing wrong with that if it takes place on the Opinion page in an editorial or a column, but it has nothing to do with news reporting.

The same fake reporting came up again last week when Trump held a townhall meeting with the Retired American Warriors PAC on Oct. 3. Trump was asked whether he would support a "holistic approach" for solving the problems of "veteran suicide, PTSD, TBI [traumatic brain injury] and other related military mental and behavioral issues" and whether he would "take steps to restore the historic role of our chaplains and the importance of spiritual fitness and spiritual resiliency programs."

Trump's answer: "Yes I would."

He then went on to explain what should be obvious:

"When you talk about the mental health problems, when people come back from war and combat and they see things that maybe a lot of the folks in this room have seen many times over and you're strong and you can handle it. But a lot of people can't handle it. And they see horror stories. They see events that you couldn't see in a movie, nobody would believe it. Now we need a mental health help and medical. And it's one of the things that I think is least addressed..."

In other words, there are many veterans who come back without post-traumatic stress disorder and others who are not so fortunate, or as Trump said, "a lot of people can't handle it," and they need mental and medical help.

This was spun by the mainstream media as Trump mocking veterans who suffer from PTSD as "weak" or "pathetic." Again, it only takes a modicum of intelligence to see that the accusation is not true. Trump was expressing compassion for our veterans who have seen things so horrible that "nobody would believe it."

But here's the Associated Press headline later that day: "Trump angers with suggestion that vets with PTSD are weak."

Huh? Say what? Yeah, I know ... the AP did talk to two people who were angry, but no one knows what role politics played in their reactions, and again, the average person is going to watch Trump's session with the veterans and see him being supportive and compassionate, not mocking or dismissive.

Even Sen. John McCain of Arizona, the Vietnam War hero who actually was in fact mocked by Trump in 2015, defended Trump from the fake reporting:

"This is kind of the classic example of the media feeding frenzy that is going on. The bias that is in the media," McCain said during a meeting with the Arizona Daily Star's editorial board. "What he is saying is that some people, for whatever reason, and we really don't understand why, suffer from PTSD, and others don't."

Trump later Tweeted his thanks to McCain for his "kind remarks on the important issue of PTSD and the dishonest media."

Heck, maybe this issue will actually bring Trump and McCain closer together as the election approaches. Now that would certainly anger the "dishonest media," and I'm not making that up!

DISHONEST MEDIA 101: 'YOUR BIAS IS SHOWING'

October 23, 2016

Two weeks ago, I wrote a column about what Donald Trump calls "the dishonest media," and I did so because as a member of the news media myself, I feel a sense of obligation to hold my profession to the same standard of accountability that I would expect for any public servants.

There are many decent, ethical highly professional people who work in journalism. I am happy to say that I work with a number of them at the Daily Inter Lake.

But sadly, the standards that we try to hold ourselves to here in Kalispell, Montana, seem to be foreign to many reporters and editors on TV and at other newspapers around the country. Because of that, I could probably write a column taking my fellow journalists to task every week and never run out of material, but honestly I didn't expect to return to the theme quite this quickly.

Unfortunately, when I was working on the copy desk putting out the Sunday paper last week, I was so shocked by a story that I changed my plans for this column.

The story, which passed muster at the Associated Press and no doubt made its way into hundreds of newspapers and probably thousands of websites, was a report on a Trump rally in Portsmouth, New Hampshire, on Oct. 13.

It was so astoundingly biased that I had to extensively edit the story to remove the reporter's personal opinions before running it on the following day's front page.

The story was headlined, "Trump challenges legitimacy of election." That was one of the few accurate statements in the report. It was all downhill from there.

I'll provide a few examples to demonstrate how the reporter inserted personal opinions into a news story, and how easy it was for me as editor to correct them.

The lead of the story was as follows:

"A beleaguered Donald Trump sought to undermine the legitimacy of the U.S. presidential election on Saturday, pressing unsubstantiated claims the contest is rigged against him, vowing anew to jail Hillary Clinton if he's elected and throwing in a baseless insinuation his rival was on drugs in the last debate."

There are three major examples of bias in this one sentence, which would have been fine if the reporter was supposed to be writing an opinion piece, not a news article. I'm sure I don't have to explain this to my readers, but apparently the trained journalist who wrote the story (and her editors) were completely oblivious to the difference between a fact and an opinion.

BIAS 1: Trump "sought to undermine the legitimacy of the U.S. presidential election."

Wait a minute! Does the "reporter" really think that Trump's speech was intended to sabotage the election? That would be quite evil, wouldn't it? But that's what "undermining" implies. In fact, Trump was saying that he does not trust the legitimacy of the election process. In my edited version, I wrote that Trump "questioned" the legitimacy of the election.

That was accurate, and substantiated as accurate by the Trump quote that followed: "The election is being rigged by corrupt media pushing completely false allegations and outright lies in an effort to elect [Clinton] president."

BIAS 2: Trump was "pressing unsubstantiated claims the contest is rigged against him." Hold on! How did the reporter determine that the claims were "unsubstantiated"? Calls to the Democratic National Committee? A Ouija board?

I easily corrected this example of bias by simply removing the conclusory word "unsubstantiated." If you are a reporter covering an election, you are supposed to write down what candidates say, not tell your readers whether you agree with the candidate or not.

BIAS 3: Trump threw in "a baseless insinuation his rival was on drugs in the last debate." There is no doubt that Trump, whether jokingly or seriously, insinuated that Hillary Clinton was pepped up on drugs during the second debate. How the reporter determined that the allegation was baseless is less certain. Did Hillary consent to a pee test for the Associated Press?

Solution: Take out the opinionated word "baseless."

Here was the result as published in the Daily Inter Lake: "A beleaguered Donald Trump questioned the legitimacy of the U.S. presidential election on Saturday, pressing claims the contest is rigged against him, vowing anew to jail Hillary Clinton if he's elected and throwing in an insinuation that his rival was on drugs in the last debate."

So when it was all over, I had a lead paragraph that was just as full of information, just as provocative, but didn't tell readers what to think about the information. It's called the difference between reporting and analysis. Or more to the point, the difference between honest reporting and dishonest reporting.

Sadly, just as the rest of that story (before being edited) was also full of bias, so too is the broad spectrum of reporting on this election in general.

Take, for instance, the shocked reaction of the media to Trump's refusal at the third debate to declare in advance that he would accept the results of the Nov. 8 election. The AP again declared that Trump was "threatening a fundamental pillar of American democracy," but that assumes the results of the election will be fair and democratic. Such an assumption ignores the possibility of a stolen election such as has been alleged in both the 1960 and 2004 presidential elections, among many others. If one of the pillars of American democracy is quietly accepting stolen elections, then we truly have devolved into a Third World country.

Another irony of the press's outrage over Trump's response is that no one has noted the parallel to the GOP primary when Trump and the other candidates were asked if they would respect the outcome of the nomination process and support the eventual nominee. Sixteen candidates said that they would, but Trump said it depended on whether the process was fair. He later agreed to support the nominee as did Jeb Bush and John Kasich, but when Trump won, it was Bush and Kasich who went back on their word and refused to support Trump.

How about we let the facts speak for themselves in both elections and reporting? But if you want my opinion (and I'm entitled to one because this is not a news story), Trump would be a chump to accept the election results before the votes have been counted. Heck, President Obama has already declared that Trump is "unfit to serve as president," so if anyone should be asked if he will accept the election results, it is Barack Obama. Does he really intend to turn the reins of power over to an "unfit" president if Trump wins? Inquiring minds want to know.

CAN'T WE ALL JUST GET ALONG?
NOT ON THE INTERNET APPARENTLY

December 18, 2016

Perhaps etiquette will catch up with the internet some day, but I am doubtful.

If Amy Vanderbilt had to dedicate 700-plus pages of her "Complete Book of Etiquette" to the rather buttoned-down manners and mores of the 1950s, just how dauntingly encylopaedic would a book have to be that catalogued do's and don'ts for the screamingly in-your-face denizens of Facebook, Twitter, Reddit, Snapchat, and the panoply of other social media apps that may not be a disease in themselves, but thrive by going viral.

Besides, there doesn't seem to be any inclination for internet inhabitants to seek the civilizing influence of an Amy Vanderbilt or Emily Post. Rules are for sissies (or you can substitute the even less politically correct words that describe people you hold in low esteem because they are polite and know how to spell).

Bottom line: Virtually everyone on the internet believes it is their God-given right to be rude, reckless and 'rong (the three R's of the digital age). In "The Treasure of Sierra Madre" the bad guys didn't "need no steenking badges," but in the virtual world of social media, the bad guys (that's all of us) don't need no steenking manners. We can say whatever we want whenever we want and that includes telling other people that they need to STFU (and if you don't know what that acronym stands for, considerable yourself blessedly innocent).

The reason for all this pondering is that I had the displeasure of wading through a couple hundred comments posted on Facebook about two letters to the editor published in last Sunday's Inter Lake. After coming up for air out of the swamp that passes for civilized discourse in the 21st century, I decided I needed to weigh in on what I had discovered —

namely, that free speech is wasted on people who don't have the education to responsibly exercise it.

The two letters in question were from local liberals who are dismayed by Trump's election, and wrote to express their opinion that Americans ought to let Congress, Trump and their neighbors know that they don't condone the president-elect's policies, tone, or supporters.

I ran these two letters in the Inter Lake not because I agree with them, but because that's what I do as a responsible newspaper editor — I provide a forum for people to talk about what's on their mind on topics of general interest. In my mind, the presidential election is a topic of general interest.

But it turns out from reading all those Facebook comments, I learned that liberals aren't supposed to talk about what they believe in any more. Apparently, you lose one election, and you lose your natural rights, too. Moreover, the Inter Lake is not supposed to publish letters from liberals any more or else rock-ribbed conservatives will whine like babies about being exposed to ideas they don't like.

Now, just a minute! I thought conservatives were the great champions of free speech and fair play. Don't I read all the time about how ticked off conservatives are that college campuses are huge echo chambers for loony liberal ideologues? Don't conservatives complain constantly that there is no room for them in the mainstream media? But when two out of a dozen letters in the Inter Lake bashed Trump, suddenly it was the conservatives who were the timid snowflakes looking for a safe space where they didn't have to confront "micro-aggressions" that made them all shivery and sad.

"The daily interlake just lost a customer," said one of these crumpled conservatives. "I imagine it's hard for you guys to stay in business when you intentionally provoke the hard working silent majority."

The same guy commented elsewhere, "The Daily Interlake is like all liberal news outlet. They never report facts. They lie to their subscribers like all liberals do."

That one made me laugh. I admit it. It's not often that I or the Inter Lake get tarred with the liberal label. Apparently, the

Inter Lake is not supposed to run letters that might offend
conservative readers. But hey, we have liberal readers too, and
they probably get offended by reading conservative letters — or,
heck, by reading this column! — so maybe we shouldn't run any
conservative letters either. How about if we just shut up and
don't talk to each other at all? That would make for some pretty
dull conversations, wouldn't it? And what the heck do letters to
the editor have to do with reporting anyway? Is it possible that
American citizens literally don't know the difference between
fact and opinion at this point?

I'm afraid so. And a lot of Americans apparently don't think
they need to listen to anyone who has a different opinion.
Admittedly, this is nothing new. Back in the old days, when you
took offense at something said by an opponent, you had a duel
and tried to kill him. Today, you just call him names and make
stuff up.

"It's what these idiot liberals do," said one commenter.
"They can't accept the outcome ... we conservatives weren't out
protesting and burning other people's buildings and properties.
Suck it up buttercup, you can suffer like we did for 8 years."

Oh yeah, right. I remember how Republicans were all about
getting behind Obama's liberal agenda in 2008 and celebrating
the "hope and change."

Ummm, no. So far as I know, conservatives weren't burning
other people's buildings to protest the election of Obama, but
there wasn't a lot of "sucking it up" going on either. Does
anyone remember the Tea Party? I thought that was a protest
movement. And as for accepting the outcome of the election of
Obama, maybe I'm getting senile, but I would swear that I
remember some folks calling him an illegitimate president and
a usurper ... Hmmmm.

But that was then. This is now. In 2008, the internet was
still a fun convenience, not a weaponized virus intended to do
harm to people we didn't like and often peopler we never met.

I do wish there was some way of putting the genie back in
the bottle, but don't count on it. It turns out we just don't like
each other all that much.

A few people do seem to know how to behave politely online, but they are easily drowned out by the screaming that comes from all sides.

Still, I prefer to end this column with a voice of sanity, so here come words of wisdom from one of our readers who also was astounded by the ugly brawl last Sunday on Facebook:

"My mind is blown... Name-calling someone who voiced their opinion? 'Idiot, moron, freak, tool' ... essentially 'Move if you don't think the way I do.' Really? I know we all hve our differing opinions ... but at the end of the day, there really are facts, actual ones, not perceived or spun ones, ones that are not 'controlled' by the media OR government ... People just please read & listen to various sources, stop garnering all your 'facts' from one source echo chambers or inherently biased sources ... the information is out there, the truth is out there, you just have to look for it ... and if you can't read or hear differing opinions or odeas or thoughts without having a melt down, maybe you should move somewhere where there is only one acceptable viewpoint ... Usually, that's where only government sanctioned ideas are allowed..."

Amen, sister!

FAKE NEWS, OR: 'THE ART OF THE FAIL'

January 8, 2016

In the old days, philosophers used to meditate about how many angels could fit on the head of a pin. These days, deep thinkers want to know how much fake news CNN can squeeze into an hour.

The answer, of course, is plenty.

I won't try to actually quantify the CNN mendacity because that would actually force me to watch an entire consecutive hour of CNN news coverage, which could potentially result in a serious condition known scientifically as mush brain.

But I did happen to have the channel turned on Thursday night when Anderson Cooper announced the breaking news that President-elect Donald Trump had broken a major campaign promise. Nightmare scenarios paraded through my head as I pondered the worst:

—DJT had a Road to Damascus type experience, and God told him not to repeal Obamacare, but just change the name to Trump Med (after first engaging in a hostile takeover of Club Med so that his friends could have access to affordable wealth care).

—DJT tore up his list of 21 potential Supreme Court justices, and on the advice of Hillary Clinton, is planning to name Barack Obama to the high court in order to protect and preserve "New York values."

—DJT has been informed that he had mixed up the Second Amendment and the Second Commandment. Trump plans to sign an executive order pronouncing himself the first president of the United States, declaring "Thou shalt have no other presidents before me."

Watching CNN for just a few minutes had left me completely unbalanced. But wait! Cooper scoop was worthy of a pooper scooper: Turns out that Donald Trump had let congressional Republicans know that he wanted to fund the border wall with Mexico through the appropriations process.

Cooper was aghast! "That would seemingly be a break from the idea of having Mexico pay for it as he said over and over again on the campaign trail."

CNN's senior White House correspondent Jim Acosta tried to reel Cooper back to earth, while at the same time maintaining the fake-news premise that Trump had somehow gone back on a promise: "We should point out, yes, that is a massive departure from what he [Trump] said out on the campaign trail. We should point out though back in October, he began to talk about this shift in this position. He talked about having Mexico reimburse the United States government for that wall, not exactly the same thing as sending over a big check across that border, Anderson."

No, Anderson, it's a totally different thing, and not one Trump voter, not one, ever expected Trump to put the wall on hold until the Mexican ambassador drove up to the White House with a $10 billion check in hand.

But that didn't stop the CNN host from going on to characterize the request for fence-building funds as a "flip-flop," or his next guest, former Treasury Secretary Robert Reich, from calling Trump a liar. You have to wonder how long the national news media will continue to question the ability of the president-elect to outwit, outplay and outlast them. As opposed to Trump's "Art of the Deal," the media seem to specialize in "The Art of the Fail."

Of course, Trump got the last word, thanks to Twitter. Friday morning, the president-elect sent out the following message:

"The dishonest media does not report that any money spent on building the Great Wall (for sake of speed), will be paid back by Mexico later!"

Actually, I am starting to think that maybe the mainstream media is not dishonest at all, just incapable of serious analysis or examination of ideas. After all, most of them probably went to Ivy League schools. That's a hard handicap to overcome.

DONALD TRUMP, HUXLEY AND THE 'ENEMIES OF FREEDOM'

March 12, 2017

It was the tweet heard round the world.

"The FAKE NEWS media (failing @nytimes, @NBCNews, @ABC, @CBS, @CNN) is not my enemy, it is the enemy of the American People!" —Donald Trump, via Twitter, Feb. 17, 2017.

Trump the counterpuncher had thrown a wicked jab at his favorite target, the "fake news media," or what he calls "the opposition party." And right on schedule, the fake news media responded by getting the story wrong.

The headline in the New York Times is one example of many: "Trump Calls the News Media the 'Enemy of the American People.'"

Um, no, sorry. He didn't. He called the "Fake News media" the enemy of the American people, and he specifically identified that as the N.Y. Times, NBC, ABC, CBS and CNN. Yet for days, the story became that President Trump had declared war on "the media" or "the press" — all brought about by convenient and no doubt intentional omission of the word "fake."

And let's face it, the inability to accurately report the contents of a 22-word post on Twitter says volumes about the agenda-driven "reporting" that we have come to expect from the guiding lights of the mainstream media.

Of course, it wasn't just the New York Times that got the story wrong. Virtually the same headline ran in the Washington Post, USA Today, thehill.com, slate.com, politico.com, the Daily Beast, New York Daily News — the list goes on and on, as if they were all eagerly self-inducting themselves into the "Fake News" industry.

This is one small example of a story that members of the national press corps got wrong (we used to call it lying), but there are dozens of them. Think of how many times you heard the president's first travel ban called a Muslim ban, even though there was no reference to Muslims in it, and it demonstrably did not affect the vast majority of Muslims. Multiply that fake story by the dozens more than have been parroted by the mainstream media, and you can begin to gauge Trump's frustration.

Add in the fact that every time the Associated Press gets a story wrong, it appears in hundreds of newspapers and is shared on thousands of websites and literally hundreds of thousands of Facebook and Twitter accounts. The impact on the American public's perceptions of the truth is immediate, obvious and damning.

We are not legitimately talking about "news media" of any kind at this point; we are talking about a propaganda machine, or at the very least, an echo chamber whose purpose is to shape opinion, policy, and even morality.

It was eight years ago that I wrote a column highlighting the prophetic warning of author Aldous Huxley about the "enemies of freedom," which the world would face as technology advanced in the coming decades.

One of the most important of those enemies was propaganda, and in a 1958 interview with Mike Wallace of CBS fame, Huxley laid out the case for how our freedom could be endangered by the mass media. The author of "Brave New World" proposed that the time might come when "television ... is always saying the same things the whole time; it's always driving along. It's not creating a wide front of distraction. It's creating a one-pointed 'drumming in' of a single idea all the time." He calls this an "immensely powerful" tool of propaganda.

This "drumming in of a single idea all the time" is exactly what Trump has recognized to be an "enemy of the American people," and anyone can see that he is right. If you hear the same refrain over and over again, you will eventually sing the song, no matter how horrible it is. The same goes for news: If you see and hear the same story over and over again, you will believe it, no matter how fake (or potentially fake) it is.

The news media celebrities on cable TV have appointed themselves the guardians of the public trust, but if you as an individual citizen are doing your duty, you must resist the "drumming in of a single idea all the time" and recognize that life in a democratic republic is binary, not singular. Question Trump, sure, but question the media, too. Question Obama. Question Congress. Question the Supreme Court. Never settle for one side of the story, and never assume that anyone in particular has your best interests at heart.

Most importantly, don't blindly trust anyone to tell you the truth, the whole truth and nothing but the truth. If you do, you have given away all your power.

Do you not believe there is any threat to your freedom? Listen to MSNBC's Mika Brzezinski, who accidentally told the truth on the "Morning Joe" show recently by saying, "And it could be that while unemployment and the economy worsens, [Trump] could have undermined the messaging so much that he can actually control exactly what people think. And that, that is our job."

Yep, today, it is the members of the news media who stand between you and the truth. In that regard, they are now more powerful than the government itself. Mika was right. They shape our perceptions, and skew our reality.

But remember that no one elected Mika Brzezinski, or Jake Tapper, or Rachel Maddow, or the New York Times or the Associated Press to the position of guardians of truth. They are self-appointed, and unlike presidents they don't go way in four or eight years. They have set themselves up to tell us what is right and wrong, and the only defense we have against them and their cupidity, arrogance and self-righteousness is eternal vigilance. Should we surrender to their dictates, we deserve the dictatorship that we get.

The Roman poet Juvenal summed up the situation aptly 1,900 years ago:

"Quis custodiet ipsos custodes?" Who watches the watchmen?

THE WAR OF WORDS OVER TRUMP AND THE CIVIL WAR

May 7, 2017

I was minding my own business driving home from Libby last Monday when my peace was shattered by a collision — not with a deer as usually happens on that stretch of U.S. 2, but with the latest vitriolic, whiny complaints of self-important conservative talk-show host Mark Levin as he once again questioned the intelligence of President Trump.

The issue at hand wasn't the Obamacare repeal or whether to withdraw from the Paris climate treaty, but rather the president's remarks in a radio interview with Salena Zito about the Civil War.

Levin, who acknowledged he was no expert on the Civil War, nonetheless was livid that Trump had ventured an opinion on how President Andrew Jackson might have averted the war had he been president sometime later than when his second term ended in 1837.

The exact quote from Trump was this:

"I mean, had Andrew Jackson been a little later, you wouldn't have had the Civil War. He was a very tough person, but he had a big heart, and he was really angry that he saw what was happening with regard to the Civil War. He said, 'There's no reason for this.' People don't realize, you know, the Civil War, you think about it, why? ... People don't ask that question. But why was there the Civil War? Why could that one not have been worked out?"

Like a bunch of liberals who also found fault with Trump's commentary, Levin argued that the matters of secession and slavery were too complicated for mere mortal man to resolve.

"So let me get this straight," he complained. "Washington, Franklin, Madison — they couldn't resolve it. Later Jefferson, he couldn't resolve it. Monroe, he couldn't resolve it. Adams, he couldn't resolve it. If only Andrew Jackson had been alive when Lincoln was alive — that is when Lincoln was president — then we would have avoided the Civil War.

"This is preposterous!"

But is it?

Andrew Jackson actually did keep the United States out of civil war — not THE Civil War, but a civil war that easily could have ensued in 1832 when South Carolina adopted the Ordinance of Nullification declaring certain U.S. laws and tariffs to be unconstitutional. South Carolina was certainly right that the tariffs were an abomination, causing the Southern states to have to pay 62 percent more for imported goods solely to benefit the Northern states that also produced the same goods, but that did not give them the right to reject federal law.

In the lead-up to that fight, Andrew Jackson made a famous retort in response to the South Carolina governor who had taunted him with a toast about states' rights. In reply, Jackson had said staunchly: "Our Federal Union: It must be preserved."

And that indeed is how he governed when the Nullification Crisis grew to a head in November of 1832. South Carolina's Gov. Hayne put together an army of 25,000 troops and yet Jackson's firm hand avoided a fight. Nor was the matter simply a fight over the tariff. Jackson wrote in an 1833 letter of his belief that "the tariff was only a pretext, and disunion and southern confederacy the real object. The next pretext will be the negro, or slavery question."

In other words, Jackson — as Trump had declared — was indeed intent on preserving the union, and although himself a slave owner, he was not willing to let the union crumble on behalf of the foul institution of slavery.

Nor do we need to rely solely on Jackson's own words to see what his fellow Americans thought about the general's resolute character and forceful nature.

The Warren Mail, in Warren, Pennsylvania, ran an editorial on April 6, 1861, that condemned Lincoln's predecessor, President James Buchanan, for his feckless leadership in the years leading up to the attack on Fort Sumter and the secession of various Southern states responding to the election of Lincoln.

The Warren paper noted "the extent to which our political disturbances have been permitted to grow, by the cowardly incompetence of Mr. Buchanan and the treachery of his counselors" and pointed to Old Hickory as the corrective antidote the country was lacking.

"The firm spirit of decision manifested by Andrew Jackson, which in 1832 checked a like ebulition of disloyalty, would, if displayed by James Buchanan in 1860, have nipped in the bud the germ of discontent that has now expanded to such ungovernable dimensions, and prevented, at least for the present, the disgraceful scenes which are being enacted throughout the southern portion of our Republic."

Likewise, the Monroe (Wisconsin) Sentinel, on March 27 of 1861, published an account of an address by Judge William Johnson of Cincinnatti, about how Washington, Jefferson and Jackson had handled cases of "armed resistance to law" similar to that which faced Lincoln. His discussion of Andrew Jackson is informative, and perhaps Mr. Levin will take time to read it before he lectures President Trump again.

"The third era of treason, and secession occurred in 1832, during the administration of General Jackson. The ostensible object of complaint then was the revenue laws, which ... were oppressive to the people of the planting States. General Jackson believed this a mere pretext on the part of the leaders ... Whatever the grievance was, they resorted for their remedy to secession and violence. They pulled down from the custom house at Charleston the flag of the Union, and trampled it under their feet, and passed laws in the Legislature of South Carolina to resist the Federal Government in the collection of the revenues. General Jackson following the example of Washington, remonstrated earnestly with them against their lawless conduct; but, when they refused to listen to reason, he ordered General Scott, with a garrison of eight hundred men, to Fort Moultrie, to see that the laws were faithfully executed. If by transmigration, the soul of Andrew Jackson had occupied the body of James Buchanan, we would have had peace to-day."

It is no accident that President Trump holds up Andrew Jackson as a role model, nor is it surprising that the same Washington elites who looked down their noses at commoner Jackson continue to be dismayed by Trump's uncouth manner of speech. But they do themselves a disservice to underestimate Trump just because he speaks imprecisely, or you might more accurately say impressionistically. He uses words as a broad brush to paint the big picture and doesn't focus on details, yet he is often proven right, as he is in this case.

Yes, Andrew Jackson died 16 years before the Civil War began, so he didn't really "get angry that he saw what was happening with the Civil War." But he did get angry at the forces in the South that were steering the country toward Civil War even when he was president, and yes, many Americans wished Jackson had been president instead of Buchanan in the late 1850s.

Let's hope this discussion remains purely academic, but with our country currently divided as much as it has ever been since the years after the Civil War, that is not a sure thing. For instance, a Calexit movement has started recently in California to separate, or secede, from the more conservative United States. It might be purely coincidental that the South Carolina secessionists of 1832 and 1860 were Democrats, and so too are the California secessionists of 2017. But then again, maybe it isn't just a coincidence.

On the other hand, we have to give credit where credit is due. Andrew Jackson, although now largely disowned by the party he helped shape, was himself a Democrat, and I'll give him the last word.

"Our Federal Union: It must be preserved."

LIBRARY PANEL PUTS FAKE NEWS IN SPOTLIGHT

May 21, 2017

The truth is I've probably written about "fake news" as much as anyone has over the past 10 years, and I've been an equal opportunity critic.

I've blasted conservatives for phony stories about President Obama, and I've blasted liberals for phony stories about President Trump.

So when Sean Anderson of the ImagineIf Libraries of Flathead County called to ask if I would participate in a panel discussion about "fake news," I jumped at the opportunity.

I was happy to see that, in a press release about the panel discussion, Anderson emphasized the importance of "information literacy" and "critical thinking skills" in sorting through published information. Those are the most important weapons against fake news, same as they are the bulwark against politicized science, political chicanery and politically correct propaganda.

Problem is you can lead a reader to information, but you can't make him or her think. I don't expect the panel, which will be held Wednesday at 6 p.m. in the Arts and Technology

Building at Flathead Valley Community College, to resolve that, but at least it's an opportunity to make a start.

One of the most annoying things about my job as editor is receiving tons of forwarded emails from people who didn't bother to check on the authenticity of the "news" before wasting my time with it. You can usually gauge just how fake these email news alerts are by how many exclamation points they use in the subject line, as well as by the use of words like URGENT and SHOCKING! Did I mention upper-case hysteria?

One of the telltale giveaways that you are dealing with fake news is that there will be a claim that it has been verified on Snopes.com or some other arbiter of authenticity, but without providing a link back to the website. Take five seconds to do a Google search and you can disprove 99 percent of these SHOCKING mass-distributed emails.

Of course, in recent months, as regular readers of this column know, I've had my hands full keeping up with the mainstream media as they worked overtime spinning more lies about Trump out of whole cloth than Rumpelstiltskin got gold out of straw.

I wrote about CNN's fake shock that President Trump was asking for funding for the proposed border wall instead of submitting an invoice to Mexico.

I wrote about the media's fake contention that President Trump's disdain for "the dishonest media" was an unparalleled divergence from what had been expressed by presidents before him.

I wrote about the New York Times' phony claim that Trump had called all news media "the Enemy of the People" when actually he had singled out the Times, NBC, ABC, CBS and CNN as the enemy.

I wrote about the narrowly scripted and intentionally biased claim that Trump's "America First" policy is anti-Semitic when actually Trump is poised to be one of the best friends Israel and the Jews have ever had.

But even before that — before the last 18 months of Trump Derangement Syndrome — I had written repeatedly of the danger of turning our beliefs over to either the government or the lockstep media, which together are the modern equivalent of the Ministry of Truth in George Orwell's "Nineteen Eighty-Four."

What I wrote in 2012 accurately predicted the echo chamber of anti-Trump media of the past two years.

"As described by Orwell ... the Ministry of Truth works constantly to update the past to bring it into alignment with the ruling party's current propaganda. They do this through a massive campaign to falsify public records and to delete opposing ideas.

In the prophetic novel, "Anything that no longer corresponded with the official version of reality was discarded by employees of the Ministry of Truth by sending it down a chute to 'enormous furnaces which were hidden somewhere in the recesses of the building.' These chutes that led to collective amnesia were known as "memory holes," and if you are starting to have the feeling that what you read and hear in the news no longer corresponds to what you remember, it may be because your old truths have gone down Orwell's Memory Hole."

The question we face as individuals is "How much responsibility do we take for looking past the headlines, asking the right questions and being eagle-eyed guardians of the truth rather than blind recipients of propaganda?"

It is not unreasonable to suppose that, on the answer to that question, hinges the future of our country. I look forward to an enlightening and civil conversation Wednesday and encourage you to attend.

Montana's original hothead in Congress (Hint: it's not Gianforte)

June 11, 2017

Greg Gianforte has been excoriated by the national media, state media, Democrats and even some Republicans for "body-slamming" a reporter the day before being elected Montana's sole congressman on May 25.

Some of those critics have gone so far as to recommend that Gianforte not be seated in the House of Representatives because of his actions, even though he has apologized to his constituents and to the reporter, and admitted the fault was entirely his own.

Admittedly, it's not a stellar way to start your political career. Scratch that. It's a horrible way to start your political career, but it's not unprecedented for a member of Congress from Montana to be involved in a violent incident and yet remain in office.

Indeed Sen. Lee Metcalf didn't just overcome a couple of violent incidents in his professional life, but is one of the most beloved politicians ever to come out of our state. He was ranked 15th on a list of the 100 Most Influential Montanans of the Century in The Missoulian newspaper.

If you don't recall Metcalf, you at least may know part of his legacy. The Democratic politician helped pass the 1964 Wilderness Act, and the Lee Metcalf National Wildlife Refuge north of Stevensville and the Lee Metcalf Wilderness near Big Sky were named in his honor. Metcalf served in the U.S. House from 1953 to 1961 and then in the Senate from 1961 until the time of his death in 1978. He also served with distinction in the U.S. Army during World War II, participating in the Invasion of Normandy, the Battle of the Bulge and more.

Nonetheless, Metcalf's record was not without blemish. Maybe it was a carryover of his Montana farm boyhood or a hallmark of his military service, but Lee Metcalf did not suffer fools gladly, meaning if you got in his way — watch out!

In 1964, during his first term, Sen. Metcalf got in some kind of a shoving match with a 24-year-old law student serving as an elevator operator in the Senate office building.

The Inter Lake carried a colorful UPI report on the incident in its Feb. 18, 1964, edition:

"Sen. Lee Metcalf, D-Mont., thought the elevator operator in the Old Senate Office Building was awfully slow Monday and told him so... The operator, Bernard O'Neill, 24, a Georgetown University law student from South Bend, Ind., claims Metcalf, a big, brawny man of 53, took a swing at him. Metcalf vigorously denies it...

"If I had taken a punch, he wouldn't have been there," said Metcalf. "I can punch hard enough for most of these elevator operators."

Substitute "reporters" for "elevator operators" and imagine the howls if Greg Gianforte had taken the same bragging approach to his attack on Ben Jacobs in Bozeman. Gianforte would rightly be lambasted, but Metcalf stood firm.

In a story the next day in the Billings Gazette, Metcalf admitted he "sort of pushed" O'Neill, but still denied O'Neill's claim that he had been punched. Whatever did take place in that elevator, Metcalf clearly acted like a self-important boor who thought he deserved special treatment.

"Yesterday," Metcalf told the Associated Press, "I was treated like anybody else — not like a senator — and I did not like it."

Metcalf admitted he got mad because the elevator operator was reading a book and not attentive enough to the senator's needs.

"I bawled him out," Metcalf said. "We had an argument, and he told me, in effect, to get out and walk if I didn't like the way he was running the elevator."

O'Neill's sponsor, Sen. Birch Bayh, D-Ind., said he told the elevator operator to apologize to Metcalf or lose his job. Metcalf, to his credit, said he was "not interested in getting the boy fired," but there is evidence he did not learn anything about his own behavior as a result of the incident.

Seven years later, while attending a Vietnam War protest, Metcalf again had his sense of privilege on display. According to a UPI story, "Sen. Lee Metcalf, a robust 60 years old, punched a policeman in the chest Wednesday when he stopped him from crossing a police line during antiwar demonstrations at the Capitol.

"Metcalf shouted that he was a United States senator and couldn't be prevented from going anywhere on the capitol grounds when [Officer M.J.] Van Fossen, wearing a riot helmet and holding a nightstick with both hands, told Metcalf he could not cross the line of policemen.

"Metcalf then jabbed out his right fist and hit Van Fossen in the left upper chest. The officer took the punch easily and did no swing back. But two other officers grabbed Metcalf's arms and started leading him toward buses where demonstrators were being arrested.

" 'You assaulted an officer,' they said to him. 'I'm not going to stand...' Metcalf said, his voice quivering. 'I'm a United States senator.' "

The Capitol Police Chief came on the scene and ordered Metcalf to be released. At that point, "Metcalf, still enraged and face flushed, grabbed a UPI reporter by the arm to get his ear. 'My name is Lee Metcalf. I've been stopped.' "

Ultimately, the "unfortunate incident," as described by a Capitol police inspector, vanished without charges being filed and without further discussion. Maybe they were worried that Metcalf would go after them if they didn't let it go.

If you talk to people who knew Metcalf back in the day, you'll discover that he had a reputation for being a hothead — screaming and yelling at staffers, as well as apparently elevator operators and policemen. He was even demoted in World War II when he threw a staff sergeant down a staircase.

Compare that to the total of one (1) incident in which Greg Gianforte is known to have lost his temper. You would think that after he was charged with assault, we would have heard a bunch of complaints about him if he had ever punched or yelled at anyone before. Maybe he has, but so far as we can tell, he is no Lee Metcalf.

TRUMP AND THE 'MEAN GIRLS' OF THE MEDIA

June 25, 2017

The preening journalists who have made a profession out of hounding Donald Trump probably see themselves as avatars of Woodward and Bernstein in "All the President's Men," but I think they are sadly miscast.

Rather, the movie that seems to best describe the media's bullying of Donald Trump and deception of the public is "Mean Girls," a 2004 comedy which showed how damaging leaks and hidden dossiers could be when put in the hands of an unscrupulous adolescent. In that film's high-school setting, rumors, whispers and "fake news" work to destroy the lives of several characters until the culprits are forced to acknowledge the damage they have done.

The only thing that separates fact from fiction is that the "journalists" who are stalking President Trump give no sign of being capable of learning from their mistakes. Give the Mean Girls in the movie credit for at least being capable of growth.

Were the kind of non-stop harassment of President Trump being carried out in high school rather than Washington, D.C., there is no doubt that it would be called cyber-bullying.

Trump has repeatedly called the year-long "investigation" into "this Russia thing" a witch hunt, and what is notable about it is the glee with which reporters (and their allies in the Democratic Party) attack Trump and members of his campaign or administration. They have proven absolutely no wrong-doing, and yet they act as though Trump is an illegitimate president. By repeating their unproven allegations over and over again, they have indeed become "cyberbullies" – spreading hateful and hurtful misinformation about Trump on the Internet 24 hours a day for more than a year.

A recent report from Harvard's Shorenstein Center on Media, Politics and Public Policy detailed the attacks on Trump. Shorenstein studied the reporting of seven news outlets on the first 100 days of Trump's presidency. Fox News had 52 percent negative coverage If Trump, which seems reasonable, but Trump was portrayed negatively in 93 percent of the coverage on CNN and NBC, in 91 percent on the coverage on CBS, 87 percent in the New York Times and 83 percent in the Washington Post.

No one could survive such an onslaught without seeing their "approval ratings" decline. Imagine if the class valedictorian were the subject of 97 percent negative gossip in the hallways at a local high school. Would you be surprised if she slit her wrists? Yet we are supposed to look the other way and pretend not to notice when the media have their knives out for Trump.

Speaking of having knives out, what about that lovely Shakespeare in the Parks production of "Julius Caesar," where playgoers get to fantasize about the bloody assassination of Donald Trump? Or the disgusting picture of "comedian" Kathy Griffin holding the severed head of President Trump? If you think either of those are OK, then surely you also think it is appropriate for teen-agers to send pictures via Instagram and Snapchat of their fellow students' heads on a platter. It's just satire, after all!

And now we have actor Johnny Depp wondering aloud when the last time an actor assassinated a president...

Essentially, our national media celebrities have established themselves as the ruling clique that judges and metes out punishment for anyone who does not meet their high and mighty standards. Their haughty demeanor (raised eyebrows, snickers, disdainful comments) on every "news" show is laughable to anyone who isn't part of their "insiders' club," but also sadly dangerous.

Any president who was subjected to 24/7 insults, rumors and gossip would be at risk of destruction — and who does that help? What true American benefits by the calculated removal of a duly elected president by means of a smear campaign? None that I can think of.

Indeed, in the ultimate irony, the biggest beneficiary of the onslaught against Trump is none other than Vladimir Putin, Russia's strongman. He can sit back and watch the growing loss of confidence in our best-in-the-world political system and know full well that his biggest ally in America isn't Donald Trump; it's the Mean Girls of the mainstream media who day after day undermine the legitimate government of the United States.

Sad.

'WITCH HUNT' TRIED TO TAKE DOWN ANOTHER PRESIDENT IN THE 1950S

July 2, 2017

What a difference 65 years makes — NOT!

The "witch hunt" under way in Washington, D.C., where every flag-waving liberal in Washington, D.C., is looking for Russian "collusion" throughout the Trump administration, is not exactly new.

In fact, it was another Republican who was the subject of a similar witch hunt in 1952 (and throughout his two terms as president). Dwight D. Eisenhower, the five-star general who was Allied commander in Europe during World War II, was targeted both by Democrats and by fellow Republicans for being too cozy with communists.

I know it's hard for liberals to see themselves playing the part of red-hunting Sen. Joseph McCarthy, but the facts speak for themselves, and just as McCarthy loved to grab headlines with outrageous allegations he couldn't always prove, so too do the Democrats in Congress seem to have a penchant for trying to destroy lives with nary a hint of evidence.

It wasn't just McCarthy who was gunning for Eisenhower though; there was a whole movement of people inside and outside the government who were after him. His Democratic opponents didn't necessarily repeat the communist smears, but they went after his character nonetheless.

In 1952, the Democratic candidate, Adlai Stevenson, said of Ike and his allies, "They are apparently willing even today to let Europe collapse. But something more than blustering words is necessary to block the Kremlin plan for world dominion."

Kind of reminiscent of the attack on Trump for his insistence that our NATO partners carry their own weight (and honor their own commitment!) as we face off against Russia in the 21st century.

Even President Truman, who in 1948 asked Eisenhower to run for president (with Truman demoting himself to vice president), could not tolerate the Republican version of Eisenhower when he ran against Stevenson.

In a visit to Cumberland, Maryland, on Oct. 23, 1952, Truman lashed out at Republicans, including Eisenhower:

"Today, freedom of thought and freedom of speech are under attack in our country. They are being attacked by the planned and deliberate use of lies, slanders and fear. A little group of people are using these weapons, on a wide scale, in an attempt to attain public office. They want to make it dangerous for anyone to express opinions different from theirs. They try to destroy the reputation of any man in public or private life who dares to stand up and oppose them."

Truman referred to the "despicable 'back street' type of campaign, which usually, if exposed in time, backfires." He said that type of smear campaign was "of a form and pattern designed to undermine and destroy the public faith and confidence in the basic American loyalty of a well-known figure."

He was referring to the McCarthy-assisted campaign for Senate in Maryland in 1950, in which Democrats were attacked by Republicans for suspicions about their loyalty, but I have read no better assessment of what Democrats have tried to do to President Trump in raising the specter of "Russian collusion."

The fact of the matter is that the campaign of 1952 and the succeeding years of Eisenhower's two terms as president were replete with many lessons for us that we have failed to learn.

First of all, the vitriol of that campaign far exceeded anything we heard in 2016. And it wasn't just Truman throwing verbal bombs. Earlier in October 1952, Eisenhower unloaded on both Truman and Stevenson while campaigning in Sacramento, declaring that they were talking "like the unintelligent people they apparently are." Not surprising he would take that tack since the day before, Truman had told a crowd in Colorado that Eisenhower had "betrayed every principle about our foreign policy and our national defense that I thought he believed in."

The Oil City (Pennsylvania) Derrick editorialized that Truman's "whistle-stop smear" campaign is "the cheapest and frowziest act of attempted character assassination in the political history of his country," bewailing the fact that Truman dared to suggest that Eisenhower had underestimated the postwar threat of communism and the Soviet Union.

As for Stevenson, the professorial Democrat, he questioned whether Eisenhower would be able to root out the communists in the federal government.

"I think we are entitled to ask, 'Is the Republican candidate seriously interested in trying to root communists out of the government or is he only interested in scaring the American people to get the old guard in?'"

Obviously, the credibility of the pundits who constantly evoke the supposedly unprecedented brash talk of Donald Trump as a candidate is hovering near zero. The problem is trying to get pundits and reporters to lower their snooty noses out of the air and into a history book — a task that may be well nigh impossible in our pseudo-literate society.

So, besides the fact that one of our nation's key allies in World War II was Soviet Russia (led by mass murderer Josef Stalin), what exactly led people to think that war hero Eisenhower was soft on communism? Trust me, the evidence was no stronger than what has been trotted out against Trump.

An advertisement in the Walla Walla (Washington) Union-Bulletin two days before the 1952 election conceded (tongue in cheek?) that "Eisenhower is not a communist," but then excoriated him for cozying up to communists while he was president of Columbia University (yes, Republicans were still allowed to head up Ivy League colleges then!).

Turns out that in 1948, Eisenhower had accepted a $30,000 grant from the communist Polish government to establish a chair of Polish Studies at Columbia. Through 1952, the chair was occupied by Dr. Manfred Kridl, who was identified as a communist.

The ad informed its readers that "The National Council for American Education stated that: 'In our opinion President Eisenhower performed for Columbia and himself a disservice when he accepted the Communist cash. Only a very naive person could think that Soviet-dominated countries have any purpose in endowing these chairs except to propagandize for their ideologies.'"

Eisenhower's connection to communists was, if anything, much more direct and obvious than Trump's connection to Russians, but — let's face it — both "scandals" are — in the words of CNN's Van Jones— "just a big nothing burger."

MONSTER SWAMP VS. SWAMP MONSTER: A D.C. ALLEGORY

July 30, 2017

Politically speaking, I'm caught between a rock and a hard place, or more appropriately between a monster swamp and a swamp monster.

The swamp is the bipartisan disaster known more formally as the federal government. The monster is President Donald Trump, whose out-sized self-caricature approach to life makes him more of a tormented DC Comics superhero (or supervillain?) than a D.C. politician.

There is no way I am going to support the swamp and its bureaucratic morass, which has a bottomless national debt and the moral code of a toothy gator. But accepting Trump on his own terms means you have to accept him as a "muck-encrusted mockery of a man," as the original Swamp Thing was characterized. Sure, he means well, but he is so elemental and so alien from what we are familiar with that he is terrifying not just to the Fake News Media whom he battles for control of the swamp, but also to the rest of us who are just distant observers on dry land.

No one likes the Twitter bombs that Trump dumps on the unsuspecting swamp creatures every morning. They are untidy and reckless. But no one liked the real bombs dropped on Dresden, Berlin or Hiroshima either. They were anything but tidy, but they got the job done.

If you know anything about Trump, it is that he is at war, and like Gens. George Patton, Ulysses S. Grant and Douglas MacArthur, he cares less about winning a popularity contest than winning the war.

The swamp creatures in Congress and the media pretend they like things nice and tidy, but that's only because they are so deep inside the mud that they have no idea just how dirty they are. I guess we'd all like things nice and tidy at some level, and that's why the swamp has survived so long. By keeping our eyes closed, we can pretend the muck doesn't stink. We can pretend that senators and congressmen are statesmen instead of power-grubbing pigs living in the muck and feeding at the public trough.

It would be awesome if someone would clean the mess up, we tell ourselves, but we forget that cleaning up a swamp means getting your hands dirty. In some measure, Trump disappoints us not because he fails, but because he makes us confront our own part in allowing the swamp to exist.

To reference a superhero who pre-dates comic books by a couple millennia, it was Hercules who was tasked with cleaning up the filthy Augean stables that housed 3,000 head of cattle.

According to Greek mythology, the stables had not been cleaned in over 30 years, a strangely fitting number since it also closely approximates the time period since Ronald Reagan tried to clean up Washington in the 1980s.

Hercules used his strength and his cunning to accomplish the seemingly impossible task of cleaning up the stable. It remains to be seen whether or not Trump will have similar success in draining the swamp, but it should be pointed out that Hercules did not get credit for his remarkable labor. Nor may Trump, but I venture to say that he will leave Washington, D.C., a fresher place than when he found it.

THE HUMAN COST OF HATE, AND THE HIGH PRICE OF LOVE

August 20, 2017

If life were as simple as the mainstream media makes it out to be, then we would have the luxury of never having to think about anything.

We could all march in lockstep from birth to death, never disagreeing, never finding nuance, never having to worry about the other side — because there wouldn't be another side.

Of course, there are such simple societies, but come to think of it, they are simply horrible. I'm talking about the nations, cultures and religions that don't tolerate diversity of opinion, ethnicity or religion. I'm talking about Germany under Hitler, China under Mao, Russia under Stalin, Cambodia under Pol Pot, the Islamic State under al-Baghdadi, Korea under the Kims.

In each of those cases, the people have been told what to think — and variance from those instructions often has meant a death sentence. Millions died under Hitler, Mao, Stalin and Pol Pot, and untold thousands under al-Baghdadi and the Kim regimes.

But, we are told, that can't happen here.

Why not? Why should we be immune? Remember that this is a country that 150 years ago found slavery to be an acceptable practice. Remember that a Democratic president locked up thousands of Japanese and Italians during World War II. How can you say that another president won't lock up his enemies and kill them?

Human progress? The perfection of the species? Don't kid yourself.

Stalin and Hitler slaughtered millions in the 1930s and '40s. Mao's reign of terror was in the 1950s and '60s. Pol Pot killed an estimated 2 million people in the 1970s. The Islamic State and Kim Jong-un are killing on a daily basis today. This is not ancient history, and unless we plan to make a completed unsubstantiated assertion that America is somehow immune from the forces of human psychology and sin that led to these other murderous tyrannies, then we have to face the fact that our democracy is precious, fragile and all that stands between us and barbarism.

That's why it is absolutely vital to recognize the threat of white supremacists, anti-Semites and all other race or religion haters. When people see the world as "us against them," it never ends well for either us or them. In Rwanda, in the span of less than half a year, the majority Hutu tribe slaughtered as estimated 800,000 of the rival Tutsis — fully 70 percent of them in the country. That is what happens when you look at a fellow human being and fail to see humanity.

It can't happen here? Can we really afford to take a superior attitude as if we were somehow better that Hutus? Do we think that somehow only Africans are subject to the insanity of tribalism? Or that somehow the scant few decades separating us from Mao and Hitler have inoculated us from the poison of hatred? Remember that Germany of the 1920s and '30s was the most cultured, most educated, most cosmopolitan of the European nations, yet it fell prey to the scourge of Nazism.

Watching dozens of young white men marching on the streets of Charlottesville chanting "Jews will not replace us" was a terrifying reminder that occluded thinking is not extinct.

But Earth to neo-Nazis: Jews do not want to replace you; they just want to be left alone to live their own lives, to raise their families without fear and to worship God (if they so choose) any way they want to. JUST LIKE YOU!

I believe Donald Trump knows that truth without being told it by me, by his daughter Ivanka, by Speaker Paul Ryan or by anyone else.

But I also believe he knows in his heart that neo-Nazis are not the only problem in America, and probably not even the biggest problem. Yes, they can easily become the scapegoat for everything that is wrong in our country, just as the left wants to make Donald Trump such a scapegoat.

But the trouble with modern-day America goes much deeper than a few men with torches and a slogan. In particular, we seem to have lost touch with our humanity. We are so enamored of our personal political ideals that we value them over and above our common humanity. We also seem to value them above common sense.

When the two sides were squaring off on last Saturday morning in Charlottesville, I watched with a growing sense of unease. Could this really be happening over a few statues placed decades ago in honor of the losing heroes of a war won by the right side more than 150 years ago? Are statues really more important than our common safety and our common humanity? Or are they just an excuse for us to devolve into dangerously divided tribes.

As I watched the neo-Nazis and Antifa soldiers pounding each other with clubs, throwing bottles and flames at each other, and bloodying each other with passionate intensity, I saw the police acting as if they had no role to play in restoring order, and I thought of Joseph Conrad's thesis in "Heart of Darkness" that the only things standing between modern man and savagery were the butcher and the policeman. If the police stepped out, then we were one step closer to chaos. God help us if we ever went hungry.

It was also obvious that what had been scheduled as a protest and a counter-protest had quickly degenerated into a riot. I recalled my mother's sage advice during the Vietnam War that when a protest turned into a riot no one was safe, and if I ever found myself in a mob, I should extricate myself as quickly as possible. Accordingly, I told my 7-year-old son that the situation was out-of-control and people were going to get hurt. Hours later, Heather Heyer died and many others were injured when an apparent neo-Nazi rammed a crowd of people in the area. James Alex Fields Jr., the accused driver, has been charged with second-degree murder, and other charges are pending. The murder of Heather Heyer was a heinous and depraved act, unimaginable, and yet it was not the only evil committed that Saturday afternoon.

If we have forgotten the lessons of Jesus, Gandhi and Martin Luther King, then we have a very dangerous path ahead.

As Jesus taught in the Sermon on the Mount, "You have heard that it was said, 'Love your neighbor and hate your enemy.' But I tell you, love your enemies and pray for those who persecute you, that you may be children of your Father in heaven." Would it not have been better for all of us if the protesters against the hate of the neo-Nazis had exhibited love instead of their own hatred? Had thrown flowers instead of punches? Had praised God instead of cursing flawed men.

I think this is what President Trump meant in his much-condemned original statement when he said, "When I watch Charlottesville, to me it's very, very sad. We have to respect each other. Ideally we have to love each other."

The president has been roundly criticized for emphasizing love rather than hate. That's not surprising. It's much easier to fight those we hate than to love them. Just ask Jesus, Gandhi and King.

STANDING FOR THE FLAG IS STANDING UP FOR OUR NATION — JUST DO IT!

October 1, 2017

President Trump did us all a great favor when he drew the nation's attention to the flag of the United States of America, the inspirational symbol of "one nation, under God, indivisible, with liberty and justice for all."

In a speech two weeks ago, the president expressed the just and righteous anger of millions of Americans that the flag was being dishonored by highly paid athletes every Sunday — supposed role models teaching America's youth that they need not pay respect to the flag, nor (as the Pledge of Allegiance puts it) "the nation for which it stands."

Those NFL football players, in ever-increasing numbers, were refusing to stand for the national anthem, "The Star-Spangled Banner," at the beginning of games. The reputed justification for their show of disrespect is that they were protesting what they perceived to be unfair treatment of blacks by our nation's police.

Whether you agree with the premise that racism has made innocent blacks targets for police shootings and harassment is irrelevant. No one has argued that the United States of America is a perfect nation. Racism is a shameful part of our heritage and cannot be excused or excised from our minds, but it does not define us. Nor is it the only part of our national heritage worthy of criticism.

But finding fault with particular people, policies or events within our broad borders is no excuse for turning your back on our flag, kneeling in silent protest of it, or linking your arms together as if you needed to build a wall to protect yourself from the red, white and blue.

Nor do you have a First Amendment right to free speech while on the job. Your boss has the right to direct your speech, and to limit it in any way necessary to accomplish the employer's goals. If you don't believe that, then try standing up on your desk Monday morning and exhorting your colleagues to walk out as a symbol of solidarity with the protesting NFL players!

The First Amendment only prevents government from restricting your speech. In fact, as others have pointed out, the ill-named National Football League has its own extensive rules spelling out how players are to respect the flag and the national anthem. Kneeling and locking arms are not included as acceptable behavior.

The NFL Game Operations Manual says that "all players must be on the sideline for the National Anthem."

It further dictates that, 'During the National Anthem, players on the field and bench area should stand at attention, face the flag, hold helmets in their left hand, and refrain from talking. The home team should ensure that the American flag is in good condition."

If teams don't get their players on the field for the anthem, they are warned that the lapse "may result in discipline, such as fines, suspensions, and/or the forfeiture of draft choice(s) for violations of the above, including first offenses."

Most importantly, the manual states, "It should be pointed out to players and coaches that we continue to be judged by the public in this area of respect for the flag and our country."

Well, duh! Apparently even Commissioner Roger Goodell and the team owners knew that it's not a good idea to thumb your nose at the American people — or the American flag!

If citizenship means anything, then it is incumbent upon all of us who live in this country to love it, to cherish it and to respect it. And yes, that goes for the flag, too. It wasn't the president who was being divisive by defending the flag; it was those players and team owners who decided that politics was more important than love of country.

Sadly, we live in an America so corrupted by selfishness that the idea of national solidarity is a foreign concept. Indeed, fear of where we are headed as a nation was in large part the explanation for why Donald Trump was elected president in the first place.

In his inaugural address, Trump told the world that, "At the bedrock of our politics will be a total allegiance to the United States of America, and through our loyalty to our country, we will rediscover our loyalty to each other."

This was not — as the mainstream media and their friends in Hollywood and the NFL proclaim — a racist sentiment. It was rather a yearning for national unity, where identity politics was shoved back into its Pandora's box, and we became committed to each other's dreams rather than to our own selfish needs. As Trump himself said, "When you open your heart to patriotism, there is no room for prejudice."

President Trump's inaugural address actually provides the remedy for the NFL calamity, if only people on the left would open their ears to hear: "We must speak our minds openly, debate our disagreements honestly, but always pursue solidarity."

It is not by coincidence that Trump also reminded us at the start of his term that the flag is not for one state, one race or one cause:

"It is time to remember that old wisdom our soldiers will never forget: That whether we are black or brown or white, we all bleed the same red blood of patriots, we all enjoy the same glorious freedoms, and we all salute the same great American flag."

What other flag would these NFL players rather salute? What other nation would they rather live in? Where else could they have the opportunities they have been afforded?

The answer is obvious. The silence is deafening.

WHITEFISH ENERGY AND BIG MEDIA'S OBSESSION WITH SCANDAL

December 3, 2017

Unlikely as it seems, Whitefish has become inextricably linked — and in a most hurtful way — to Puerto Rico, to scandal and to hurricanes.

That's because the little start-up company called Whitefish Energy (yes, with its two employees) had the audacity to offer its services in restoring power to the island in the wake of Hurricane Maria. Moreover, Whitefish Energy secured a $300 million deal with the Puerto Rico Electric Power Authority, and by all accounts quickly had hundreds of subcontractors on the ground in Puerto Rico working to overcome the devastating infrastructure crisis.

But because Whitefish Energy is based in, yep, Whitefish, Montana, and because it only has two employees, the national media decided to go full kamikaze on the little company and blame it for every downed power line in Puerto Rico (forget about those 100 mile per hour winds!). Plus, because Whitefish Energy is two words, the reporters and headline writers around the world opted to blame just simply "Whitefish" for everything that went wrong in Puerto Rico. It didn't hurt that Secretary of the Interior Ryan Zinke, a go-to boogeyman for the mainstream media, also lives in Whitefish, or that his son had briefly worked for the company one summer.

Now, I'm no expert on energy, power lines, hurricanes or disaster recovery, but I do know something about news, and I have to say that the Whitefish Energy story has been blown so far out of proportion that it's stretched to the point where it can only be called fake news.

The underlying supposition of all the reporting about Whitefish Energy is that the company did something wrong. And why? Because the two-man operation nailed down a $300 million contract to perform vital and necessary services under horrible conditions for the Puerto Rican people. If you believe in class warfare, like most left-wing journalists do, then Whitefish Energy is guilty of exploiting the poor people of Puerto Rico. How dare they seek to get paid for restoring power!

But from what I can tell, no one has claimed that the company pocketed the money and then didn't deliver the services it had promised. Actually, CEO Andy Techmanski and his little team in Whitefish ratcheted up their storm response almost immediately after getting a signed contract. They put together a team of 300 subcontractors and started putting boots on the ground within days.

Remember, virtually 100 percent of the power was out on the island, and the ancient infrastructure was already seriously inadequate, so the task was by no means simple.

If the mainstream news industry were not playing favorites and constantly trying to invent the scandal of the week, the Whitefish Energy story could easily have been played up as a positive can-do role model of American entrepreneurship.

While the rest of us, and most importantly the rest of the power companies, were sitting around doing nothing, Techmanski was actively pursuing a deal with the Puerto Rico Electric Power Authority, even before Hurricane Maria devastated the island on Sept. 20.

Remember, Hurricane Irma had crashed through the Caribbean weeks earlier, knocking out power to approximately 1 million people on the island. Techmanski thought he could help (and, yes, make a profit at the same time) and he reached out to the Puerto Rican power authority through LinkedIn. Thus, by the time Maria had hit, Techmanski already had a relationship with PREPA.

Since the few other companies that were interested in working with Puerto Rico were demanding huge up-front payments of $25 million, and Techmanski wasn't, he got the contract. Imagine that! And then he started to fulfill the contract ... and then, the national media caught the blood scent and tried to destroy him.

But think about it. Have you heard any evidence that anything improper ever took place? I haven't. No evidence that

Ryan Zinke had anything to do with the contract being issued, so rumors of corruption were fake news. No evidence that Whitefish Energy ever pretended to have more than two employees, so efforts to make the company look like some kind of scammer were presumably fake news as well. Has there been any evidence of Whitefish Energy NOT fulfilling the terms of its contract? None that I have seen.

What we know for sure is that some competitors of Whitefish Energy didn't like the fact that they didn't get to bid on the $300 million contract. Sorry, Charlie. Better luck next time.

I can't vouch for everything that Whitefish Energy did in Puerto Rico, and I have no connection to the company or Andy Techmanski, but I do respect the initiative, hustle and zeal with which Techmanski got the job — and apparently got the job done, despite the baying hounds of the media nipping at his heels.

As a matter of fact, Techmanski announced last week that Whitefish Energy had just completed work on the main north-south power line in Puerto Rico, allowing PREPA to restore power to much of San Juan, one of the hardest hit areas. You probably won't read about that in the national media because it doesn't fit the scandal narrative they've been pushing, but whatever you read, make sure you analyze it carefully down to the tiniest details. Sometimes the big picture is just a big lie.

WHAT WOULD G. WASHINGTON MAKE OF D.C. WASHINGTON? (SOME DARE CALL IT A SWAMP!)

December 10, 2017

Once again it has become apparent that the partisan divisions within our nation have strained our patriotic foundation to the point of crumbling.

Turn on the TV news any day and you will see competing narratives that seem to have nothing in common. On CNN and MSNBC, the lead story every day is that President Trump or someone close to him did something wrong — horribly wrong — impeachably wrong. On FOX News though, the story is more likely to be that President Trump is the victim of a political conspiracy, and you will learn about a lot of exculpatory evidence that never seems to show up on CNN or MSNBC.

I watch all three news channels, plus Fox Business and C-SPAN, so I get a pretty well-rounded view of what the nation is being told by the opinion-makers. In addition, I read news from the New York Times, the Washington Post, the Wall Street Journal and Breitbart.com every day, in addition to the AP coverage in the Daily Inter Lake.

What I see is frankly terrifying. First of all, the news media no longer make any effort to be unbiased or neutral reporters of fact. You can't even talk about left-leaning media any more; it is now left LEADING. The entire national conversation is being directed by unelected, self-selected arbiters of right and wrong sitting in anchor chairs at "news" channels. Politicians now take their signals from TV talkers, and since they know where the real power lies, they don't dare stray from the party line as defined by those talk-show hosts.

This has been most obvious in the daily onslaught of stories about the Trump candidacy, the Trump transition and the Trump presidency. On one channel, you will hear that Trump colluded with Russians, obstructed justice, broke the law and will probably go to jail. On another channel you will hear that

Hillary Clinton and her Democratic allies used the FBI and the corrupt Justice Department as political weapons to first try to disgrace Trump and then to destroy him with manufactured evidence.

Yet it is not only the political future of the country that is in the balance, but the economic future and ultimately the existential future as well.

How exactly can it be, for instance, that a matter of such import to the nation as the tax-reform plan can be decided entirely on a partisan basis? Is there no Democrat who sees the advantage of lowering taxes in order to stimulate the economy? Do Democrats not have any small businesses in the states they represent? Yet when the Senate voted on the tax reform plan recently, it was on a straight party-line vote except for one lone Republican who voted with the Democrats.

Moreover, because of the echo-chamber news outlets, a large majority of Americans reportedly oppose the tax cuts being offered to them because they are being told they are actually tax increases. Huh? How did a tax cut become an increase? That's easy. Because of what Mark Twain called "lies, damned lies and statistics." Most of the statistics being used to show a tax increase for middle-income Americans actually plug in numbers from 2027, the first year after the tax cuts are set to EXPIRE! That is just plain dishonest, but you can't expect the folks in Congress, let alone the folks watching the news on TV, to figure out the truth, can you?

The tax cuts are going to benefit most (not all) Americans, rich and poor, but more importantly, the lower corporate tax rates would stimulate growth in our economy like we have not seen for 30 years. That would result in money flooding back into the country, higher wages and more jobs, and it really doesn't have to be partisan at all. Democrat John Kennedy did the same thing five decades ago.

But this isn't about one vote or one tax plan or even one president. It is about the very nature of our country and our freedom.

George Washington warned, among many other cogent points of advice, in his 1796 "Farewell Address" that partisanship had the capacity to destroy the nation by blinding us to what had brought us together in the first place.

The first president assured us that "the unity of Government, which constitutes you one people" is a "main pillar in the edifice of your real independence, the support of your tranquility at home, your peace abroad; of your safety; of your prosperity; of that very Liberty, which you so highly prize."

In other words, it is our unity of purpose that underlies all our success, yet somehow, miraculously, just eight years into the American experiment, Washington had already foreseen that this "unity of Government" would be under attack for nefarious purpose.

"It is easy to foresee, that, from different causes and from different quarters, much pains will be taken, many artifices employed, to weaken in your minds the conviction of this truth; as this is the point in your political fortress against which the batteries of internal and external enemies will be most constantly and actively (though often covertly and insidiously) directed, it is of infinite moment, that you should properly estimate the immense value of your national Union to your collective and individual happiness; that you should cherish a cordial, habitual, and immovable attachment to it; accustoming yourselves to think and speak of it as of the Palladium of your political safety and prosperity; watching for its preservation with jealous anxiety; discountenancing whatever may suggest even a suspicion, that it can in any event be abandoned; and indignantly frowning upon the first dawning of every attempt to alienate any portion of our country from the rest, or to enfeeble the sacred ties which now link together the various parts."

I doubt whether Sen. Chuck Schumer, D-New York, or Sen. Mitch McConnell, R-Kentucky, have given much if any thought to these words of George Washington, but surely they are living out the worst nightmare of our first commander in chief. The "immense value of our national Union" is apparent to me and millions of Americans, but sadly I am losing hope that it will withstand the current "attempt to alienate" the red states of Trump Country from the blue states of Clinton Country. God save us.

SWAMP CRITTERS TARGET RYAN ZINKE, BUT I'M BETTING ON THE SEAL

December 17, 2017

If anything speaks authoritatively on the partisan mess that is Washington, D.C., it is the vilification of Interior Secretary Ryan Zinke, seemingly the left's favorite target after President Trump himself.

Just last week, former government ethics chief and serial Trump critic Walter Shaub made headlines when he called Zinke "the poster child for this lawless administration's misuse of governmental authority and resources."

Well, pardon my disbelief, but when Zinke was a member of the Montana Legislature, he was the "poster child" for moderate Republicans. In the preceding 30 years, he was also the "poster child" for over-achievers (He was a 4.0 student at Whitefish High School, as well as class president and football star). Later he was a "poster child" for military heroes, serving as a Navy SEAL in both Iraq wars, Bosnia-Herzegovina and Afghanistan. Then he was Montana's lone congressman, elected twice by the people who know him best.

Here at the Inter Lake, we got to know him as a state legislator, a local businessman, and even as a member of our editorial board for a brief tenure. In every instance, we saw in Ryan Zinke a willingness to look at both sides of an issue, but not to talk out of both sides of his mouth. He was plainspoken to the point of being brutally honest and he made it his personal mission to "restore trust in government."

It is therefore with considerable bewilderment that I have watched the Democratic establishment and the national media try to paint Zinke as some sort of Neanderthal jet-setter criss-crossing the country with a club in one hand and an arsonist's match in the other.

A lot of the issues raised about Secretary Zinke do seem to revolve around travel — taking charter flights on several occasions, bringing his wife with him on flights while he was traveling on official business, selling a campaign-related RV to a friend and fellow Republican at a favorable price. Really? Do you really think other Cabinet members have not used charter flights in the past? Besides, Zinke says that his office is spending less on noncommercial air travel than the previous two secretaries. What's wrong with that? As for the RV, it's up to buyer and seller what price a vehicle is worth. Zinke is not the first person to offer a friend a good deal on a vehicle.

How about this headline from Mother Jones magazine: "The Interior Department Is Giving Business to Secretary Zinke's Billionaire Pal." Wow! That's scandalous! Until you read the story and find out that the business amounted to three night's lodging at Whitefish Mountain Resort for 99 bucks a night. An Interior Department official needed a place to stay while attending the Western Governors Association meeting in Whitefish last June. Sure, Bill Foley, the majority owner of the resort, is a friend of Zinke, but who cares? Has Mother Jones ever been to Whitefish? It's a small world, and probably every hotel owner in the town of 5,000 people knows Zinke. And do we really think that Foley became Zinke's "pal" so that he could somehow get the corner on that $297 of hotel lodging income?

And we wonder why most Americans have no interest in running for office or serving in government! As for Lola Zinke traveling with her husband, why exactly should the Cabinet secretary's wife NOT travel with him? Considering all the stories coming out of D.C. about the antics of other men, we think it might be a good idea if more men in high office traveled with their wives.

Finally, the high crime that drove Walter Shaub crazy was that Zinke had retweeted a message from the House Natural Resources Committee about a squabble over President Trump's decision to shrink several national monuments.

As interior secretary, Zinke had recommended that Trump greatly reduce the size of the Bears Ears National Monument in Utah, among others. The outdoor retailer Patagonia took offense at this move, and sent out an online message that "The President Stole Your Land." Zinke told reporters the claim was "nefarious, false and a lie." He also retweeted the House committee's claim that "Patagonia Is Lying To You."

Shaub said, Zinke had "misused his official position by re-tweeting this wildly inappropriate tweet," and that his "thuggish interference with a business is outside the scope of his duties," suggesting that Patagonia should sue him for libel.

Well, sorry, but if Patagonia wants to engage in a debate about public policy, they had better be prepared for a fight. We know Ryan Zinke is, and we suspect he is better armed.

TRUMP'S YEAR OF LIVING DANGEROUSLY

January 7, 2018

The Associated Press delivered its traditional Top 10 list last month and while the choices actually made more sense than usual, they were particularly antiseptic — as if the AP were afraid to give context to the stories.

What was missing, it seems, is politics. Every story on the list is a bone of contention between liberals and conservatives, between Democrats and Republicans, between Trumpists and Never-Trumpers.

Here's the AP list, from No. 1 to 10: Sexual misconduct, Trump's first year, Las Vegas shooting, hurricane onslaught, North Korea, Trump-Russia probe, Obamacare, tax overhaul, worldwide terror attacks and Islamic State.

When you think about every one of those stories, the first thing you think about is how they are lightning rods of political divisiveness. The media proved this year they could spin anything into a complaint about President Trump, his Cabinet and his policies. Trump is to blame for mass murder. Trump is to blame for climate change. Trump is to blame for that little guy in North Korea being off his rocker. Trump is to blame for Obamacare sucking. Trump is to blame for you paying less in taxes (not sure how this one works!). Trump is to blame for

Muslims hating America, and Obama is to get full credit for ISIS getting its butt handed to it by Trump.

As for the No. 1 story of the year, sexual misconduct, that was a story that broke across the entire spectrum of American society last year, but the involuntary poster child for the "me-too" accusations was Republican Senate candidate Roy Moore, who was tepidly endorsed by President Trump, as the mainstream media mentioned every 10 minutes during the final weeks of the campaign. Disgraced movie mogul Harvey Weinstein probably considered sending the GOP an anonymous donation in thanks for Moore taking the heat off Hollywood for its longstanding culture of sexual predation.

As for "Trump's first year" ... if that was only the second biggest story of 2017, why is it that CNN and MSNBC spent 90 percent of the time talking about it? If you lump Everything Trump (including Never Trump) all together, it should definitely be the No. 1 story of the year, and if you break it down into its component parts, it probably should take up at least five of the Top 10 slots, maybe more.

Here's a reasonable list of 10 significant stories from Trump's first year that will have a major impact on the country for years to come:

1) First and foremost, exposing the national news media as the opposition party. It was not the Democrats who rallied citizens against the president; it was CNN, MSNBC, the New York Times and the Washington Post. Remarkably, President Trump remained standing despite having sustained numerous bites to the ankles during repeated attacks by swamp creatures.

2) Putting Neil Gorsuch on the Supreme Court plus appointing conservative judges to the top federal courts. If Hillary Clinton had been elected, the courts would have been a rubber-stamp for unconstitutional policies for decades to come.

3) Revamping U.S. energy policy and opening the Arctic National Wildlife Refuge to oil drilling. Don't forget: Trump also kept his promise to withdraw from the bogus Paris climate agreement.

4) Overhaul of tax policy, resulting not just in tax cuts for most Americans but also an incentive for corporations to invest in this country and its great workers.

5) Trump's Twitter account rattled the NFL, North Korea, Democrats, and establishment Republicans, among many others. Bravo!

5) The economy and stock market soared under President Trump, in large part due to the massive deregulation that took the shackles off most of our major industries.

6) ISIS is on the run. (Oh wait, I forgot — that was President Obama's plan all along!)

7) Trump took on the "corrupt" leadership of the FBI and the Department of Justice for failing to do its job. Does anyone remember how FBI Director Jim Comey, after being fired by President Trump, broke the law by leaking classified documents to the New York Times in order to get his buddy, Robert Mueller, appointed as special counsel in order to dig up dirt on Trump? "Twilight Zone" rerun maybe?

8) Repeal of the Obamacare individual mandate, which is probably the death knell for Obamacare, which itself was an affront to the liberty-minded principles on which this nation was founded.

9) Fulfilling the promise of not just himself, but also Presidents Clinton, Bush 43 and Obama, to order the U.S. embassy in Israel moved to Jerusalem. That's something new. Call it reality-based foreign policy.

10) Of course, the so-called Trump-Russia probe got its own spot on the AP list. I'll go along with that, but for me the reason it is news is because it represents the bloodless coup d'etat being sponsored by the mainstream media against President Trump and the forgotten men and women who voted for him. When it was revealed that the Hillary Clinton campaign had paid for the Fusion GPS "Russian dossier" that was used to brand Trump a traitor, it should have been enough for any honest American to acknowledge that it was Trump who was betrayed and targeted for removal from office

The fact that he has nonetheless gotten so much done in the Year of Long Knives is a testament to his endurance, vision and intestinal fortitude. Whether he can survive another year of living dangerously remains to be seen, but my money remains on Trump for the win.

HUFFINGTON POST SMEARS RYAN ZINKE WITH FAKE CHARGE

January 27, 2018

The fake news media took another scalp this week, er, I mean, they distorted another story in order to smear the Trump administration.

What else is new, right?

This time it was Interior Secretary Ryan Zinke's turn in the barrel. Oh wait, he's already had his turn in the barrel. Oh wait, multiple turns.

There was the fake story about Zinke's role (none) in getting Whitefish Energy a contract restoring power to Puerto Rico after Hurricane Maria. There was the fake story about Zinke's campaign selling an RV to a Montana politician at a discounted rate (anyone ever heard of depreciation?) There was the fake story about Zinke flying from Las Vegas to his hometown of Whitefish, Montana, aboard a charter flight so that he could attend a meeting of the Western Governors Association hosted by Montana's Gov. Steve Bullock.

It's no accident that Zinke has been a favorite target of the left-wing media for their fake scandal-mongering. Rather, it's because the interior secretary has been one of Trump's most effective surrogates — throwing out harmful regulations, rolling back politically motivated programs, cutting staff and moving programs out of D.C. It's all been very scary for the Swamp Monsters.

But the latest attack on Zinke may be the lowest blow yet.

The Huffington Post broke the news Monday that "Zinke held onto undisclosed shares" in Proof Research, a Whitefish-based company that specializes in production of lightweight rifles using carbon fiber technology.

The story began with this announcement: "Interior Secretary Ryan Zinke is a shareholder in a private Montana company that manufactures and sells firearms and advanced weapons materials, a financial interest he did not disclose when nominated last year."

It is not until seven paragraphs later that the Huffington Post author, Ital Vardi, reveals that the shares held by Zinke are worth so little that they were exempted from disclosure, which isn't required until the value hits (wait for it!) $1,000.

Turns out that Zinke's 1,000 shares (out of nearly 57 million outstanding) are worth somewhere between $250 and $850. That's not $250 each. It's $250 for all of 'em. Yep, a quarter per share.

In other words, Zinke didn't do anything wrong. Oh wait. He met with Proof Research executives for a few minutes on April 11, 2017, for what his calendar called a "Brief Update of Proof Research." To the Huffington Post, that is evidence of skullduggery and "questions of access."

To the rest of us, it is evidence that Zinke is supporting a local business that provides local jobs. And what the Huffington Post does in stories like this is more evidence (as if we needed it) that the fake news media doesn't care about the facts — just the headlines insinuating (in this case, falsely) that conservatives are corrupt.

Who needs a real scandal when you can just invent one?

WHY WOULD A JOURNALISM SCHOOL BE AFRAID OF FREE SPEECH?

February 03, 2018

If there are two institutions that should support free speech without reservation, they would be journalism and higher education.

True journalism cannot exist without freedom of expression, and particularly the freedom to speak openly about any topic without fear of reprisal.

Likewise, the college campus only has meaning as something more than a steppingstone to a salary if we acknowledge that the free exchange of ideas is the fundamental raison d'etre for "the academy."

It was, therefore, doubly disturbing to find out last October that the dean of the University of Montana Journalism School had weighed in against the appearance of conservative columnist Mike Adams that was planned for this month.

Adams, who is a criminology and sociology professor at the University of North Carolina, was invited to be the featured speaker at the 10th annual Jeff Cole Distinguished Lecture Series. Cole was a journalist for the Wall Street Journal, and his widow, Maria, is a major benefactor to the J-school in Missoula. It was she who invited Adams, who writes for Townhall.com and has been widely condemned on the left for his outspoken defense of traditional values. Cole said she doesn't agree with everything Adams writes, but she admired his opposition to censorship and vigorous defense of free speech on college campuses.

"I could hear my husband going 'Now it's time to step up. I was about freedom of speech. I was about the First Amendment I lived opposing censorship every day," Cole told NBC Montana.

So, in honor of her husband, Maria Cole stuck to her guns and insisted on Mike Adams giving the Jeff Cole Distinguished Lecture even when the journalism school backed out of its co-sponsorship.

Larry Abramson, the dean of the Journalism School at the University of Montana, told Cole in an email: "I think we can find a speaker who will talk about free speech issues, without running the risk of offending students."

Abramson told KGVO-AM in Missoula that "the J-school does not have to invite people that we think don't match our priorities or our values as a tolerant, welcoming school."

That discordant justification of intolerance didn't sit well with either Adams, who has written three subsequent columns about "Grizzly bigotry" (referencing the school's mascot), or Maria Cole, who has donated more than $1.2 million to the journalism program over the past 15 years. She opted to shell out a bit more money and booked the 1,100-seat Dennison Theater on the university campus for the night of Feb. 13.

To her credit, the university's interim president Sheila Stearns early on said she disagreed with Abramson's decision, but had not been involved in it.

"Fear of controversy I don't think is and never should be a characteristic of a university," she told the Missoulian. "We're never afraid of ideas. I would say ... make sure the event is well-planned and safe."

Nonetheless, Stearns gave Abramson considerable cover when she issued a joint statement with him saying that the School of Journalism opted not to co-sponsor this year's Jeff Cole Lecture because, according to the Missoulian report, "Adams is not a journalist and is not addressing any specific journalism concerns."

That was a cop-out. Adams is a nationally recognized opinion columnist, an essential element of journalism, and he is addressing restrictions on learning and fighting bias, two issues which are essential not just to journalism, but to a free society.

So what makes Mike Adams such a lightning rod for criticism on the left? Well, he's smart and a good writer. That's a combination that is intolerable to the tolerant left, which promotes diversity of gender, religion and skin color but is terrified by diversity of ideas.

Most notably, Adam drew the ire of Social Justice Warriors at the University of North Carolina and beyond for his 2016 column entitled "A 'Queer Muslim' Jihad?" That column told the story of how the Secret Service had been called to the campus in Wilmington prior to an appearance by Donald Trump because of a Facebook post that raised concerns for the candidate's safety.

Adams pointed out with some humor and a lot of derision that the supposed threat emanated from a woman who was both the founder of the Muslim Student Association and the former president of the university's gay PRIDE group. Considering that homosexuality is not tolerated by fundamental Islam, it was Adams' implicit thesis that the woman was more a danger to herself than anyone else, yet she had been empowered by the university's policy that students have a "right to be unoffended."

The conclusion of that column by Adams can easily fit as the conclusion of this one as well:

"Despite what the diversity proponents tell you, all ideas are not equal. Some are more dangerous than others. Thankfully, the chickens of diversity appear to be coming home to roost."

Let's hope that Dean Abramson got the message. His students deserve to hear from all sides, and as future journalists they should insist on that opportunity.

FEMA FLIP: MAYBE WHITEFISH ENERGY WASN'T SO BAD AFTER ALL!

February 11, 2018

Whitefish Energy probably won't say so, but the power contractor won vindication of sorts last week when it got a shout-out from a FEMA official for its work restoring power in Puerto Rico.

You'll no doubt remember that Whitefish Energy spent time in the dock as public enemy No. 1 last year after it won a

$300 million contract from the island territory to restore power in the wake of Hurricane Maria.

Perhaps you also recall that we never heard that Whitefish Energy wasn't doing the job it had promised to do. What people complained about was that the company was making a lot of money to do a job that desperately needed to be done.

As a result of the public outrage, Whitefish Energy lost the contract after just one month and completed its work in late November after restoring power to approximately 50 percent of the devastated island.

Lo and behold, it is now two and a half months later, and according to the Voice of America, power has been restored to just 60 percent of the island (https://www.voanews.com/a/puerto-rico-electric-grid/4241096.html). In other words, work has slowed to a crawl since Whitefish Energy was removed from the project.

Maybe that's why, in hindsight, an official with the Federal Emergency Management Agency now is singing praises of the tiny company that could.

FEMA Region 9 Deputy Administrator Ahsha Tribble was attending a Puerto Rico Financial Oversight and Management Board meeting in New York on Feb. 1 when she made this shocking statement:

"Without getting kicked from my attorney, Whitefish was there early. They did a good job. They took a risk. That risk is still being weighed."

In other words, the only reason why Whitefish Energy lost the contract was politics.

Tribble was refreshingly candid in her statements, and obviously didn't get the memo that Whitefish Energy was to be treated as an enemy of the state.

"It's been a challenge for the last 128 days that we've been there, but I also want to thank people who took a risk to be there in the beginning," Tribble said in her remarks. "This is different, it's complex and the elephant in the room — PREPA doesn't have a lot of money, as we know, so there was a challenge getting people to want to come there in the beginning."

PREPA is the Puerto Rico Electric Power Authority, and it was that organization which hired Whitefish Energy in the first place. They did so because Whitefish Energy did not demand a fistful of cash up front just for showing up. Yes, Whitefish Energy was going to make a lot of money, but if the lives of Puerto Ricans are truly important, then paying the money should not have turned into the main issue.

Getting power back to the island was what Whitefish Energy promised to do, and the company delivered much more efficiently than whoever picked up the job after Whitefish was unceremoniously kicked off the island by self-righteous know-it-alls.

Tribble's comments are part of a three-hour panel discussion available on YouTube at https://youtu.be/HmyQIj3JC8g

ARE CONSERVATIVE BLACK WOMEN REALLY 'UNSAFE' TO HEAR? OR JUST ON FACEBOOK?

April 15, 2018

Mark Zuckerberg may be a master of the universe, but there are two things even he shouldn't have done — one, allowing Facebook users' private information to be shared with Cambridge Analytica, and two, getting on the bad side of Diamond and Silk.

Error No. 1 is what brought Zuckerberg, the baby-faced founder of Facebook, to the halls of Congress last week to be grilled by politicians who can condone any political sin except the cardinal one —getting caught. Cambridge Analytica supposedly used its analysis of Facebook data to help Donald Trump get elected president. If we are being honest, most politicians' first thought on hearing the news was probably, "Why didn't I think of that?" Their second thought apparently was how can we use this news to make ourselves look morally superior in nationally televised hearings?

That explains why for hour after hour on Tuesday and Wednesday, the nation was gripped with insomnia as we listened to 70-something-year-old senators shame 30-something-year-old Zuckerberg for doing what he's been doing publicly for 14 years — collecting our most private and intimate thoughts and broadcasting them to the world for all to see.

Watching all those preening and precious senators and congressmen searching for some way to capitalize on billionaire Zuckerberg's distress was yet one more reminder of how quickly a politician will turn into a block-sucking leech if there are news cameras on hand to record the feast.

The highlight though had to be Zuckerberg being grilled about Facebook deciding to label "Diamond and Silk" as "unsafe for the community."

Now, most of you probably never heard of Diamond and Silk before last week, which probably tells you everything you need to know about how "dangerous" they are. But for the record, they are a couple of middle-aged African-American sisters from North Carolina who became famous during the last presidential campaign for posting YouTube videos to defend "their man" —Donald Trump. They went viral when they savaged then Fox News anchor Megyn Kelly for daring to question Trump about insulting women. Rosie O'Donnell had it coming, they assured Megyn Kelly ("or Kelly Megyn whatever your name is") for daring to start a feud with Trump in the first place. Clearly these were two women who were willing to turn the heat up on liberals and self-important news anchors ... but does that make them "unsafe for the community"? Really?

That's what Facebook accused Diamond and Silk of being after the political comedy duo complained that the social media giant was restricting traffic to their page. Here was the message from Facebook, as reported by Diamond and Silk:

"The Policy team has came to the conclusion that your content and your brand has been determined unsafe to the community. This decision is final and it is not appeal-able in any way."

The bad news for Zuckerberg was that this story broke just a few days before he was scheduled to appear before Congress. That means he had to answer the tough questions everyone wanted resolved:

Exactly what "brand" was unsafe? The brand of being black women who proudly and loudly support Trump? And what exactly is "the community"? Is it everyone on Facebook? Is it white people who are afraid of black conservatives? Is it liberals?

Whoever it is, they obviously don't have much of a sense of humor.

Of course, Zuckerberg back-pedaled away from the official Facebook statement, claiming that there had been an "enforcement error." The official response from Facebook spokeswoman Sarah Pollack said the message was "inaccurate and not reflective of the way we communicate with our community."

Actually, as anyone who has tried to get an answer out of the nameless, faceless behemoth known as Facebook can tell you, the company doesn't really communicate at all ... they just share their "terms of service" with you and use them as a cudgel to force you back into line.

If you are outspoken conservatives like Diamond and Silk, that means you are supposed to shut up and, well, shut up ... in order to protect the "safe space" that Zuckerberg built.

Fortunately, "outspoken" when applied to Diamond and Silk means that "the community" had better get used to being "unsafe" because these two women clearly have no intention of shutting up. You go, girls.

STRANGE DR. HALPER:
OR HOW THE LEFT LEARNED TO STOP WORRYING & LOVE THE CIA

May 27, 2018

The ability of the intelligence community to shape public opinion through both overt and covert means was never more obvious than in the 10 years following the JFK assassination.

Likewise, there has never been a period when the mainstream media's abject failure to hold government agencies accountable was more apparent than in the years following Dallas.

Until now.

Watching Anderson Cooper or any other CNN host smirk their way through an interview with supporters of President Trump cannot help but bring back memories of Dan Rather dissing proponents of assassination conspiracy theories. But whereas CBS only spent an hour or two every year defending the CIA and the FBI, our own beloved CNN does so 24 hours a day, seven days a week (barring the occasional intrusion of a royal wedding).

Thank goodness that in the world where CNN lives, the CIA and FBI can do no wrong. Unfortunately, in the world where the rest of us live, the intelligence and police agencies of the United States are entirely capable of demonstrating the truth of Lord Acton's dictum that "absolute power corrupts absolutely."

Last week, the vast chasm between the facts and the left-wing media widened even further than ever before. As story after story demonstrated a well-orchestrated campaign within the Obama administration's highest levels to target Donald Trump, the mainstream media took the side of former Director of National Intelligence James Clapper, who argued (on "The View" no less) that Trump should be happy that the FBI was spying on him! Yippee!

Meanwhile, the news media geniuses thought they were being good citizens by not revealing the identity of the Cambridge professor who had reeled in three low-level Trump campaign aides to get the Russia collusion story rolling. In fact, most of the media parrots were being disingenuous by not trumpeting the fact that Stefan Halper had close ties to the CIA for at least four decades and that he was almost certainly running a disinformation campaign that was aimed at protecting the intelligence community from the threat that Trump represented as an outsider who would never go along with the dirty tricks that had become so commonplace in the Deep State's protection of its own power base.

There's no doubt that Halper met with those three Trump aides during the summer of 2016 and apparently reported back to his bosses in the Obama administration about what he learned about the Trump campaign's connection to Russia (pretty much zilch).

I say that his bosses were in the Obama administration because we know that from May 2012 until September 2016, Halper was paid more than $900,000 by the Department of Defense for "classified" work. He also got paid $129,280 in July 2017 (the smallest of his five checks), which may have settled up his account for "work" done during the final year of the Obama administration, and yes, by work I mean spying on Trump.

In July 2016, Halper met in London with Carter Page (the foreign-policy and energy adviser who was additionally spied on with a FISA warrant starting in September 2016).

In August 2016, Halper met with Trump campaign co-chairman Sam Clovis and offered his own services as a foreign-policy adviser to Trump — an offer which wisely was never pursued.

Then, shortly after the meeting with Clovis, Halper reached out to another obscure Trump campaign aide named George Papadopoulos and offered to pay him $3,000 and an all-expenses-paid trip to London to write a paper about energy issues in the Middle East. Both Halper and a young woman identified as Halper's assistant quizzed Papadopoulos about his knowledge of Hillary Clinton's emails and a Russian connection to the campaign. Papadopoulos denied any knowledge of any interference in the campaign.

Apparently, Halper reported to someone in the FBI or CIA or both about his contacts with the three campaign aides, and shortly thereafter the report by British spy Christopher Steele was shopped around to the news media with information alleging connections between Trump and Russia. We won't know more about any of this, or what it proves, until Congress uses its subpoena power to force testimony from Halper and others, but we can certainly be suspicious.

That's because Halper is not just a "Cambridge professor." The Oxford Ph.D. got his start in politics in the Nixon White House, but it was his association with Gerald Ford's CIA director George H.W. Bush that launched him into the national spotlight. Halper's support of Bush in the 1980 presidential campaign resulted in him being named Director of Policy Coordination for the Reagan-Bush ticket when that team was running against Jimmy Carter. Halper is widely believed to have run the plot to gain access to Carter's briefing book prior to a critical debate. Although Halper has long-denied involvement, the plot apparently involved former CIA agents inside the White House with ties to Bush. Carter blamed "Debategate" for his loss to Reagan.

At this point, it might be worth noting that Halper's father-in-law at the time was Ray Cline, the former deputy director of the Central Intelligence Agency. Halper, who was in charge of Bush's opposition research team, also employed a CIA veteran named Robert Gambino. Although Halper remained a paid adviser to the Department of Defense, he left his official government job in the early 1980s to become the founder and chairman of Palmer National Bank in Washington, D.C.

Palmer was funded by a Dallas, Texas, real estate developer named Harvey McLean Jr. who also had ties to George Bush, but according to "Inside Job," an account of the savings & loan scandal of the 1980s, the real money behind the bank came from Herman Beebe Sr., who reportedly had extensive connections to organized crime figures such as Carlos Marcello, who himself has been linked to the assassination of President Kennedy.

"Inside Job" called Beebe's thrifts "potentially the most powerful and corrupt banking network ever seen in the U.S." Beebe later went to jail for bank fraud, but Halper, the chairman of Palmer National Bank, was never caught up in any banking scandal. He was however caught up in another spying scandal when Palmer National Bank was used by Oliver North to funnel money to the Contras during the Iran-Contragate scandal, though which the Reagan administration sent missiles to Iran in exchange for money to secretly fund the Contra rebels in Nicaragua.

Was it just an accident that Halper was involved in the second of two "gate" scandals, or was he part of what historian James Canham-Clyne called the "national security state"? And looking forward, can Halper's involvement in the 2016 "Spygate" scandal be considered anything other than proof that what is now called the "Deep State" is nothing less than the latest manifestation of that CIA-FBI-Defense nexus that Eisenhower warned against as the military-industrial complex?

One thing is certain. You won't get any answers to these questions from the New York Times, the Washington Post, CNN, CBS or NBC. As far as they are concerned, the "intelligence community" is beyond reproach. That is, if you ignore the Kennedy assassination, the overthrow of Salvador Allende in Chile, the wiretapping of Martin Luther King Jr., the failure to stop the 9/11 attacks, Iran-Contra, drug trafficking, lying to Congress, etc.

Yet the geniuses in the national media want you to believe that you have nothing to fear from the CIA or FBI except fear itself. There's no way we should be worried about the national security apparatus of the United States spying on a presidential candidate of the opposition party.

Except, wait a minute, what about Watergate?

Wasn't that a case of a president spying on the headquarters of the opposition political party? And weren't the five Watergate burglars all associated with the CIA? James McCord was a former FBI and CIA agent, and the other four burglars were all tied to the CIA's operations against Cuba after the Castro revolution. The two top dogs were G. Gordon Liddy, a former FBI agent, and E. Howard Hunt, a longtime CIA agent whose own connections went back to the Bay of Pigs and the Kennedy assassination.

So yeah, you can just nod your head and go along with the mainstream asleep-at-the-wheel media while they drive off a cliff, or you can pay attention and start connecting the dots for yourself. We're not in Kansas any more, Toto. This is a Crossfire Hurricane (look it up!) aimed not just at President Trump but at anyone who dares to challenge the establishment elite who have run things for far too long.

PARDON ME, CNN, BUT TRUMP IS THE PRESIDENT, NOT YOU

June 3, 2018

Let's just say that there is this thing called the Constitution, and let's pretend that it is the supreme law of the land.

Now imagine that for years people have ignored this Constitution — which divides power up between a legislative branch, an executive branch embodied by the president, and a judiciary. Over the years, various branches have claimed powers for themselves that are not assigned to them by the Constitution, or have exercised powers in ways that are convenient, but not necessarily responsive to the Constitution. To make it even more interesting, let us assume that various presidents have acceded to the power grabs and allowed their own authority to be taken over by others.

Now, ponder what would happen if years, decades, perhaps centuries after the ratification of the Constitution, a statesman decided to go back to the original document — to the "supreme law of the land" — and acted in accordance with the dictates of that document rather than in the manner to which the times have become accustomed — what would happen to such a man or woman?

Enter President Donald J. Trump, the man of destiny —
who like Samson before him is determined to tear down the
temple of the false gods, whatever fate befall him. Day after day,
week after week, month after month, Trump has demolished
the shibboleths of the swamp and stood on the solid ground laid
down for him by the Founding Fathers.

There are many examples of how Trump acts as president
in the manner envisioned for him by the founders — much to
the astonishment and horror of those who stand on squishy
custom rather than the cold, hard rock of the Constitution, but
this week let's consider the pardon of Dinesh D'Souza.

This was the sixth pardon exercised by President Trump so
far compared to the usual practice of presidents to save up their
pardons for their last day or two in office. Let me ask you: If the
pardon is intended to correct an injustice or to acknowledge
redemption, what exactly is the point of waiting years for justice
to be done?

Didn't Jack Johnson, the black heavyweight boxer who was
sentenced to jail for crossing state lines with his white girlfriend
in 1913 — didn't Jack Johnson wait long enough for justice? Did
he really have to wait for the end of Trump's presidency in 2021
or 2025 to have his name cleared? Trump didn't think so, and
he didn't wait for the Justice Department's Office of the Pardon
Attorney to tell him it was OK to do the right thing. That's what
the feckless fake news media wanted him to do. But Trump just
did what he thought was right without getting "permission."
Just a guess, but maybe that's why he's president and the
Pardon Attorney isn't.

Oh dear, then the president drove Jake Tapper and his
friends at CNN into a tizzy when he speculated on possibly
commuting the sentence of former Illinois Gov. Rod Blagojevich
or pardoning style maven Martha Stewart for their "trumped
up" (sorry, but it's appropriate) charges. But CNN isn't the
president either!

As for D'Souza, he is a conservative author and activist,
which makes it hard for some of our liberal friends to
understand why he wasn't still in jail, let alone why he deserved
a pardon! I won't go into the details of the case here, but suffice

it to say that he donated too much money to a losing political campaign, and instead of being fined (as would usually be the case) he was made an example of by U.S. Attorney Preet Bharara, who was confident he could convince a liberal New York jury that D'Souza was really a scary ham sandwich.

Bottom line: Trump did what we elected him to do — act as president. Here's what the Constitution says about the president: "... he shall have Power to grant Reprieves and Pardons for Offences against the United States." Hmm, sorry Jim Acosta. Looks like Trump wins again.

IMMIGRATION 'CRISIS' BROUGHT TO YOU BY THE MEDIA MATRIX

June 24, 2018

You can either see what the Deep State Media Matrix wants you to see or you can look behind the cable charade and see the truth.

It was pretty obvious that the leftist media and their Democratic pawns were worried about President Trump's rising popularity after his successful Singapore summit with Kim Jung-un and then the release two days later of the inspector general's report demonstrating conclusively that the FBI's so-called Russia investigation was headed up by people who shared Hillary Clinton's belief that Trump and his supporters were a "basket of deplorables."

So who could be surprised really when one day later the topic in the national media had changed from "Trump is winning" to "Trump is an evil monster"?

Starting a week ago Friday, the media discovered (surprise!) that the Trump White House is taking a hard line on illegal immigration — and the pharisees of CNN and MSNBC began dressing themselves in sackcloth and ashes to impress us with the sincerity of their shock and dismay at finding out that children coming across the border illegally are separated from the adults who accompanied them (not necessarily their parents).

Honestly, if you need a give-away (a "tell" as they say in poker) that the left-wing media is conspiring to damage this president, all you need to do is click back and forth between CNN and MSNBC for about three hours. If every time you turn on one of these channels they are parroting the same story back at you with different talking heads pouring ashes on each other and cursing Trump, then you know you are in the middle of a feeding frenzy. Of course, I'll admit that President Trump does throw Twitter chum into the water to rile up these media sharks, but watching their bloodlust take center stage 24/7 is truly astounding, especially to someone such as myself who knows just how much other news is going on at any given moment in time.

Think about it. For one full week, you would be hard pressed to turn on either CNN or MSNBC or watch a late-night "comedy" monologue without catching one more manifestation of the "party line" that Trump is Hitler. In fact, Trump is doing exactly what Trump said he would do when he was elected — enforce immigration policy and do anything he can to discourage illegal immigration into the United States. That's what the people who elected him expected, and it is what the open-borders left-wing establishment will do anything to prevent.

The main arguments against Trump's border policy are all emotion-based, not logic-based. It all boils down to this bit of wisdom: It is sad to see children separated from their parents, and therefore we must not do so. But the facts can easily dismiss this emotion-based argument:

— First of all, the government separates children from their parents under all kinds of circumstances — almost all of which are to benefit the children. Yes, children inevitably cry when separated from their parents or put into a strange new environment, regardless of whether that environment is an improvement over their previous living conditions or not. That is called human nature, and does not prove anything one way or the other. Child Protective Services takes children away from parents to protect the children. People in prison are separated from their children as a matter of necessity. The claim that taking children away from parents is by its very nature cruel or inhumane has no validity.

— Moreover, about 10,000 of the 12,000 immigrant children being held in care facilities by the United States were sent here without their parents. In other words, they were put in the hands of dangerous smugglers by thoughtless parents who — in a sane world — should not have parental rights in the first place.

— The remaining 2,000 children in custody came across the border with some adult who claims to be a parent, but in many cases these "parents" are just other border-crossers trying to take advantage of the system by having a minor in tow. How would we know otherwise? Most of them have no documentation.

— In any case, the law prevents the children from being imprisoned for crossing the border because we are a caring society. Therefore, we have two choices: either house these minors in a separate facility from their arrested parent figures or else release both the minors and the adults into the general population where they will in most cases never be heard from again.

That is not a solution; it is a surrender — and if it sounds familiar, that's because it is the same policy of capitulation that has been followed by both the Bush 44 and Obama administrations. It is also the policy of the European Union, which is facing collapse as a result of willfully opening its borders three years ago.

There is a solution, which is to return families of illegal immigrants to either Mexico or their home country as a unit, quickly and safely. Sen. Ted Cruz, R-Texas, has introduced legislation to do just that, as well as to create family housing options where such illegal immigrants can remain together until their asylum claims are adjudicated. Of course, if Democrats wanted solutions to the problem of children being separated from their parents, they would seize on this compassionate solution, but we all know they won't. What the

Democrats want is an issue to elect more Democrats in the mid-term elections, and that means a solution to immigration is an impediment to their emotion-charged campaign to vilify Republicans.

President Trump, on Wednesday, switched course and signed an executive order to allow illegal immigrant families to stay together while their cases are being litigated. It remains to be seen whether this will satisfy anyone, Republican or Democrat, but at least the president has once again shown that he is interested in solutions, not just talk like so many other politicians. And, of course, the Democratic leadership immediately pivoted away from their argument that children should not be separated from their parents, now saying it is inhumane to hold the children at all. Oddly, the media did not exhibit any hysteria when Democratic President Barack Obama ordered children held in custody after they crossed the border illegally! Again, if you drink the media Kool-Aid, you will never get the straight story — just the spin cycle.

President Trump said last week that he will not allow the United States to become a "migrant camp." Let's hope so. But he also should not do anything to give false hope to foreign citizens who want to escape their own wretched countries to invade ours. Allowing migrants to escape punishment for illegally crossing the border would just encourage more of them to use children as political pawns and put more children in danger as they make the 2,000 mile trek from Central America across Mexico to our porous border.

If you want to end the prospect of children sitting in detention centers in Arizona, Texas, New Mexico and California, there is only one real, permanent solution. Build the wall.

TRUMP GOES TROLLING FOR EAST COAST LIBERALS IN MONTANA!

July 7, 2018

Two weeks ago, Donald Trump Jr. went fly-fishing in Montana. Last week, his father went fishing on Montana, too, but with a different target in mind.

President Trump's stemwinder of a speech at the Four Seasons Arena in Great Falls was all the bait he needed as he went trolling for East Coast liberals and he hauled in a larger than usual catch with a masterful performance in front of 6,600 Montanans.

Trump, of course, has it down to a science how to reel in his favorite species — liberalis journalisticus — but he doesn't have to work too hard since they tend to bite down on any shiny object he throws their way, as if convinced that finally, this time, the fish will outsmart the fisherman. Fat chance.

It's hard to know just where to start cataloging the fake outrage (which is itself a subspecies of what is now called "fake news") that the liberal state media purveys in the wake of any public appearance of the president, but as always CNN provides the textbook example of what it looks like to be at the wrong end of being trolled.

Chris Cillizza, the fake politics editor at CNN, turned in a hysterical (yes, both funny hysterical and crazy hysterical) review called "The 11 most dangerous things Donald Trump said in his Montana speech."

Cillizza claimed that "Trump's speech on Thursday night contained a number of genuinely dangerous lines, lines no president before Trump would even considering [sic] uttering among a small group of friends — much less in front of thousands of people."

The fake moral arbiter then declares that he will explain "why each one poses a real risk to the body populace." (I'm sure Chris knows that it should either be "body politic" or "populace" but not a mash-up of both, so let's give him a pass on that one.)

I wish I had room to go through all 11 of these things that keep Chris Cillizza awake at night to assuage his fears, but I can only pick out a few of the biggies — most of which are also scaring the folks over at MSNBC and the New York Times. Someone has to help these people sleep better at night, and I guess it must be up to me.

One of the biggest worries for Cillizza and his East Coast cronies is that Trump has a "dangerously naive view of the Russian president [Vladimir Putin]." Why? Because Trump made fun of the media for believing that he is "dangerously naive." Yeah, you read that right. Trump's big sin was that he challenged the national media to actually pay attention and not parrot left-wing talking points.

So what exactly did Trump say? Well, the only part that Cillizza quotes — and the part you probably heard played over and over on CNN and MSNBC — is this: "You know what? Putin's fine. He's fine. We're all fine. We're people."

Well, that's not exactly damning evidence, but as reported by the dishonest media, Trump said that he thought Putin was a "fine person." No. He said that Putin was "fine" and he said that Putin was a person ("We're people.") But he never said that Putin was a fine person as a character endorsement.

Trump was trolling the media and Democrats for their patronizing view that somehow Donald Trump missed the Cold War and would be taken advantage of by the crafty Russian during their upcoming meeting in Finland.

The context, which was entirely omitted by the fake news media, was that Trump had just finished discussing the press coverage of his meeting with Kim Jung-Un in Singapore, where it was claimed that President Trump had "lost" in the summit simply by meeting with Kim in the first place.

It also came after Trump had described the situation in Europe where NATO members are doing trade deals with Russia while demanding that the U.S. keep them safe from Russia...

Dismissing reports that he is "angry at NATO" or that "he loves Russia," Trump then made this statement:

"I will say this ... I'm meeting with President Putin next week and getting along ... with Russia and getting along with China and getting along with other countries is a good thing, it's not a bad thing ... it's a good thing."

And then continuing to make fun of the Democratic meme that Trump is "soft" on Russia, the president said, "I will say this, I'm gonna have to ask them [the Russians] this question: How bad has it been since Trump has been in? Take a look. We've just increased our military spending by 700 billion dollars. We've become a nation that is exporting energy for the first time, so many things, and you look at all the money NATO is getting now [thanks to Trump's pressure on Europe to pay its fair share] ... they're probably saying in Russia "You know if we did like this guy we made a big mistake; we'd rather have crooked Hillary Clinton!"

The president then stated the obvious — a principle which seems to have been the main victim of the "Russia collusion" hoax — that it is better as Winston Churchill once remarked to meet "jaw to jaw" than to wage war.

"Getting along with other countries" — the president said Thursday — "and you're talking nuclear powers in all fairness ... getting along is really a nice thing, it's a smart thing ... we're going to beat everybody ... we have the greatest military and hopefully we'll never have to use it... You know the only way you're never gonna have to use it? If it's so powerful, so good, so strong that nobody wants to play games and that's what we're doing..."

The president then circled back to the theme of the elite media and their complaint that just meeting with an enemy like Kim Jung-Un means you have lost.

"Now they are saying it with Putin ... [Speaking in a pretentious voice meant to mimic the media's talking heads] 'Well Putin is highly prepared, and Trump — will he be prepared for the meeting?' ... Trust me, we'll do just fine. Fake news. Bad people. [Resuming pretentious media voice] 'Will he be prepared? Will he be prepared?' and I might even end up having a good relationship, but they're going, 'Will President

Trump be prepared? You know President Putin is KGB and this and that.'"

And after this long dismissive, discursive one-man colloquy, Trump hits his stride to the cheers of the crowd, and finally resolves not that Putin is a "fine person" but that he is fine as an adversary, that Trump understands him, and will not be intimidated. He's just one more opponent like all the others that have underestimated Trump: "You know what, Putin's fine. He's fine. We're all fine. We're people. Will I be prepared? Totally prepared. I've been preparing for this stuff my whole life. They don't say that ... And you really do. You really... I'll tell you what... because I see the way they write... they're so damned dishonest and I don't mean all of them because some of the finest people I know are journalists. Really. Hard to believe when I say that, I hate to say it, but I have to say ... but 75 percent of those people are downright dishonest ... They're fake."

Which brings me to my final point. Cillizza takes offense at the president continuing to call out the press in the wake of the massacre at the Annapolis Capital Gazette, even though the reporter begrudgingly admits that the president's rhetoric had nothing to do with the murders of five people. Cillizza says, nonetheless, "the responsible thing" for the president to do would be to not challenge the press to be fair and honest. Sorry, Chris, but the responsible thing to do as journalists would be to tell the truth, the whole truth and nothing but the truth. Then you would have a shield against all claims of bias or dishonesty. But maybe that's asking too much.

JOURNALISTS USED TO FIGHT FAKE NEWS; TODAY THEY PRETEND IT DOESN'T EXIST

August 12, 2018

How — I am sometimes asked — can a journalist like me question the ethics of a fellow journalist reporting about the White House? Shouldn't all reporters and editors stick together?

Well, no. They should stick with the truth.

Consider if the question were turned around. What if we asked: How can a politician question the ethics of a fellow politician? Shouldn't all politicians stick together?

Obviously, some of them would like to. That would make it easier for them to lie, cheat and steal — what we now call "living in the swamp."

But fortunately there are some politicians who insist on holding each other accountable; by the same exact token, one hopes there are a sufficient number of journalists who will hold each other accountable when members of their trade do shoddy work — which, in our case, means either getting the facts wrong or intentionally misleading the public about what the facts mean.

In fact, the term "fake news" — popularized to the consternation of the media by President Trump — was first put in wide use hundreds of years ago. Nor is Trump the first president to question the veracity of press reports. No less a personage than Thomas Jefferson, who valued the free press as highly as anyone, nonetheless found many of its practitioners to be wanting in judgment and ethics.

In a letter to John Norvell in 1807, Jefferson wrote: "To your request of my opinion of the manner in which a newspaper should be conducted, so as to be most useful, I should answer, 'by restraining it to true facts and sound principles only.' Yet I fear such a paper would find few subscribers. It is a melancholy truth, that a suppression of the press could not more completely deprive the nation of it's benefits, than is done by it's abandoned prostitution to falsehood. Nothing can now be believed which is seen in a newspaper. Truth itself becomes suspicious by being put into that polluted vehicle."

I doubt many of those who attack the president today would be comfortable calling Jefferson by the same rude names they use against Trump, but you never know. In any event, as I discovered by looking at several hundred references to fake news over the last 200 years at newspaperarchive.com, there is no greater critic of fake news than the legitimate press — which rightfully yearns to distinguish itself from the unethical work of lesser journalists. I found more than 4,000 citations for "fake news" from before 2015 when Donald Trump announced his presidential bid. Throw in the more generic "false news" and you get another 13,000 citations. They range from false reports on various economic markets (possibly intended to manipulate profits) to fake news from the frontier (exaggerating the danger of Indian uprisings) to the rumor spread by the Associated Press in 1895 that President Grover Cleveland had been assassinated at his summer home. About the latter report, the Daily News of Milwaukee wrote, "The poor old Associated Press is again in a peck of trouble. It gets involved in so many fakes that it keeps one busy to follow them."

Same could be said about the current Associated Press, except there are few editors who have the temerity to call them out for their mistakes, whether intentional or otherwise.

It should be noted that not all of those thousands of citations of "fake news" in the historical archives of newspapers are aimed at the press as the culprit. There can be other sources of false news than newspapers, but a large portion of the references to fake news in the past 200 years or more are cases of journalists defending the reputation of their chosen profession by admonishing those among them who do not live up to the common standards of fairness and truth.

No surprise. The credibility of newspapers and of journalism in general depend on our ability to get the story right in the first place, and to admit our mistakes promptly in the second place. That's what we stress at the Inter Lake. Our reporters take seriously their responsibility for getting both sides of the story, and for keeping their own opinions out. We aren't perfect, and when we fall short, we admit it.

Unfortunately, it seems that some big-name journalists today consider themselves and their chosen profession above reproach. When President Trump calls them out for publishing fake news, they merely put their thumbs in their ears and shout back petulantly "NOT FAKE NOT FAKE!" no matter how obvious it is to an objective observer that it was indeed fake.

A prime example of that occurred last Sunday morning when President Trump's tweet about the Trump Tower meeting held by Don Jr. in 2016 was widely trumpeted as some kind of new (and damning) revelation when actually the president had said the exact same thing (in virtually the same words) a year earlier. Someone was asleep at the switch, but it wasn't Trump's tweet manager.

Another tweet by President Trump last weekend also elicited shock and outrage from the usual suspects in the media when he said, "The Fake News [outlets] ... purposely cause great division & distrust. They can also cause War! They are very dangerous..."

All over the "vast wasteland" (look it up) of cable news, the talking heads either feigned ignorance or just plain showed their ignorance as they claimed that there was no way a newspaper could cause a war. How dare Trump say otherwise?

The only problem is that newspapers and in particular fake news have caused wars, most notably the Spanish-American War, which was sparked in part by the "Yellow Journalism" reporting of the newspapers of William Randolph Hearst and Joseph Pulitzer, especially when the U.S.S. Maine naval ship mysteriously exploded and sank in Havana Harbor. "Remember the Maine! To hell with Spain" became the rallying cry and the newspapers urged the U.S. to war even though the cause of the explosion was never resolved.

The Philadelphia Times, on April 19, 1898, had this to say about the tactics of Hearst and Pulitzer and fake news:

"In periods of great public excitement, and especially when a nation is convulsed by the apprehension of war with all its countless horrors, the public press has an exceptionally responsible duty to perform. It should resolutely print the truth, the whole truth and nothing but the truth.

"Since the beginning of our severely strained relations with Spain, some of our public journals have done more to degrade American journalism than has ever been done in the same period in the history of our country. The most reckless sensationalism has been adopted and continued from day to day, until the more intelligent portion of the reading public has ceased to respect newspaper publications relating to the war, because of the unparalleled extravagance of the fake news given in some of the leading journals of the country. They have not only brought an ineffaceable stain upon the journalism of the nation, but they have wantonly and maliciously inflamed public sentiment by the most atrocious perversions of the truth."

That indictment of the New York World and the New York Journal and the other Hearst and Pulitzer papers stands as one of the high-water marks of American journalism. It is so easy for a newspaper to call out the unethical antics of a politician, but much more courageous to challenge one's own peers to a higher standard. May the spirit of the Philadelphia Times prevail as journalism lives through another period of "reckless sensationalism" and, yes, regrettably, "fake news."

'I AM PART OF THE RESISTANCE INSIDE THE NEWS MEDIA,' AND I'M NOT ANONYMOUS

September 9, 2018

Over the years, I've been asked to run anonymous letters dozens of times, but I've never done so. The explanation is always the same: Our readers have a right to judge the validity of a submitted opinion based on who you are and whether you have an ax to grind against the subject of your letter.

The opinion editors of the New York Times obviously feel differently. On Sept. 5, they ran a hyperbolic op-ed entitled "I am Part of the Resistance Inside the Trump Administration" that the newspaper said was written by a "senior official in the Trump administration."

The op-ed told us nothing new. It merely confirmed what has been obvious for a long time — that many figures in the Washington, D.C., establishment fear President Donald Trump and are working to undermine his administration. That doesn't justify giving the op-ed's author the privilege of speaking under cover of darkness. If there is someone in the White House working to subvert the president's agenda, the rest of us — the American people who elected President Trump — have a right to know who that is, and the president has a right to hold that person accountable.

Of course, the New York Times could have just turned their anonymous op-ed into one more of their anonymous sources that they quote daily in their own tireless efforts to subvert the president. That would have been more fitting, since at least we already know what the Times' agenda is.

The smartest thing former grey eminence Steve Bannon ever said was when he called the national mainstream media "the opposition party." The Democratic Party barely has a presence on the national stage these days; it is CNN, MSNBC, the New York Times and the Washington Post that carry forward the left-wing banner these days.

The word treason has been thrown around recently to describe the attempts to undermine the presidency of Donald Trump, and though treason as a crime has a very narrow definition in the United States, it also has a broader meaning that is certainly appropriate to describe the betrayal of the president and the Constitution by various powerful people and institutions.

In some ways, we are living through a new and more intense version of "The Treason of the Intellectuals," described by French author Julien Benda in his book of that name in 1928. "Our age," he wrote, "is the age of the intellectual organization of political hatreds." Anyone who watched the Senate Judiciary Committee's disgraceful hearing on the confirmation of Judge Kavanaugh to the Supreme Court knows that we are still living in such an age, only more so.

Benda wrote at the beginning of the age of mass communication, and yet he already saw that "political passions have attained a universality never before known. ... Thanks to the progress of communication and, still more, to the group spirit, it is clear that the holders of the same political hatred now form a compact impassioned mass, every individual of which feels himself in touch with the infinite number of others, whereas a century ago such people were comparatively out of touch with each other and hated in a 'scattered' way."

The internet has accelerated these changes in ways that Benda could never have imagined, but he did state that these "coherences" of passion "will tend to develop still further, for the will to group is one of the most profound characteristics of the modern world."

It seems that we are now living out Benda's worst nightmare — an age of manipulation of the masses by those who think they know better — whether you call them the "deep state," the "opposition party," "the national elite," "the entrenched bureaucracy," or just "the establishment."

Benda's conception of the intellectuals, which he distinguished in the original French text as "clercs," is in opposition to the laymen or the masses, and thus should be understood as a class of people who envision themselves as superior to what we now call "the deplorables." It is these intellectuals who envision themselves as the guardians of policy and politics, and who work to protect the status quo against any inversion that threatens their power.

There is no exact parallel between Benda's assessment of the 1920s and our own situation as we approach 2020, but it is enough to understand that there exists a duality between the common man and the "intellectual," and that the intellectuals seek to dominate political thought and use political passions as their weapon of oppression.

As Benda put it, "the 'clerks' now exercise political passions with all the characteristics of passion — the tendency to action, the thirst for immediate results, the exclusive preoccupation with the desired end, the scorn for argument, the excess, the hatred, the fixed ideas. The modern 'clerk' has entirely ceased to let the layman alone descend to the market place. The modern 'clerk' is determined to have the soul of a citizen and make vigorous use of it."

It is the fixed ideas of the establishment against which Donald Trump arose like a modern-day iconoclast, and there is no wonder that the establishment is terrified of him. They conspired against him in the halls of the Justice Department and the FBI before he was elected, and thanks to a fake Russian dossier funded by the Hillary Clinton campaign, they have worked to sabotage him through the Mueller "investigation." There's no doubt they could very well destroy him because they see no bar on their authority — not the Constitution, not the law, not common decency.

As Benda described a similar phenomenon in his own time, we "see men of thought, or men giving themselves out as such, professing openly that they would not submit their patriotism to any check on the part of their judgment, proclaiming ... that 'even if the country is wrong, we must think it is right,' denouncing as 'traitors of the nation' those of their compatriots who retain their liberty of mind, or at least of speech, in regard to their country."

As someone who has been similarly denounced, let me conclude by saying that "I am Part of the Resistance Inside the News Media." To paraphrase the Times' anonymous op-ed, I believe my "first duty is to this country" and that the news media "continues to act in a manner that is detrimental to the health of our republic." I am not loyal to the news industry but to the truth. Anonymous sources, biased reporting and smirking superiority in the newsroom should be decried by everyone who works in this business. We can only get to the truth by putting aside our personal beliefs and telling stories fairly and without an agenda of our own.

The news media should not be "the opposition party" to Republican presidents; rather, it should be the umpire that fairly calls balls and strikes. Is that too much to ask?

A WORD TO THE WISE: OVERTHROW YOUR TECH OVERLORDS WHILE YOU STILL CAN

September 16, 2018

When the history of the 21st century is written, odds are that it will be the story of the slow but willing enslavement of the masses by the tech overlords.

Sure we love our smartphones, but is that any reason to surrender our freedom to think for ourselves? The more dependent we become on Google, Twitter and Facebook for information, the less certain we can be that we are looking at the real world and not the manufactured Matrix deemed suitable for adult consumption by Silicon Valley.

What price are you willing to pay for the convenience of unlimited access to limited truth?

These questions arise this week, as they have almost every week for the past decade, as the evidence mounts that search engines and social media are not just a conduit of reality, but a filter of it. There is the whole truth, and then there is the Google Truth. More and more, we are getting the Google Truth, and the devil take the hindmost.

Of course, the whole truth is there to see for anyone who takes the time to look for it, but in an age where critical thinking is a lost art, and where the day is easily filled with comforting distractions, it is even harder for those "with eyes to see" to remember to use them discerningly than it was back when Jesus warned us to do so.

Breitbart.com released a leaked video last week that showed Google executives meeting with staff members on the Friday after Trump's election on Nov. 8, 2016, and lamenting their failure to elect Hillary Clinton.

Among the many shocking comments, Google cofounder Sergey Brin consoled his crew:

"Most people here are pretty upset and pretty sad. I find this election deeply offensive, and I know many of you do too. It's a stressful time, and it conflicts with many of our values. I think it's a good time to reflect on that. ... So many people apparently don't share the values that we have."

Google insists that nothing at the meeting suggests that the company would let its employees' obvious bias affect "the way we build or operate our products." That would be reassuring if it were not so laughable. Just repeat the experiment made by PJmedia.com, when they found that 96 percent of the Google results about Trump were negative. Do your own search on Google for the phrase "Trump news" and study the results. When I did it, every result on the first page was anti-Trump, including headlines such as "House GOP 'screwed' as bad political numbers pile on Trump," "Fox News hosts blast Trump for 'distasteful' remarks on Puerto Rico," and "What if Trump has been a Russian asset since 1987?"

The first positive story about Trump came on the fourth page of Google results (39th on the list) when a CNBC story reported on Trump's claim that "Facebook, Twitter, Google 'have to be careful'" not to rig the news. Kudos to reporter Ryan Browne for telling the story straight when so many other outlets used the occasion as one more opportunity to bash Trump.

Of course, it's not just Google that is deciding what you should and shouldn't read. Twitter, which also denies that it has a political agenda, is one of the worst offenders.

Last week, Twitter rejected four ads proposed by the Center for Immigration Studies because they supposedly contained "hateful content" in the form of either "hate speech" or "advocacy against a protected group." The so-called hate speech was advocating in favor of enforcing current U.S. immigration laws that target "criminal aliens" or "illegal aliens." So are we to assume that "illegal aliens" are now a "protected class"? Not by federal law, but only by Twitter law, which sums up the problem nicely. Are we comfortable letting Big Tech dictate to us what we can and cannot say (or see) in the modern town square?

I'm not, and yet I suspect that most Americans, especially conservatives, will demur against trying to regulate access to information on the internet. Why? Because we also support the free market and want to limit government regulation of private enterprise. Therein lies the rub.

Even though the behavior of Twitter and Google is inexecrable, the argument will be made that no one has to use Google or Twitter, so they do not deserve regulation. Moreover, you could make the case that Google's filtering of information is a form of protected "free speech" in that no one is obligated to tell the "whole truth" except when sworn to do so. Just as I pick and choose what information to include in a column, so too Google could argue that it is free to pick and choose what information to provide to the public — and civil libertarians are likely to accept such an argument.

This is a perfect example of the most insidious of Saul Alinsky's "Rules for Radicals" — "Make the enemy live up to its own book of rules."

Alinsky's "Rules" are a Machiavellian roadmap for anyone who is willing to do anything to gain power. For the most part, those who have embraced the "Rules" are — like Alinsky himself — radical leftists who are intent on restructuring American society into a socialist utopia like Venezuela (sarcasm intended).

It is rather obvious, as you go down the list of the rules that they are constantly in play as the progressive movement inside both the Democratic and Republican parties works to undermine the conservative movement embodied somewhat paradoxically by President Trump. This is true in attacks on Trump himself, as well as attacks on targets that are associated with Trump such as Judge Brett Kavanaugh or Interior Secretary Ryan Zinke.

• "Ridicule is man's most potent weapon."
• "Keep the pressure on."
• "Pick the target, freeze it, personalize it, and polarize it."

But "Make the enemy live up to its own book of rules" is the most dangerous of the "Rules" because, as in jiu jitsu, it turns the enemy's strength into a weapon against him.

In this case, those who wish to control the flow of information (and thus control the culture) have asked conservatives to surrender their voices as the price for keeping a free market. Should they accede to this Hobson's choice, conservatives will soon find they have neither a voice nor a free market.

Google is no different than any other public utility. It is not an accident that we originally referred to the Internet as a superhighway, and just as the public has a vested interest in protecting the neutrality of highways, phone service, and power transmission, so too do we have a right to demand neutrality in how the storage and transmission of information to the public takes place.

If we surrender that right, then we have no one to blame but ourselves for the dystopian nightmare that will follow.

JIM ACOSTA AND THE HUBRIS OF CELEBRITY JOURNALISM

November 19, 2018

When do Jim Acosta's 15 minutes of fame expire?

Has there ever been anyone less deserving of the spotlight who has managed to hog it quite so thoroughly as CNN's White House show horse? Most recently, on Nov. 7, Acosta gave President Trump a moral lecture in the form of a loaded "question" about why Trump called the migrant "caravan" an "invasion." According to Acosta, it is not an invasion because the migrants were hundreds of miles away, and besides, the migrants aren't going to be "climbing over walls and so on."
One week later, as we all know, members of the caravan (and of course it's not really a "caravan") were sitting astride the border wall and invading U.S. territory. So much for Acosta's credibility.

Mind you, the president answered Acosta's "When are you going to stop beating your wife?" question, and acknowledged that he and the reporter have a difference of opinion about what an invasion is, but Acosta was pressing his left-wing agenda and not actually trying to elicit information with his "fake question." Moreover, Acosta then tried to commandeer the press conference and ask another unrelated question even after the president had called on someone else. It wasn't until Acosta refused to turn over the microphone to a White House intern and insisted on sparring with the president that Trump called him a "rude, terrible person." Later, the White House withdrew Acosta's press pass on account of his jostling with the intern when refusing to hand over the microphone, resulting in CNN suing the Trump administration to protect its preening, petulant reporter.

Face it, if Acosta were a grandstanding lawyer, he would have long since been found in contempt of court by the presiding judge, but because he is instead a grandstanding TV journalist he apparently has a constitutional right to do and say anything he wants so long as CNN is willing to sign his paycheck.

Really? Have we actually reached the point where the First Amendment enshrines the right to be rude? And if Jim Acosta has that right, then what is to stop every so-called journalist in the world from showing up at the White House with a whoopee cushion and a demand for a press pass?

Pardon me for not joining the journalistic pack and defending the divine right of reporters to act as buffoonishly as possible without suffering consequences. I know that is the response de rigueur for editors when someone like Acosta goes out of bounds, but I bring nearly four decades of experience in community journalism to the table, and to me Acosta is just one more self-important reporter who gives a bad name to the hard-working journalists who take their job more seriously than their haircut.

Truth be told, I have hired a couple of reporters and photographers over the years who thought they could be rude to the subjects they were covering. But unlike CNN I didn't sue the sources who objected to the bad behavior of my employees; instead I sat down the culprits and told them that a repeat performance would not be tolerated. That, in a nutshell, seems to be the difference between community journalism and celebrity journalism. No one wants to sit Jim Acosta down and tell him the truth. He is a pretentious boor who needs to settle down and do his job — respectfully!

This entitlement mentality of his (and others in the TV pack) seems to be a manifestation of the mistaken belief that journalists have been granted some kind of hereditary nobility endowed to them by Woodward and Bernstein of Watergate fame. It's almost as though these celebrity journalists consider themselves the Sun Kings of democracy and that everything else, including presidents and paupers, revolves around them.

But wait! Bob Woodward himself last week withdrew his blessing from CNN and Acosta. According to a series of tweets from NBC's Dylan Byers, Woodward said at the Global Financial Leadership Conference in Naples, Florida, "In the news media there has been an emotional reaction to Trump. Too many people for Trump or against Trump have become emotionally unhinged about this." The legendary Washington Post investigative reporter also complained about CNN suing the White House: "This is a negative ... Trump is sitting around saying, 'This is great.' ... "When we engage in [Trump's strategy] we're taking his bait." ... "The remedy [isn't a lawsuit], it's more serious reporting about what he's doing."

Say what you will about Woodward, and I don't always agree with him, but he is on the right side of this debate. No one in journalism has earned the right to claim the rewards of celebrity journalism more than Woodward, but yet he has actually managed to remain somewhat humble and seemingly unimpressed with his own accomplishments. More power to him.

Meanwhile, Jim Acosta and CNN continue in their endeavor to modernize the 1813 complaint of Thomas Jefferson to the age of cable TV news:

"The newspapers of our country, by their abandoned spirit of falsehood, have more effectually destroyed the utility of the press than all the shackles devised by Bonaparte."

Or as Donald Trump said more pointedly in response to being accosted by Acosta, "When you report fake news, which CNN does a lot, you are the enemy of the people" — and also, he might have added, the enemy of the free press's utility and reputation.

REAL FEARS ABOUT FAKE NEWS:
A WARNING FROM GOLDWATER

December 17, 2018

I recently received a reminder that the concept of fake news didn't just spring fully formed out of the forehead of Donald Trump in 2015, but has been a real specter in American politics for decades.

Roseann Quinn, a reader from Kalispell, Mont., sent me a letter from the late Sen. Barry Goldwater, dated Sept. 19, 1974, that laid out a perfect case for its existence long ago.

It was written by the Arizona Republican to Orion T. Quinn, a World War II veteran who had used his piloting skills later in life to transport politicians such as Goldwater and Gov. Ronald Reagan to their political and campaign stops throughout California and elsewhere. Roseann's husband, David, had inherited the letter from his father, who died in 1983, and Roseann came across it recently when rummaging through family mementos. It's a reply to a letter from the elder Quinn, which from the context must have been a complaint about biased and unethical news reporting.

"Believe me," Goldwater responded, "your concern about the press and media is shared by many of us in public life. I have been talking with editors around the country and particularly with the editor of the biggest paper here in Washington" – presumably Ben Bradlee at the Washington Post, fresh off the Watergate story – "pointing out that unless something is done to reinstill the American's [sic] faith in the news media, they could well lose the freedom of the press."

That is a significant admission by Goldwater — that he was worried an irresponsible press might somehow provoke such a backlash that it would eventually lose the protections afforded by the First Amendment. That is a worrisome prospect, one we have not yet reached even today, and it should be emphasized that Goldwater made the statement soon after Watergate, which arguably was the high-water mark of American journalism.

The next line is particularly interesting: "To really appreciate the abuse that news is receiving, you have to live in Washington where the news is made and you hear it made on the Floor of the Senate or the House or the remarks of the President and then read what is said about it the next day, and you wonder if you really heard what you thought you did or not."

That phrase "the abuse that news is receiving" may sound at first like a complaint of Jim Acosta that he is being mistreated by scary Sarah Sanders, but it is far different. Here, Goldwater is according "the news" a kind of revered status as something that exists not as the work product of CBS or CNN but as a truth, an ideal — the objective facts of what really happened. In Goldwater's formula, it is the journalists themselves who are abusing the news — by stretching it or slanting it or just not understanding it. I don't know if anyone working in the celebrity news business today would even recognize the possibility of such an objective truth in politics, but if they do, then the rest of us can attest to the fact that this truth is being abused by agenda-driven reporters who don't revere "the news" as much as their own ascendant careers.

Although it is natural for 21st century news consumers to see Goldwater's complaint through the prism of Donald Trump's war against "fake news," it should be noted for the record that Goldwater presumably found fault with the news media of the 1970s without consulting Trump. It is certainly not surprising that the conservative icon was wary of the mainstream media since it had savaged him during the 1964 presidential race. Most famously, Goldwater's credo that "[e]xtremism in the defense of liberty is no vice" was twisted into a dangerous confession of extremism as some shadowy threat to the government instead of what it was — a straightforward pledge to do everything in his power to protect American freedom, the same pledge you would hope to hear from any presidential candidate. The media also somehow forgot the second half of Goldwater's statement: "Moderation in pursuit of justice is no virtue."

In retrospect, Goldwater probably offers the closest parallel to the savage treatment accorded to Donald Trump, with the exception that the attacks against Goldwater were more effective. He was a dismal loser in the 1964 race against President Lyndon Johnson, thanks in large measure to such "abusive" reporting as the article in the misleadingly named Fact magazine titled "1,189 Psychiatrists Say Goldwater Is Psychologically Unfit to Be President."

By 1974, however, when Goldwater sent his letter to Orion Quinn, he had undergone the image makeover the media reserves for Republicans who speak out against fellow party members (think John McCain or Jeff Flake, to name a couple of other Arizonans). It was well known that just a month before writing the Quinn letter, Goldwater had told President Nixon that he had one choice — resign voluntarily or be impeached and removed from office — which meant Goldwater had started to make the transition from dangerous firebrand to elder statesman.

Still, he never surrendered his integrity, nor his insight, and the Quinn letter demonstrates incontrovertibly that the conscience of the Republican Party would have understood and applauded President Trump's war against fake news. Like Trump, Goldwater seemed to know it was a losing battle, but one worth fighting. As our current president has repeatedly said, it's not about being hurt by negative news, but about expecting fair news.

"I am going to keep trying to get them to straighten out," Goldwater concluded. "All I ask is objectivity: I don't want the news slanted at any direction, just toward the truth."

More than four decades later, we are still waiting.

Afterword

"FROM COUNTRY EDITOR TO AMERICA'S DIARIST"

BY RICHARD L. SPENCER

I began reading Frank Miele quite fortuitously some 10 years ago and have never regretted it since I was attracted to the title of one of his columns while searching the internet. I forget which article it was, but I do remember how immediately astonished I was that something as sophisticated came from a Mid-Western editor of a small town newspaper called the Daily Inter Lake published out of Kalispell, Montana. As one begins reading these weekly articles from the past decade, you will find them still true, even more so. They are forever prescient, and a stark warning to our Republic: Follow the Constitution. One can ignore reality, but one cannot ignore the consequences of ignoring reality; and, that is the style you will find in Mr. Miele's fundamental thinking and comments, and that is what makes them so valuable for all of America. They are now to be published in the first three volumes of "The Heartland Diaries," entitled "Why We needed Trump," and in subsequent volumes critiquing the media, studying the history of the Progressive movement's subversion of the Constitution, and praising America's heartland values.

I quickly became a consistent reader and also was leaving comments. After that I was sending the articles to friends who replied, "they were going to become a follower." My Sunday mornings soon became one of coffee, Frank's article of the week, and my wife reading to me followed by discussion of its content. We were always amazed at the deepness of his thoughts as they went beyond the political realm and were loaded with Common Sense that is a rare commodity in journalism, especially when it relates to problem-solving policies

What is so alluring about Mr. Miele's "Heartland Diary" entries is that they come from the soul, they are thoroughly researched, and they always have a critical point that causes the reader to evaluate his own opinions. That is one of the major clues of a solid thinker — soul in his writing that stands the test of time. Now, as the decade has passed, I seldom read other editors because when it comes to philosophic intent or critical thinking, Frank is the master. I am always astounded by how rich his mind is and how he has had the energy and intellect to produce such readable articles week after week for the better part of two decades. No one can match him. However, his readers are the winners, as they have the wisdom needed to appreciate such work.

It is a feather in Frank's cap to be known as one who pursues the truth, week after week, no matter the public derision. Mr. Miele has been the country's most courageous editorial writer through some of our most troubled times and a fine example of the best that journalism has to offer.

The difference between Frank and the national herd of editors is clear — that when he speaks of the principles of government he knows that of which he speaks. The others speak merely of their own bias rather than the principles elucidated by our Founders.

Most journalists have lost their way to the detriment of our country; Frank never has, and that is a difficult public road for him to travel. Courage and truth are his first line of defense against the naysayers, as it should be for all. Unless we honestly admit, as a whole, to the "why" we have allowed our country and its society to be slowly devoured by this monster of Moral Relativism, we will never come close to resolving our political divide.

This basic conflict about governance in the "Heartland Diaries" that you are about to read has been the fuel for the best of mankind and the worst; and, it is at the forefront of our democratic world that struggles to govern mainly through political parties. However, the folly of the argument between the two views of governance lies in the fact that the U.S. Constitution is largely one of a constrained view of the people to be governed, not an unconstrained view. "Heartland Diaries" is clear on that point.

There should be no argument that our Founders' goal was to construct a governance system that allowed man his individual freedom to be all that he can be. The constrained vision sees freedom as finite and argues that government power is accumulated at the expense of private freedom. It is not a living Constitution as many progressives believe it should be. One must never underestimate a country's inability to imagine its own destruction fostered by its political elite through their selfish quest for power with means that are morally unjustifiable, but best serve their desired outcomes. The Constitution, as written, is Frank's map — forming the basis for his thinking and writing as highlighted in the "Heartland Diaries."

That single attribute of a principled search for truth is so lacking by others in journalism, even though they have been given a special constitutional mandate to protect the public, that Frank comes to the party almost alone in his efforts to inform. And, that in my opinion, makes him one of the outstanding and finest examples of his profession. He, unlike others, never blinks at the truth! Frank is only conservative in his protection of the U.S. Constitution and strives for resolutions to problems that have to be pulled like weeds from the garden and replanted with workable policies.

The readings in "Heartland Diaries" are a serial history beginning with the advent of the 9/11 terrorist attack that briefly united all of America and then fell apart because of the Progressive lust for power. Mr. Miele writes from the point of view of a serious, honest, patriot of America's founding and its growth to become a world power. Now, we are faced with the current Progressive movement by the left to embrace socialism, and no clear distinction can be drawn between "socialism" and "communism." That comment is certainly to be heeded by the country at large.

The historical outcome defining socialism is how the few have managed to plunder the many through the sophistry that persuades the victims that they are being robbed for their own benefit. It belies the basic foundation of all that we believe, all that we cherish, and all that the goodness of American citizens has provided for the world.

Progressives are degrading Western Civilization from inside our democratic walls through the "Political Correctness'" that destroys Good and substitutes Evil. They have set out to recreate America and Mr. Miele takes that head-on throughout the "Heartland Diaries" within the administrations of Bush, Obama, and Trump. Reading Mr. Miele's articles will give you great insight into our country from the Middle of America which is the backbone of all that is good and sane, but continually rebuffed by the Elites of the Far West Coast and the Northeast corridor.

Frank Miele has written a true history of the political thoughts of the American people since 9/11 with the publishing of the "Heartland Diaries." It is far and beyond the scope of anything else that I have seen published or read. It is educative, truthful, and helpful to all in sorting out their thoughts about the political time-bombs that we harvest now in keeping with the divisiveness we have sown during the past decade.

Lastly, enjoy Mr. Miele's critical writing and analysis that form the first three volumes of the "Heartland Diaries" about the last three presidential administrations and the vast change of heart since 9/11 concerning the impact of that terror attack upon our soil. It has turned into a political battle among our governing bodies, and the radical left with the American people. A quote by Thucydides the Greek (471-400 B.C.), "... Peace is an armistice in a war that is continually going on...." Many reject that, but it has been world history forever, and some forget that.

"Heartland Diaries" will make excellent reading and should encourage productive discussion as it is a picture of our country in political turmoil. Mr. Miele has created a Tour de Force with his "Heartland Diaries," a multi-volume book that once one begins to read it they w_ll not want it to end. It is really that good.

— RLS, November 2018

Richard L. Spencer, Ph.D., is a retired lieutenant colonel in the U.S. Air Force, who served as a combat navigator during the Vietnam War delivering needed military supplies, ammunition, tanks, helicopters, etc., to every hot spot in the world. Counting his reserve service, Spencer devoted 27 years to his military career. As a civilian, Spencer has focused on an academic career as an economist and administrative professional, including stints as vice president of the Community College of Philadelphia and the Community College of Delaware County. He resides in Delaware with his wife Susan, and they have four grown children. Spencer is a devoted student of history. You can read more of his analysis and critiques in book reviews he published on his old squadron's webpage at http://cargomasterraster.blogspot.com/

ABOUT THE AUTHOR

Frank Miele is a conservative columnist at RealClearPolitics.com. He is also the moderator of www.HeartlandDiaryUSA.com. He worked as an award-winning community journalist for most of four decades, including 34 years at the Daily Inter Lake in Kalispell, Montana, where he was managing editor from 2000 to 2018. Miele's "Editor's 2 Cents" column was a regular feature in the newspaper from 2004 to 2018 and won him a broad following among conservatives across the nation. He lives with his wife and children in Kalispell